3

MEMORY AND HOPE

by Dietrich Ritschl

A THEOLOGY OF PROCLAMATION
CHRIST OUR LIFE
DIE HOMILETISCHE FUNKTION DER GEMEINDE
NUR MENSCHEN
ATHANASIUS

DIETRICH RITSCHL

Memory and Hope

AN INQUIRY CONCERNING
THE PRESENCE OF CHRIST

❧ ❧ ❧ ❧

THE MACMILLAN COMPANY · NEW YORK

COLLIER-MACMILLAN LTD. · LONDON

Library of Congress Catalog Card Number: 67-22732

FIRST PRINTING

The Macmillan Company, New York

Collier-Macmillan Canada Ltd., Toronto, Ontario

Printed in the United States of America

To

Paul M. van Buren *and* James A. Wharton

my friends and former colleagues at
Austin who first introduced me to the
American theological mentality and have
continued to stimulate me, even if one
may have, like Lot's wife, glanced over
one's shoulder for a while

Contents

Foreword

THE ALUMNI ASSOCIATION and Board of Trustees of the Austin Presbyterian Theological Seminary established a lectureship in 1945 to bring to the seminary campus some distinguished scholar each year to address an annual midwinter convocation of ministers and students on some phase of Christian thought.

The Thomas White Currie Bible Class of Highland Park Presbyterian Church of Dallas, Texas, in 1950, undertook the maintenance of this lectureship in memory of the late Dr. Thomas White Currie, founder of the class and president of the seminary from 1921 to 1943.

The series of lectures on this foundation for the year 1965 is included in this volume.

David L. Stitt
PRESIDENT

Austin Presbyterian Theological Seminary
Austin, Texas

Preface

AT THE TIME of my changing from the pastoral ministry to a teaching position, I wrote a book directed to the preaching task of the minister. The present book, directed to the teaching task, marks the transition from seven years of studying and teaching in the fields of New Testament and History of Doctrine to concentration in the field of systematic theology. The traditional division of theology into various disciplines has become problematical and systematic theology has become a very difficult science in our time. The period of preparation for responsible work in this field cannot be long enough. It is therefore with some hesitation that I here present a critical view of our Western theological tradition and a christological thesis which I hope will help us to overcome our present impasse in theology and especially in Christology. What I present here cannot claim to be more than a suggestion and a stimulus toward new thoughts in a time of crisis in Western Church life and theology.

I have tried to formulate my christological thoughts in such historial (Part One) and systematic (Part Two) fashion that the burden of our Augustinian heritage and the new tasks for the future of the Church may be understood and become of concern to the reader who has basic theological training. I have therefore kept to a minimum the quotations in languages other than English, and I refer the more scholarly inclined readers to my publications in various journals and to my German study on Athanasius.

It seems to me that a considerable helplessness is characteristic of Western theology in our time. I intend to propose that the real problem of Western Christology—the heart of theology—does not lie at the point of concentration and focus in the present scholarly discussion. Exegetes and dogmaticians are presently in large measure preoccupied with modifications of Martin Kähler's problem of the his-

torical Jesus and the post-Easter Christ, although in reality the problem lies in the relation between the "historical-risen" Christ and the
Christus praesens.[1] By the term "historical-risen" I mean to refer to
the fact that, in the mainstream of Western theology, the post-Easter
Christ was and is conceived to be a *Christ of the past*. Consequently,
the affirmation of Jesus' resurrection did not really solve the problem
of his contact with us today. In other words, *the ultimate problem
which has caused our theological helplessness lies in the separation
between Jesus Christ and the Church*. It is at this point that the problem of Scripture and tradition becomes most obvious and relevant;
discussions about this problem (e.g. between Protestants and Catholics) will remain fruitless as long as it is not understood as a corollary
of the overarching problem of the conception of Jesus Christ in his
relation to the Church. It is also here that the so-called subject-object
split becomes most noticeable; but I consider it philosophically naive
and theologically unnecessary to aim at the "overcoming" of the
subject-object split, which is a true description of the reality of human
life in history. The philosophical attempts to overcome this split for
the benefit of theology have resulted in a de-historicized understanding in personalistic categories. The theological discussion about hermeneutics of the last two decades has made this more than clear. My
thesis is that *this attempt represents a prolongation of a modified
Augustinianism which cannot solve the problem of the relation between the historical-risen Christ and the present Church, but which,
on the contrary, has caused that problem*.

It should not be denied that a variety of christological approaches
are possible in order to articulate the Church's confession. But in
facing the question why the Church must and can make such confessions in the first place, we are compelled to make a fundamental
decision. The legitimate beginning of theological thinking is at stake.
My thesis is that the only legtimate starting point is the *Christus
praesens*, connected with the "memory" and "hope" of the Church,
and is neither Scripture nor the historical Jesus nor the historical-
risen Christ. It is only under this "umbrella" then that various types
of Christology can be unfolded. I realize that, in order not merely to

---

[1] I prefer the use of the term *Christus praesens* to the English phrase "the presence of Christ," since in the latter phrase "presence" is the subject and "Christ"
the genitive object. I realize, however, that it is somewhat artificial to continue
with the use of Latin terms in theology. But a correct rendering in English like
"Christ here and now" is even worse than the use of an old Latin phrase.

present this thesis as a stimulus but also to prove it step by step exegetically and historically, one would have to give more than a lifetime of work. But it is my firm conviction that academic theology, aided and criticized by the so-called secular sciences as well as by the local congregations, must involve itself in nothing short of this work. It will entail a reexamination of our Western Augustinian heritage, a new search for the correlation of prayer and thinking and a more radical understanding of the priestly or vicarious task of the Church for others. The present book cannot be more than a pointer in this direction, but it is written with the conviction that our present theological helplessness and ecclesiastical confusion must not be suffered in vain. Political and ecumenical events of the last decade have made it unmistakably clear that Western theology is at the crossroads. An inquiry concerning the *Christus praesens* must take seriously our present helplessness; for it is obvious that *nature and grace, reason and faith, scholarship and piety, theology and doxology, historical past and existential present have been separated from each other.*

It is this emphasis on the *Christus praesens*, who is received in the memory and hope of the Church, which determines the direction of the present book. Our study is indeed concerned with Christology. But if the thesis of the *Christus praesens* has any merit, it follows that our discussion will also be concerned with part of the content of the contemporary hermeneutical controversy. Yet it does not seem helpful to discuss hermeneutical problems in a merely methodological fashion. The separation between dealing with hermeneutical problems and the actual process of exegesis, typical of our present time,[2] is unfortunate and does not do justice to the origin of the problem itself. Neither an isolated systematic or philosophical investigation nor a one-sided exegetical approach will help to overcome the present hermeneutical problem. Only a historical-christological study corresponds in content to the background of our present questions and can shed new light on the problem itself. It is only in this sense that the present book will also deal with hermeneutical questions. This is to say that hermeneutics enters the picture in only a secondary

---

[2] A recent example of this is the learned and yet depressing discussion in the collection of essays *The New Hermeneutic*, ed. James M. Robinson and John B. Cobb, Jr. (*New Frontiers in Theology*, Vol. II, New York: Harper & Row, 1964), of which the historical study by James M. Robinson (pp. 1–77) is by far the most helpful.

way. Hermeneutics is by the very nature of its task and by its location within the whole structure of theology a subcategory of Christology.

In correspondence with the nature of the problems at stake our study will attempt to combine both historical investigations and systematic reflections. Following the introductory chapter, which states the problems, the *historical part* will advance the thesis that Augustinianism has led Western theology into its present state of affairs. In criticizing Augustinianism, i.e. the effect of a rightly or wrongly understood Augustine, one will not be able to avoid criticizing Augustine himself. However, such criticisms, in order to avoid injustice to Augustine and unexplicated statements, would demand a monograph on Augustine. The brevity of the treatment of Augustine may be a shortcoming of the present book. Our criticism of Augustine, however, is meaningful and tenable only by admitting that the difficulties within our contemporary theological situation have determined the analysis of Augustine and Augustinianism. It seems to me that this is a legitimate reason for having an interest in a Church Father. The present study, therefore, will approach Augustine simultaneously from two different angles: from an examination of our discontent with much of contemporary Western theology and from having found valuable theological insights in the theology of the Greek Fathers,[3] obscured and badly misconceived by Augustine himself and by later Western theology. In order to be fair, a monograph on Augustine himself would have to limit such discussions. But our interest is in the excessive adherence of the Western tradition to Augustinian categories and in the corresponding neglect of the real point of Eastern thought. Instead of a detailed study of Augustine's thought, the present book makes use of the results of Augustine-research of the last four decades and relates these results to the development of Western theology on the whole and especially to contemporary problems. This procedure seems justified since our main thesis is not historical but christological. Moreover, Augustine and Augustinianism, though being the first and probably the decisive influence upon theology in the West, are not the only part of our theological tradition that deserves critical reexamination. Augustine's influence permitted the impact of various theological forces, either by preparing their ac-

---

[3] Cf. my studies "Hippolytus' Conception of Deification," in *SJT*, Vol. 12, No. 4 (Dec. 1959), pp. 388 ff., and the brief programmatic article "Athanasius, Source of New Questions," in *JES*, Vol. 1, No. 2 (Spring 1964), pp. 319 ff., and especially, *Athanasius, Versuch einer Interpretation*, (Zürich: EVZ-Verlag, 1964).

ceptance or by calling for a reaction. It suffices to mention such different forces as Dionysius the Areopagite (whose system was fully introduced to the West by the Augustinian Bonaventura), the theological Aristotelianism of the Middle Ages and of Protestant Orthodoxy, medieval and also Protestant mysticism, even the Reformers themselves (Luther was an Augustinian monk and Calvin quoted Augustine more often than any other Church Father) and also theological liberalism and historicism of the nineteenth century. They all are connected with Augustine's overwhelming influence and each of them deserves separately a radically critical reexamination. The historical part of our present study, however, will be restricted to the exposition of the main aspects of Augustinianism: The first chapter attempts to show that we are in difficulties concerning the Bible and history because of our neglect of the understanding of the *Christus praesens*; the second chapter suggests that the West, due to its addiction to Augustinianism, has not received the best part of Eastern theology; and the third chapter draws lines from Augustine's thought to certain trends in contemporary Western theology.

The *systematic part* works toward an answer to the basic christological question. It is less historically oriented than the first part and deals with the various attempts to leave behind the traditional "platonic" or "metaphysical" framework. I am inclined to take these new attempts seriously, e.g. Paul van Buren's suggestion, at least insofar as they show evidence of scholarly knowledge in exegesis and the history of philosophy and of doctrine. It is by reason of this restriction that I am not interested in entering into a discussion with the dilettantish advocates of the "God-is-dead" movement. The systematic part consists also of three chapters: the first deals with an extreme Western answer to the basic christological question, the dogmatical forms of "Atheistic Christology" (represented in the form of an epistemological restriction by Herbert Braun and Paul van Buren); the second chapter discusses the ethical version of the dogmatical content of the first; and the third takes up the questions of the opening chapter of the historical part on the *Christus praesens* and utilizes the findings from the other chapters in the attempt to outline my christological thesis. (My manuscript was almost completed when two important new books came to my attention: Jürgen Moltmann's *Theologie der Hoffnung* and Eberhard Jüngel's *Gottes Sein ist im Werden*. I find myself greatly stimulated by both books and share with the authors at least the questions and analyses of our contemporary problems. Some footnotes will refer to these new approaches.)

The major part of the content of this book was delivered in the Thomas White Currie Lectures at Austin Presbyterian Theological Seminary in February, 1965. I am most thankful to the president and my former colleagues at Austin for having invited me to this lectureship. Part of the material was also presented in the form of lectures at the universities of Rostock and Greifswald in East Germany in December, 1964, and the substance of the chapter on Augustine and justification has been expounded in German in my contribution to the *Festschrift* for Karl Barth's eightieth birthday (*Parrhesia*, Zurich: EVZ-Verlag, 1966).

I should like to acknowledge with gratitude the encouragement, criticism and help received from Paul L. Lehmann of Union Theological Seminary in New York, who read the draft of the book and made most valuable suggestions, from Ernst Wolf of Göttingen, Albert C. Outler of Perkins School of Theology in Dallas, my Roman Catholic friends in Pittsburgh and various friends in Eastern Europe, especially J. M. Lochman of Prague. I cannot objectively measure the influence upon my thinking through the regular discussions and exchanges with Markus Barth at Pittsburgh, and with my two mentors in Old Testament theology, James A. Wharton of Austin and James Barr of Manchester. Nor should I omit mentioning the stimulus I have received from my colleagues Edward Farley and George H. Kehm and from my students at Pittsburgh in two seminar courses, one on Augustine's *Enchiridion* and another on the theology of Gerhard Ebeling. Moreover, I am especially grateful to two graduate students, Charles C. Dickinson III, who in a selfless way studied the manuscript and carefully improved my use of the English language, and Milton Aylor, who examined the style of the final draft and helped me by making useful suggestions. Finally, I want to express my indebtedness to Pittsburgh Theological Seminary for a sabbatical semester and to the American Association of Theological Schools for a grant which enabled me to stay longer than usual in our home in Switzerland.

Reigoldswil, BL   Dietrich Ritschl
Switzerland   PITTSBURGH THEOLOGICAL SEMINARY
Fall 1965

List of Abbreviations

CD	Karl Barth, *Church Dogmatics*, Engl. transl. ed. T. F. Torrance (Edinburgh: T. & T. Clark)
Denz.	Henricus Denzinger, *Enchiridion Symbolorum*, Edition 31, ed. Carolus Rahner, S.I. (Freiburg: Herder, 1957)
EvTH	Evangelische Theologie
FN	Footnote
HThR	Harvard Theological Review
JES	Journal of Ecumenical Studies
JR	Journal of Religion
JThS	Journal of Theological Studies
Migne	J. P. Migne, *Patrologiae cursus completus, Series Graeca* (PG), *et Latina* (PL)
RelLife	Religion in Life
RevBen	Revue Benedictine
RevMet	Review of Metaphysics
RGG	*Die Religion in Geschichte und Gegenwart*, 3rd edition, ed. Kurt Galling, (Tübingen: J. C. B. Mohr, 1957–1962), Vols. I–VI.
SJT	The Scottish Journal of Theology
ThBL	Theologische Blätter
ThLZ	Theologische Literaturzeitung
ThRu	Theologische Rundschau
ThSt	Theological Studies
ThToday	Theology Today

ThZ	Theologische Zeitschrift, Basel
TU	Texte und Untersuchungen zur Geschichte der altchristlichen Literatur
WA	*Weimarer Ausgabe* of Martin Luther's works
ZKG	Zeitschrift für Kirchengeschichte
ZNW	Zeitschrift für die neutestamentliche Wissenschaft und die Kunde der älteren Kirche
ZThK	Zeitschrift für Theologie und Kirche

NOTE

The references in the footnotes to the locations of patristic, medieval and Reformation texts do not include indications of specific editions or translations. The chapter and verse divisions of these classical texts are standardized and can be located in any edition. The translations are my own.

Introduction
The Impasse of Present Western Theology

THE DIFFICULTIES in contemporary theology are frequently attributed to modern man's awareness of the new *Zeitgeist*. The fact that significant sociopolitical and philosophical developments have become generally recognizable realities since the end of the Second World War is taken seriously by the younger generation of theologians. Some of them go as far as to proclaim that the determining factors in our time are unprecedented, unique and radically new, almost as though a new creation had occurred, the implications of which have now become obvious to their analytical mind. This discovery of the "secular world," of "modern, scientific man" and of the "secular university" has, especially among American theologians, some overtones of an awakening and of repentance and culminates in the use of the expression "the post-Christian Era." This term indirectly suggests a certain theological position: *an orientation toward the past which is embarrassingly challenged by a new analysis of the present.* It is at this point that the aforementioned difficulties come into focus. If theology finds its orientation by referring to events of the past as they are available through past interpretations and if it is the declared task of theology to make revelant to today the essence of those past events and their interpretations, certainly an analysis of a supposed radically new situation in the present will constitute a major crisis for theology.

But even if this basic theological position should be found to be faulty (because it is still determined by the Western preoccupation with "mass-conversion" or with the general applicability of the Gospel to every person), it should of course not be denied that our time presents us with radically new tasks. Yet that expression "post-Christian Era" is to be theologically regarded as faithless and historically it is obviously nonsensical. It shows little more than the "Constantinian" grounding of its advocates and at best their regret for having remained uncritical for such a long time. Indeed, the term "post-Constantinian Era" (or post-Christendom) is the only meaningful designation which points to some helpful insights. The long, almost unbroken development of the identification of Church and culture, beginning with the fourth century, was not shaken radically enough either by the mind of the Renaissance or by the theological work of the Reformers, but rather by the Enlightenment and by subsequent events in intellectual and political history. After the Second World War it should have become clear to most thinking Christians that the period was gone in which the identification of Church and Western culture appeared possible. The next lesson which we must learn, however, is harder and more costly because it requires theological thinking and not merely historical observation. We must now learn to accept and even to welcome the challenging fact that the long period from Constantine or Theodosius to the eighteenth century did not represent the "norm" of the existence of the Church but rather the exception. We are now returning to the "normal" form of existence, which is that Christians are a minority group among the citizens of the world and that much of what they say is not appreciated by their fellowmen. This is the "norm." The difference between the present situation and that of the Early Church is nevertheless fundamental. The Church and theology today carry the burden of almost two thousand years' history of actions and omissions, of thoughts and doubts.

It cannot be denied that the theology of our time shows indications of a certain helplessness. Our "theological helplessness" is not only reflected by the often discussed tension between systematic theology and Biblical exegesis but also by the uncertainty, or at least the lack of optimism, regarding our respective theological traditions and their validity and adequacy in the linguistic dress in which they have been handed down to us through the centuries. Philosophical linguistic analysis[1] as well as less sophisticated forms of investigation have

---

[1] For a helpful introduction to linguistic philosophy of the Anglo-Saxon type (as distinct from the theologically perhaps more exciting language philosophy of Heidegger and his followers), see J. O. Urmson, *Philosophical Analysis* (Oxford: The Clarendon Press, 1960; first edition 1956, Oxford University Press), and Frederick Ferré, *Language, Logic and God* (New York: Harper & Row, 1961), and Kent Bendall and Frederick Ferré, *The Logic of Faith, A Dialogue on the Relation of Modern Philosophy to Christian Faith* (New York: Association Press, 1962), or William P. Alston, *Philosophy of Language* (Englewood Cliffs, N.J.: Prentice-Hall, Inc., 1964).

taught us to be more careful in the use and evaluation of theological formulations. This challenge is more radical than the mere admonition of the historian always to see a formulation or statement in the light of its historical setting. We really can no longer escape the challenge of examining what happens theologically when we use old statements or formulate new ones in the form of a given language. When one faces these tensions and complications and, in addition, the overwhelming complexity of the political and ideological situation of our world in relation to the task of the Church, one should not be surprised at indications of a theological helplessness.

Indeed, Church members, theological students and ministers do not radiate much confidence and joy in matters of theology. Theological authors on both sides of the Atlantic have not yet succeeded in overcoming the hardening of past positions or in showing ways out of our helplessness. Moreover, many representatives of the older generation, e.g. men of the Confessing Church of the thirties, have disappointed the present generation. Their courageous "confessional" language strikes us today as overly straightforward and optimistic. Thus, a helplessness and lack of direction is becoming characteristic of many of the younger theologians and their students, not to mention the pastors and members of local congregations.

The true *danger* to Church and theology in America, however, is not in this present helplessness but rather in the premature and often non-theological *attempts to overcome it.* A new theological intelligentsia, frequently consisting of exegetically and historically ill-trained or uninterested theologians, pointedly prides itself upon its antichurch and artificially this-worldly attitude.

For many decades, academic theology in America has depended slavishly on European theological scholarship. It is understandable and also fortunate that often the same theologians who have received part of their training in Europe now call for a halt in transporting European, especially Continental, theology to the American scene. But recent developments seem to indicate that the new approaches of these theologians are not as free and independent as they were intended to be. Many mistakes of Continental theology are unconsciously or uncritically repeated, and the basic questions of Continental European theology obviously still dominate the inquiry of even the most outspoken advocates of a new, i.e. often anti-European, theology. Moreover, the unity of the theological enterprise, which collapsed in Europe in the eighteenth century, has by no means been regained by the new attempts on this side of the Atlantic. On the contrary, within a few years of relatively independent theological productivity, two distinctly different theologies have begun to emerge: the outcome of the oversimplified heritage of the christocentric theology of the Reformers and of Karl Barth in the form of the "God-is-dead" suggestion and the more Anglo-Saxon–oriented philosophical theology which tends toward a rehabilitation of theism (advocated, not surprisingly, by some former Bultmannians) aided by Alfred N. Whitehead's and Charles Hartshorne's highly respectable philosophical metaphysics and resembling to some degree discussions of the ideas of Leibniz.

It can hardly be said that these new trends in theology show a competency in or deep concern for exegesis, despite the ancestry of Bultmann to parts of this new development. The observation is not very encouraging that many post-Bultmannians in Anglo-Saxon theology are merely systematizing and modifying the results of Bultmann's later writings without being able or willing to enter into Bultmann's most competent and demanding exegetical work. Originally, a call for help was extended to Heidegger and later to Collingwood, but what was meant to be of structural help has become today, in many quarters, almost a source of content.[2] Nevertheless, terms such as "Gospel" or "Good News" are still used with amazing frequency and seem to occupy a central place. The traditional Augustinian theological ideology, i.e. the feeling of being under the compulsion to apply to the present eternally true ideas, values and insights, seems to constitute the focal point of these theological approaches.

Yet it would be unwise to overlook or belittle the value of the stimulus that comes from the theological contemporaries just mentioned. There is even partial agreement in many points between their views and the position elaborated in the present study.[3] But here (it seems), the real impasse of present Western theology becomes clear: those with whom one is inclined to agree, as far as their flexibility and intellectual honesty is concerned, do not really provide

---

[2] Cf. Hans Jonas' critical address "Heidegger and Theology" at Drew University in April 1964, publ. in *RevMet*, Vol. XVIII, No. 2 (Dec. 1964), pp. 207–233.
[3] This is the case concerning Paul M. van Buren, *The Secular Meaning of the Gospel* (New York: The Macmillan Company, 1963).

an alternative to the traditional forms of theology.[4] They either sacrifice inalienable aspects of the Good News by approaching Scripture (and tradition) with narrow and artifically "modern" questions or they merely restate in seemingly modern terms the ancient formulations or else they combine both approaches. The concepts of these most recent writers are often indebted to the somewhat obsolete theological employment of what is known among philosophers as "personalism." Slogans like "personal categories" and "encounter" are again being used with surprising liberty by both Protestant and Catholic authors.[5] These thought-forms may have their merit, but they could also deceive us and become bases for superficial approaches toward the solution of the fundamental theological dilemma. Moreover, they uncritically perpetuate the Western theological obsession with personal salvation, expressed in individualistic categories.

The fact of the matter is that all these approaches, intended to

[4] What appears on the surface to be an observation of the obvious, namely, that a theology with which one does not agree nonetheless provides a "stimulus," is in reality a very complex problem. Some remarks can briefly illustrate this and also explain the critical evaluations advanced in this introductory chapter.

Theology is by its very nature time-bound and situation-bound. (For the application of this to biblical theology, cf. Ernst Käsemann, "The Canon of the New Testament and the Unity of the Church" in *Essays on New Testament Themes* [Nashville: Alec R. Allenson, Inc., 1964], SCM Studies in Biblical Theology, No. 41, pp. 95 ff.) This insight was not known to scholasticism or to positivism of the last century, nor was it taken seriously in Karl Barth's earlier writings. An example is the enormous stress on the "doctrine of justification" in the theology of the Reformers (and partly of Augustine). This emphasis was necessary and possible within the Constantinian self-understanding of the Church, that is, at a time when the "good works" of non-Christians were merely a theoretical problem at the periphery. But times have changed and a repetition or reapplication of Luther's statement that only the justified Christian can do "good works" would be quite misleading (a point neglected by much of post-Bultmannian theology). But the demand for a *new* doctrine of justification does not suggest that the Reformers' concept *was* false, or even that it *is* false. Provided that one's environment is that of the Constantinian self-understanding, as is the case in many of our Churches, one must perhaps for the moment also share the old doctrine which is appropriate to this understanding, although one does not "agree" with it. In other words, several different and even contradictory theological understandings and articulations are possible at the same time. Thus, theological statements have their proper places on certain *levels*. The "space" within which theological thinking occurs is, so to speak, a multistoried building. The academically trained theologian differs from the rest of the Christians in being obliged to think on several levels simultaneously. He should be able to think and speak vicariously-interpretatively for other Christians. It goes without saying that this necessary "double talk" be radically new and appropriating the analysis of man's condition and self-understanding in the last third of our century, do not yet show signs of the advent of a theological language and the grasp of a theological content that could replace the traditionally European theological enterprise. This is all the more discouraging since theology in Europe is to a large measure still preoccupied with hermeneutical questions. There are good reasons for the assumption that the seemingly new and often anti-Continental theological experiments in American theology are only the less sophisticated version of the predominantly German discussion of hermeneutics. The connection between the two can be demonstrated biographically in the cases of many scholars.

We propose the thesis that Augustinian categories in Western theology are of such overwhelming weight and importance that even the newest and most radical theological attempts are shaped by their influence. Augustinianism, i.e. the concept of a timeless God (or the denial of it), the negative evaluation of "ordinary" world history, the idea that God's decisive actions lie in the past (a thought which is quite basic to William Hamilton's deistic suggestion that God has

---

presents great problems regarding the integrity of the theologian. Unquestionably, mutual understanding despite disagreement should be especially intense among academically trained theologians and it is tragic if they are only capable of *either* understanding *or* disagreement. But this sectarian attitude unfortunately dominates much of the current theological discussion in America. It not only contradicts the ancient academic tradition of being able to disagree with each other and yet maintain a strong sense of solidarity but it blocks the way to what I would like to call a new "piety" which we will have to learn among scholars as well as between different denominations: the *confidence* in each other *despite disagreement* and—in the extreme cases, such as in our contact with Eastern Orthodoxy—even *despite* the lack of full intellectual *understanding*.

Thus, a "stimulus," to say the least, can come from those theologians whose conclusions one does not find acceptable, mainly because one does not agree with their starting points, i.e. their analysis of the situation and their understanding of theology's and the Church's task. For it is theoretically possible to "agree" with any consistent theology, provided one agrees with its starting point and goal.

5 The category of "personal encounter" had a liberating effect upon Catholic theology and should not be judged prematurely in the same way as its Protestant utilization. Cf. E. Schillebeeckx, O.P., *Christ the Sacrament of the Encounter with God* (New York: Sheed and Ward, 1963); but somewhat disappointing is his employment of the category of "encounter" in his critique of Bishop Robinson's *Honest to God* in his book *Personale Begegnung mit Gott* (Mainz: Matthias Grünewald Verlag, 1964).

died in recent times) and the emphasis on personal justification (leading to "authentic existence") is the platform of both the advocates of a new theology for the secular age and their critics. Thus one cannot freely agree with the critics of the most recent theologies, since their own presuppositions are similar to those which have made possible these new experiments which differ from more conventional academic theology mainly in the radicalism of putting the questions and in the daring onesideness of formulating answers. It is of course true that the relatively modern, though tradition-bound, types of theology on both sides of the Atlantic present a very heterogeneous picture.[6] The common denominator, however, which permits the statement that the criticism of new radical theology on the basis of these more conventional theologies is really not promising, is the almost general helplessness or silence concerning the relation between the present Church and the presence of Christ. This outgrowth of the manner in which Augustine and Augustinianism shaped the most decisive theological questions unites in many ways the different theologies of our time.

[6] The following classification seems reasonable:
  a) Strictly historical-critical work, both in biblical exegesis and in history, often indebted to nineteenth-century historical positivism and connected with crypto-apologetic tendencies, dogmatically and denominationally tolerant or unconcerned, though not interfering with the personal piety of its adherents (to be found especially in American Old Testament circles, but also in some places in Eastern Europe; the recent tendencies in America toward the development of a highly critical philosophical reexamination of dogmatics and ethics, i.e. the revival of "philosophy of religion," will perhaps represent the Anglo-Saxon form of the originally European textual and historical scholarship).
  b) "Reformation theology" molded and revived by the political turbulence of the twentieth century, partly growing out of the Confessing Church in Germany and influential upon the ecumenically oriented "international" Protestant theology of a Reformed type (though with Anglican elements); it is politically alert and intends to be concerned for both the Church and "the world" (its finest form exists in Eastern Europe, modifications of it in the World Council of Churches and its agencies); it strikes the younger generation as impressive and naive at the same time.
  c) The postwar personalistic-existentialistic systematization of historical critical exegesis, fighting the "subject-object split," searching for thought and language forms to "make relevant" the ancient message (represented exegetically and systematically in Europe, systematically and practically in America, especially in the sphere of influence of Methodist theological schools, perhaps as a stopgap for obsolete conversion-theology).
    It would not be difficult, of course, to enumerate other forms of theology, e.g., the remnants of Protestant Orthodoxy, strictly denominational theologies defending a system and remaining ethically reactionary, pietistic non-

This unsuspected unity of different types of theology is the case although a seemingly most important dividing line is felt by many to separate all theological work into two conflicting parties. Ever since the revival of Reformation theology, and especially since the impact of Karl Barth, a radical division has seemed necessary and meaningful: the separation between a theology which intends to clarify and verify the meaning of all possible theological statements by testing them over against the empirical situation (stressing understandability); and a theology which, in the opposite direction, intends to clarify and verify the meaning of all possible theological statements by testing them over against the *viva vox evangelii*, i.e. the living word of God, which does not necessarily imply a limitation to the biblical texts. Whether these two types are mutually exclusive depends upon the understanding of the "living voice of the Gospel." In the present study we will at times make use of these two categories of verification, which constitute two apparently irreconcilable types of theology, but we will eventually depart from these fixed alternatives, especially when it becomes clear that the second type *is* in fact limited to the "voice of the Gospel" as contained in the Bible. Ultimately we cannot agree that theology must decide between the two extremes of regarding as its criterion either the biblical texts or the present reality, although it is evident that this seems to be the alternative when reviewing the present theological situation. In the last analysis we will avoid the exaggerated categorization which makes Bultmann's or Ebeling's theology begin with man's self-understanding and Barth's theology with God's self-disclosure.[7] Nor will we concede that Paul Tillich's concept of "correlation" adequately describes what is apparently a dilemma and that his concept truly shows a third way.[8] Least of all is the not officially accepted attempt of the

---

systematic biblical theology and the prolongation of the Social Gospel, whose representatives do not like to be classified as theologians. But none of these groups can rightly be counted among the academically respectable theologies mentioned in the first three categories, which is not to say that some of the other approaches do not also have their merits.

[7] Jürgen Moltmann makes this provocative categorization the basis of his criticism of Western theology's preoccupation with the revelation or the disclosure of "being," in his *Theologie der Hoffnung* (Munich: Chr. Kaiser Verlag, 1964), *passim*.

[8] Paul Tillich, *Systematic Theology*, Vols. I and II (Chicago University Press: 1951 and 1957), e.g., Vol. I. pp. 8 ff., 59 ff., Vol. II, pp. 13 ff. The concept of correlation is either a truism, i.e., a method not as new as it sounds, since there was scarcely a good theologian in the history of the Church who was not aware of both man's questions and the Bible's message; or, more probable, it is

early "Innsbruck theology" of recent Catholic writers of any help. Their distinction has classified as "scientific" the theological investigations of the *essentia* and the *verum*, and as "kerygmatic" the thoughts about *existentia* and the *bonum*.

Therefore, since a clear-cut division (and consequently a choice) between an anthropologically or empirically oriented and a biblically verified theology does not appear to be acceptable and since the suggestion of a complementarity or "correlation" cannot seriously be considered as bridging the two, one will have to recognize that Western theology faces an impasse on the level of rather fundamental questions. Not only the recent radical attempts to construct a "new theology" but also the perpetuation of the more conventional and often academically quite respectable theological approaches are caught within the awkward dilemma of deciding (or defending the decision) between a situational and a biblical orientation. The former tries to do justice to the situation in which the theologian finds himself, but it reduces or neglects the biblical witness and with it important formulations of the tradition, and it accuses the opposite party of Platonism or Biblicism. The latter, on the other hand, takes the early witnesses seriously and accepts their judgment over present theological formulations, but it does injustice to the present situation of contemporary man and of the world in general, and accuses the other party of having sacrificed the center of theology. Thus, despite its heterogeneity, contemporary theology—in both its "radically new" and its more traditional forms—faces the Scylla of contextualism and the Charybdis of Biblicism.[9] The ancient philosophical

---

Tillich's expression of an ontological unity which overarches or precedes the difference between philosophy and theology, a view which is indebted to the later systems of Schelling. If this is the case, correlation cannot be considered a *theological* answer to a fundamental theological dilemma.

One may also think in this connection of Bartholomäus Keckermann's (1571–1609) careful elaboration of the distinction between the synthetical and the analytical method in theology. This comes closer to a helpful solution, and his categories will be utilized in modified forms in the present study. Keckermann's categories, however, do not go beyond the structural and merely methodological realm and cannot directly produce insights in matters of theological content.

[9] Any objective survey, e.g. the article by Gene Reeves, "A Look at Contemporary American Theology," *RelLife* (Autumn 1965), pp. 511 ff., or the spectrum represented in the thirty-three articles in *New Theology Nos. 1 and 2*, ed. Martin E. Marty and Dean G. Peerman (New York: The Macmillan Company, 1964 and 1965), confirms the above evaluation. Cf. also the analysis of tensions and dangers in Catholic theology by Karl Rahner, S.J., *Nature and Grace, Dilemmas in the Modern Church* (New York: Sheed and Ward, 1964).

tension between nominalism and realism has finally become manifest in the form of a basic theological impasse.

However, this is only a structural and methodological description of the impasse in Western theology.[10] The material reason for the impasse must be seen in *Western theology's embarrassment over the ongoing function and work of the risen Christ*. The situational theology, which we shall call "world-verification" type theology, considers the speech about the resurrected Christ to be sadly mythological and metaphysical. The more this type of theology moves away from this originally central affirmation, the less "theological" it becomes, *viz.* moving gradually toward the philosophy department (in its academic location) and toward humanism (in its ethical expression) it struggles to maintain its identity as "theology." The biblically oriented theology, on the other hand, which we shall call "revelation-verification" type theology, maintains in seemingly full theological integrity its point of orientation as well as the expression of its content—though in modernized forms—in accord with the ancient biblical texts; but it refers to the resurrection of Jesus as an event of the past and it is as embarrassed as is world-verification theology when it comes to *theological interpretations* of current events. It is primarily the "meaning" of the resurrection which is being interpreted and the presence of the resurrected one is theologically affirmed almost in restriction to actual Christian worship. If it is not clear how world-verification theology is really based on the ancient witness to the election of Israel and to the advent, death and resurrection of Jesus, it is certainly not any more clear what revelation-verification theology can say about God's ongoing work in Christ. Should the theological interpretations of historical events be restricted to those that took place during the period which later was designated by the writing of the canonical books, e.g. to the Exile or to the fall of Jericho or of Samaria, concluding with the events recorded and interpreted in the book of Acts? And is theology really

---

[10] It is interesting that Heinrich Ott, the only direct pupil of both Barth and Bultmann, in a definition of the task and method of systematic theology consciously tries to do justice to both points of orientation: "Dogmatics watches over the Church's proclamation [materially] regarding its faithfulness to Scripture and [formally] regarding its understandability" ("Die Dogmatik überwacht die kirchliche Verkündigung (materiell) hinsichtlich ihrer 'Schriftgemässheit' und (formell) hinsichtlich ihrer Verständlichkeit"), in *RGG*, 3rd ed., Vol. III, p. 1253.

adequately defined as basically being a "dialogue with the Bible?" If the task of theology is based on an axiom which is analogous to the ancient rabbinic saying "No revelation after Ezra," it would indeed be tempting to forsake the narrow gate and the steep path of revelation-verification theology and to enter through the wide gate to the broad avenue of world-verification theology. But this must not be permitted as a choice.

The absence of the *Christus praesens*, and that includes the virtual lack of the *hope* that the greatest things are still to come, is in varying degrees typical of both types of theology. The reason for this absence of the balance between memory and hope must be seen in the inherent handicap with which Western theology had to work: the Western Church always adhered to the conclusions of the great christological councils that were the product of Greek theology, which theology was interpreted by the Westerners with Augustinian categories. In other words, the theology of the Western Church operated with the results of Greek theology without really having a firsthand knowledge of it and without sharing the Greek understanding of worship and of the presence of Christ. This is not to say that the Greek Fathers could today provide the solution to our problems, but it does mean that our theological thinking has been greatly influenced by inadequately or wrongly understood results of a complex theological process in the Eastern part of the Early Church. One would suppose that historical scholarship of modern times has grasped the magnitude of this influence. But it can be shown that the great scholars of the nineteenth century, both Catholics and liberal Protestants, were unable and unwilling to depart from the Augustinian tradition. Both Newman and Harnack read the Greek Fathers and the New Testament through "Augustinian glasses." A *radical reexamination of our whole historical tradition* including the history of Biblical interpretation and political developments is, therefore, the only way toward a solution of this historically conditioned impasse.

After this description of the cardinal problem within Western theology, it remains to be said that the awareness of our difficulties concerning the ongoing work of God in Christ and the necessity of interpreting theologically current political events is not totally absent in contemporary publications. The fourth volume of Karl Barth's *Church Dogmatics*, especially the second half of IV, 3, presents an impressive attempt to do justice to the ongoing work of Christ and to

the hope of the Church, under the heading of the doctrine of reconciliation.[11] If this is read over against the background of the relatively strong "consensus" in matters of Christology in ecumenical
(often not strictly academic) theology, one must admit that there is
not only consistency with but also progress beyond previous valuable
theological insights. For it is quite obvious that there was more of a
consensus regarding Christology at the conferences in Amsterdam in
1948 and in New Delhi in 1961 than at the beginning of ecumenical
discussions in Edinburgh in 1910. But this valuable consensus has not
really solved the problem, nor has it enriched the academic theological
discussion from which it originally came. Instead, new problems
have arisen which seem to direct attention away from Christology.
There are many voices demanding a "new doctrine of the Holy
Spirit."[12] This demand demonstrates the awareness of the helplessness regarding the relation between the present Church and the presence of Christ. But is a new pneumatology really what we need?
Berkhof himself denies that the Holy Spirit is a "person" distinctly
different from the risen Christ. If this is true, how can pneumatology
become the new avenue toward a helpful solution? The same remark
would apply to those who advocate the necessity of elaborating a
new "doctrine of the Church," including the problematical subcategories of "liturgical renewal" and a new investigation of the "meaning of the sacraments." Necessary as these studies may be, is it not
obviously true that they will remain hanging in midair and will have
to be dealt with in the abstract if they are still based upon the
understanding of the "historical-risen Christ" as a mere event of the
past?

---

[11] Cf. also the publications of John Knox, e.g. *The Church and the Reality of Christ* (New York: Harper & Row, 1962).

[12] E.g. the 19th General Council of the World Alliance of Reformed Churches, Frankfurt, 1964; and in relation to it, H. Berkhof, *The Doctrine of the Holy Spirit* (Richmond: John Knox Press, 1964); cf. his article "Come Creator Spirit!" in *Bulletin* of the Dept. of Theol. of the World Presby. Alliance, Vol. 4, No. 4 (Summer 1964), pp. 1–12. Cf. also the report on conversations with the Russian Orthodox Church in 1963, *Vom Wirken des Heiligen Geistes*, ed. Aussenamt der Evangelischen Kirche in Deutschland (Witten: Luther-Verlag, 1964), and the more traditional study by George S. Hendry, *The Holy Spirit in Christian Theology* (Philadelphia: The Westminster Press, 1956). In this connection one may also think of the enormous increase in publications on ecclesiology by Roman Catholic authors since Vatican II.

Christians will face tremendous challenges in the remaining three decades of this century. And theologians, it seems, have the special task of reexamining with radical honesty our Western-Augustinian theological tradition. Only then can we claim to serve and to strengthen one of the main purposes of the Church today. This purpose can be summarized in the following formula: In our divided world filled with fear, hatred and prejudice, Christians are called to do what non-Christian humanists can at best do in a broken way; they can face openly and interpret honestly the past, i.e. political and ecclesiastical history, without fear, because they know forgiveness; and they can face the future, without fear and without false idealism, because they have hope. Honest and concerned *memory* is possible because of the *hope* that decisive things in the relation between God and the world are still to come and *hope* is possible because of the *memory* of what has already happened and of what is understood and accepted as a promise. Theology, i.e. the reflection upon these dimensions in the light of the present situation, is obliged to extend and constantly renew the invitation to "hope backward" into the realm of memory and to "remember forward" into the realm of hope. *Memory and hope are the dimensions of faith in the Christus praesens* and it is only because of the *Christus praesens* that these dimensions are open to our perception. Hope provides not only a "mood" but the matrix of future events; it "creates the reality of tomorrow." It is for those who hope that the fullness of history is present. It is this formula that will be expounded in this book in order to reach an understanding of the presence of Christ and of the task of the Church. This theological concept, set over against the Augustinian tradition, which is concerned with applying to the present the essence or "meaning" of past events, may provide an alternative to the helplessness of today's theology and to the approaches represented by the new theological "intelligentsia," whose lack of historical knowledge and concern is to be lamented but whose discontent with our theological situation is in many ways to be shared.

Part One

HISTORICAL CONSIDERATIONS

The Burden of the Augustinian Heritage

I

The Presence of Christ: The Problem of Scripture and Tradition

A TWOFOLD PROBLEM would have to be faced if the principle "No revelation after Ezra" were applied to the New Testament as being distinct from later events and texts. Firstly, the meaning of the term "revelation" would have to be clearly defined in relation to and distinction from the possible assertion that "God is present." For in the era "after the revelation" this assertion could only be meaningful if it did not imply that "God's presence" also means his "revelation." This is precisely what Western theology, especially in its Protestant forms, felt compelled to elaborate; while the decisive revelation was conceived as an event of the past, it was nevertheless maintained that God can be present in the era "after the revelation." Obviously, the effect of such presence could hardly be more than a reenactment and confirmation of what God had already revealed in the past. And correspondingly, theology cannot do more than God himself is ready and willing to do, namely, explain, confirm and apply the ancient news to ever-new generations. But, if this is the mode of God's presence in Christ, and if the task of theology consists in bridging the gap between the time of revelation and the present time, God must actually be spoken of in deistic categories: this means, among other consequences, that the world is deprived of its hope. Only the individual's future life after death remains as a legitimate realm of hope. But is it really necessary and meaningful to speak of God's or Christ's presence without implying that he continues to reveal himself in ever-new ways?

Secondly, if this axiom concerning a revelatory mode of presence as distinct from a silent or merely reaffirming presence of God is maintained, the meaning of the concept of revelation[1] itself must necessarily be expounded on the basis of the already asserted difference between ordinary times and revelatory times or events. This categorization-in-retrospect, it seems, gives a metaphysical or trans-historical character to revelation before any clarification or definition is attempted. "Ordinary world history" is of another, lower quality than revelatory history. The events that take place in the era "after the revelation" are as such not capable of being interpreted since it is certain that they cannot enrich the knowledge of God, who has ceased to reveal himself. All that is left to be done with these later events is to categorize and evaluate them; they cannot speak the language which was assumedly spoken by the revelatory events of the past or the texts which interpreted them. Thus, a conclusion which would strive at "overcoming" the realm of these ordinary events of history is understandable.

These two problems have determined, in large measure, theological work in the West, but the second of them has received less attention than the first. It is the second, however, which, in the form of its typically Western treatment, shows alarmingly the departure from the Old Testament[2] and the subsequent first- and second-century Christian understanding of historical events.[3] The difference

---

[1] H. Richard Niebuhr, *The Meaning of Revelation* (New York: The Macmillan Company, 1941; 3rd printing, 1964, Macmillan paperbacks), gives a lucid description of the problem and suggests a solution with the concept of Christianity being a "permanent revolution" and ongoing *metanoia*.

[2] Cf. the most valuable results of Old Testament research of the last few decades, as presented, e.g. by Gerhard von Rad and Walther Zimmerli, and recently in the form of daring suggestions by James Barr, *Old and New in Interpretation* (London: SCM Press, 1966), esp. chaps. 3 and 5 (cf. "Revelation through History in the Old Testament and in Modern Theology," *New Theology*, No. 1, pp. 60 ff.).

[3] Cf. K. Stendahl, "The Apocalypse of John and the Epistles of Paul in the Muratorian Fragment," in *Current Issues in New Testament Interpretation*, essays in honor of O. A. Piper, ed. W. Klassen and G. F. Snyder (New York: Harper & Row, 1962), which shows that the post-Apostolic Church did not apply the "No revelation after Ezra" principle, as we have called it. Cf. also Markus Barth, *Conversation with the Bible* (New York: Holt, Rinehart and Winston, 1964), pp. 288–292.

between "inspiration" regarding prophetic words or texts related to events and "illumination" regarding later authentic interpretations of such texts cannot possibly be supported biblically; it is an invention of the theologians. The reason for this invention must be seen in the theologians' difficulties concerning the ongoing work of God in Christ in history. While they rightly pointed to the uniqueness of the so-called Christ-event, they were usually inclined to equate God's revelation with this unique event, though not excluding prior promises leading to it. The thought is precious to Protestant theologians that the "once-and-for-all character" of Jesus' advent and death forbids the idea that God continues to reveal himself by "adding" anything to what he has already made known. Strong arguments and convincing reasons have been advanced in support of this dogma, especially in defense against the seemingly opposite, but ultimately rather similar, Roman Catholic concept of the continuing incarnation in sacramental form. Could it not be that this equation of Jesus' coming and God's "last revelation" is heavily indebted to a static and timeless concept of God and, consequently, to a necessarily metaphysical/trans-historical understanding of revelation as it was held, for instance, by the Gnostics?

Yet recent Old Testament scholarship has taught us that Yahweh is not the name of a static being, however transcendent, but a "roadname." And he is not timeless or unchangeable; rather, his faithfulness to Israel will not change as time goes on. What is "unchangeable" is his "revealed" pledge that he will continue to "go before them" (Ex. 13:21); Yahweh's unchangeability is *not* his "nature" or life as though he were detached from history. Why should the chain of promises and fulfillments (that were again turned into promises), which is not merely characteristic of, but which *constitutes* the history of Israel, suddenly end in the first century with the coming of Jesus, the fulfillment of Israel's promise? The broadening of the realm of God's people from Israel to the Gentiles was not the end of *one* activity of God and the beginning of *another*, more static and timeless kind of activity. But it would appear that for much of Western theology the high respect paid to Scripture as distinct from tradition was necessarily connected with a diminuition of the significance of the presence of God in Christ in our time. The choice, however, between the emphasis on the "revelatory" character of Scripture at the expense of the *Christus praesens*, and a spiritualistic reliance upon divine revelations through the Spirit at the expense of exegesis,

is most unfortunate. It would leave us with the alternatives of traditional Biblicism (including the reaction to it in the form of the "God-
is-dead" suggestion) or modern hermeneutics, *viz.* the attempt to do
justice to both the authority of the ancient biblical texts and the
"meaningfulness" (*Bedeutsamkeit*) of their basic content to the
modern reader. But in either case the relation between Jesus (or God
in Christ) and the Church is conceived as a prolongation, reapplication or reenactment of a revelatory event of the past. Thus the
theologians' difficulties with the presence of Christ are manifest in
the various attempts to define the relation between Scripture and
tradition.

a) Jesus and the Church

We begin with a brief description of the theologian's "pain of
christological thinking": Jesus Christ cannot become the object of
our investigation as if he were not the subject of our lives. How then
can he be the content and criterion of Christology? Being aware of
this question, the whole tradition of the Church in the East and West
has directly or indirectly given an answer to this question by pointing
to the fact that Jesus Christ "makes himself present." The ongoing
worship of the Church through the centuries is the indirect answer to
the question. But what does it mean that Jesus Christ "makes himself
present"? This question is the center of Christology. But Christology
is by its very nature and function, in the "multistoried" house of
theology, an "impossible" undertaking since its object is at the same
time the subject of our lives.[4] Moreover, Christology cannot be a
separate part of theology, and yet it is this since one cannot think
and speak of everything simultaneously. Ultimately, one can only
speak either *to* God in Jesus Christ in prayer or *from* him in the
sermon. Every thought and statement *about* him is only justifiable in
a derived manner. But clarification, examination and verification of
consistency, which are the task of theology, necessitate thinking and

---

[4] "Teaching about Christ begins in silence." It is with these words that Dietrich
Bonhoeffer, in the summer semester 1933, opened his remarkable lectures on
Christology which at last have appeared in English translation, *Christ the
Center* (New York: Harper & Row, 1966). This brief but powerful book is
unique among the Christologies of the mid-twentieth century in that it begins
with the presence of Christ; *vide* the Introduction, pp. 27 ff., and Part I, "The
Present Christ—the 'Pro Me,'" pp. 43 ff.

speaking *about* Jesus Christ. This necessity, in the awareness of its basic impossibility, is the pain of christological thinking. The more christological thinking is separated from worship, the greater is its pain; conversely, the more it is identified with worship, the lesser is its clarity.

Traditional theology has provided several alternatives for under-standing the relation between Jesus and the Church. Despite the danger of oversystematization, it may be permissible to categorize the basic alternatives in the following groupings:

a) The strictly platonic-realistic understanding, which asserts that Jesus Christ is now living as a part of the triune God and is building up his heavenly Church, the earthly Church being merely a reflection of heavenly realities; the sacraments seal or cause the earthly Church's union with the heavenly Christ, whereby the Church has a certain power over the realization of this union (medieval theology presented this view in its purest form).

b) Reformation theology's emphasis on the Word of God as the peculiar mode of the presence of Christ, culminating for instance in Bullinger's summary statement in the Second Helvetic Confession that the proclamation of the Word of God *is* the Word of God;[5] the Word, according to this understanding, has priority over the Church and the individual; a certain intellectualism can develop on this basis, and the real issue of the presence of Christ is somewhat obscured or at least limited to the gathered congregation.

c) The reliance on the strength of the mere memory of Jesus' words and works, typical of eighteenth- and part of nineteenth-century liberal theology, but also basic to what seems quite different, *viz.* mysticism with its emphasis on personal unification with Jesus (e.g. Bernard and trends in pietism); the individual, according to this understanding, has priority over both the Word and the Church.

d) Existentialist theology, which in perpetuation of at least one part of the Reformers' concern, works out the "meaningfulness" (*Bedeutsamkeit*) of the original kerygma and shows how it liberates

---

[5] Bonhoeffer in 1933 clearly elaborated his Christology on this basis, "Christology is the science of the Word of God. Christology is *logology*" (*op. cit.*, p. 28). And, summarizing his statements on the mode of the Word's presence: "This one, whole, person, the God-man Jesus Christ, is present in the church in his *pro me* structure as Word, as sacrament and as community" (p. 49). (The early) Bonhoeffer's strong emphasis on the *pro me* is a Lutheran legacy which is vulnerable to misinterpretation.

man toward a full acceptance of world reality and of his own future existence within it; this understanding not only presupposes a time-less concept of the kerygma but also the necessity of a never-ending repetition of its appropriation on the part of the believer; the Church is merely the platform on which this can happen, since the individual has priority over the Church, though not over the kerygma.

A more radical view of God's ongoing work in Jesus Christ is necessary if his relation to the Church is not to be restricted to a reenactment, however sacramental or word-centered, of his life in the past, and if the understanding of this relation is not to be dissolved into mystical-personal experience. Our "more radical view of God's ongoing work" will have to take seriously the question concerning the difference between the Exodus and the coming of Jesus. If the latter is not a repetition or reenactment of the former, and also if the latter does not devaluate and make obsolete the former, but if both are connected by God's ongoing work, we cannot escape the task of examining the relation between "earlier and later," "old and new," "past and present." The uniqueness of Jesus' resurrection is not to be sought in its violation of the laws of nature nor in its discontinuity with the events in the history of Israel, but it lies precisely in the unique *relation* to these events. In historical-exegetical language the difference between the Exodus and the coming of Jesus is this: what was perceived and declared to be true for Israel in and after the Exodus is now perceived and declared to be true for Jews and Gentiles. *This* is the significance of the "Christ-event." To say less than this is to conceive of the Christ-event as a mere stage in the quantitative increase of man's "knowledge of God," the coming of Jesus being of merely epistemological importance. But to say more than this is to declare the Christ-event to have been an ontic change of such dimensions as would be intolerable within the permissible limits of our understanding that God, while indeed "changing" or having a "history," nevertheless maintains his sameness. Such an excessive interpretation would invalidate the election of Israel and invite such meaningless questions as "What happened to people's salvation before the time of Jesus?"

Thus the relation between Jesus and the Church is inseparable from the question of the relation between Israel and the Church. It follows that a mere examination of post-Easter occurrences will not suffice. Nor will the broader (post-Bultmannian) quest concerning the continuity between the historical Jesus and the witness to the resurrected Christ sufficiently prepare for an answer to the question concerning the relation between Jesus and the Church. For our inquiry concerning this relation, our attention is indeed first focused upon the theological significance of the early post-Easter witnesses. But the texts make unmistakably clear that the earliest Easter witnesses understood what had happened in Jesus as related to what had happened to Israel in the past. Their memory of this past enabled them to understand the present occurrences which, however, in turn compelled them to correct their understanding of this memory. Moreover, the texts also make clear that the earliest witnesses' understanding of what had happened in Jesus was not such as to suggest that what had taken place was the end of God's activity. On the contrary, the expectation that Yahweh leads into ever-new stages of history, an expectation restricted before the coming of Jesus to Israel, now becomes the expectation of both Jews *and* Gentiles. There is no doubt that the earliest Easter witnesses understood what had happened at Easter in the categories of memory and hope: Jesus had become to them the *fulfillment* of Israel's hope (reinterpreting the history of Israel's specific articulations of promises) and also a new *promise* (demanding new articulations of specific promises). The resurrection marked the point in God's history with mankind at which Jesus became not only the fulfillment of what *Israel* had been permitted to hope for but also the promise to the *Gentiles* to share Israel's new hope.

This theological pre-consideration directs our attention to some basic aspects of recent New Testament research. The exegetical basis for the insight that the biblical texts do not lend themselves to the nineteenth-century "historical Jesus approach" has found the widest possible agreement since the rise of the method of *Formgeschichte* in the twentieth century. It is agreed that the post-Easter kerygma[6] is not a commentary on the historical Jesus; rather, the Pauline epistles, the (post-Pauline) Gospels and the rest of the epistles are a *commentary on Easter*. In other words, the early Christian kerygma is based upon the resurrection of Jesus. The surprising observation

---

[6] Usually I try to avoid the term "kerygma" for reasons to be explained later; cf. the warning not to overload the term by K. Goldammer, "Der Kerygma-Begriff in der älteren christlichen Literatur," ZNW, Heft ½ (1957), pp. 77–101.

must be made that Jesus himself had preached the coming of the Kingdom of God, whereas the Primitive Church made Jesus himself the content of the kerygma; his resurrection *is* the decisive act of salvation,[7] the fulfillment of the eschatological expectation of the Kingdom of God. But "resurrection" is a notion peculiar to later Jewish anthropology and theology and it may not be without danger of misunderstanding to focus our attention today on this notion rather than on the ongoing work of God in Christ. Reserving for later discussion the question whether after Easter Jesus "became" what he had not "been" before, bracketing as it were the fundamental theological question, we must now review some exegetical results.

Utilizing the views of Eduard Schweizer,[8] and partly also of Ernst Käsemann,[9] we can say that early post-Easter theology pointed in two directions. It stressed the insight that God himself has entered into history in Jesus, but it also pointed to the manhood of Jesus himself who in many ways changed the various preconceived concepts of the Messiah. The content of the first statement cannot be "proved" historically[10] but is a statement of faith, while the content

[7] See below, Chap. VI, for a reformulation of the term "salvation." Reginald H. Fuller, *The Foundations of New Testament Christology* (New York: Charles Scribner's Sons, 1965), presents an overly systematic categorization of the steps that led from Jesus' own proclamation to ever more amplified Christologies in the first few decades of the earliest Church. He centers his inquiry around christological titles almost as though these were the only point of entry into the New Testament's (implicit) Christology. Fuller also shows a dislike for "functional Christology." We will not here utilize Fuller's findings, although there are parallels between the way he sets out to ask about the resurrected Christ and our initial interest.

Cf. the interesting consensus between Protestant and Catholic New Testament research as manifest in the Catholic collection of essays *Who is Jesus of Nazareth?* Vol. 11 of *Concilium*, ed. Edward Schillebeeckx, O.P., and Boniface Willems, O.P. (New York and Glen Rock, N.J.: The Paulist Press, 1965).

[8] Eduard Schweizer, *Erniedrigung und Erhöhung bei Jesus und seinen Nachfolgern* (Zurich: Zwingli-Verlag, 1955); Engl. transl., *Lordship and Discipleship,* "Studies in Biblical Theology," No. 28, (London: SCM Press, 1960); and "Der Menschensohn," in ZNW, 1959, pp. 185 ff., and "Die historisch-kritische Bibelwissenschaft und die Verkündigungsaufgabe der Kirche," in *EvTh,* No. ½ (Jan.–Feb. 1963), pp. 31 ff.; "Die theologische Leistung des Markus," in *EvTh,* No. 7 (July 1964), pp. 337 ff.; "Die Frage nach dem historischen Jesus," in *EvTh,* No. 8 (Aug. 1964), pp. 403 ff.

[9] Ernst Käsemann, *Exegetische Versuche und Besinnungen,* Vols. I & II (Göttingen: Vandenhoeck & Ruprecht, 1960 & 1964), partly contained in *Essays on New Testament Themes,* "Studies in Biblical Theology," No. 41 (Naperville, Ill.: Alec R. Allenson, Inc., 1964).

[10] Wolfhart Pannenberg has attempted to challenge this kind of thinking in

of the second is at least to a large degree merely historical, though of course it presupposed the faith of previous generations in the coming of the Messiah.

New Testament scholarship has observed it to be highly significant that Jesus himself avoided the use of fixed titles with regard to his own person.[11] Jesus was not "his own dogmatician." Moreover, there is also widespread agreement that Jesus is not depicted in the New Testament writings as a "model of true Christian faith" or as an "example of a good Christian" (this, however, is the basis of Ebeling's Christology; one may of course think of passages such as Hebr. 5:8, 9 and 12:2, "the pioneer and perfecter of our faith," or Rom. 5:18, etc., but these refer to Jesus' vicarious obedience rather than to his "authentic existence" as the first of all believers). The majority of the earliest congregations lived exclusively by the Old Testament, by sermons, narratives, exhortations or other forms of writings based upon the Easter proclamation. Even Luke, who is suspected of having thought otherwise, reflects this fact in the first chapters of Acts, which provide summaries of early resurrection sermons.

The content of the Easter sermons may have varied according to the background of the preachers and the hearers. Though not unchallenged, Eduard Schweizer distinguishes[12] the Hellenistic congregational theology from Paul's proclamation by observing that the "exaltation of Jesus over principalities and powers" is characteristic of the former and that "the Cross and Resurrection as foundation of freedom from law, sin and death" is typical of the latter type of Easter theology. Be this as it may, the statement as such indicates what we have attempted to say in the Introduction, namely, that theology is time- and situation-bound and that one and the same question can be answered in different ways.

If it is true that the earliest congregations lived by the Old Testament and Easter sermons, why then were the Gospels written? It is

---

Offenbarung als Geschichte (ed.) (Göttingen: Vandenhoeck & Ruprecht, 1961) and now in his Christology, also to appear in a shorter version in English, *Grundzüge der Christologie* (Gütersloh: Gerd Mohn, 1964).

[11] The latest publications, dealing also with earlier works, are Werner Kramer, *Christos Kyrios Gottessohn* (Zurich: Zwingli-Verlag, 1963), and Ferdinand Hahn, *Christologische Hoheitstitel im Neuen Testament* (Göttingen: Vandenhoeck & Ruprecht, 1963).

[12] *EvTh*, No. 7 (July 1964), p. 337; and No. 8 (Aug. 1964), p. 404. Cf. also Willi Marxen, *Die Auferstehung Jesu als historisches und theologisches Problem* (Gütersloh: Gerd Mohn, 1964).

historically clear that the Synoptic Gospels began to appear in written form for the wider use of the Church about a decade after the Easter-theology epistles had already fed the congregations. Why was this new form of theological expression necessary? Why did not Paul sense the necessity of mentioning the "historical Jesus"? The answer is summarized by Eduard Schweizer—and this is not challenged—that " the witnesses of the New Testament fall back on the life of the historical Jesus wherever faith was in danger of deteriorating into mere theory."[13] In other words: the "post-Pauline" Gospels are a commentary on the early Easter kerygma and a corrective to a possibly half-understood Pauline theology or to other types of early Easter theology. Dogmatically speaking, this means that the earliest congregations saw themselves as constituted by the resurrected Christ and sufficiently fed by a theology based upon his resurrection. The emphasis on the true humanity of Jesus became necessary only after this, i.e. only after it had occurred to some to question the reality of his humanity. And it is obvious that those who provided this new emphasis as a corrective did not find themselves in disagreement with Paul and the other "Easter theologians." The absence of "disagreement" does not imply that one emphasizes the same point. We can omit at this point a discussion of Luke's theology, of which some say that it has a different emphasis and intent.[14] This omission is justified, for it is not disputed, not even by Conzelmann, that Luke also stressed the importance of the presence of Christ in the Spirit, which is our primary interest here. There are some open questions, however, which spring from these observations. What happens to the post-Easter Jesus Christ and to the Church when his presence is proclaimed? What does this proclamation mean christologically and ecclesiologically? And what is the outcome of this when looking at it historically?

Pannenberg, attempting to do justice both to history and to the post-Easter Jesus, advances the thesis that God's final revelation is still to be expected at the termination of world history. If this view should endanger the once-and-for-all character of the "Christ-event" by making history itself identical with revelation, the only other

---

[13] *EvTh*, No. 8 (Aug. 1964), p. 415.
[14] E.g. Hans Conzelmann, *Die Mitte der Zeit* (Tübingen: J.C.B. Mohr, 3rd ed., 1960); Engl. transl., *The Theology of St. Luke*, by Geoffrey Buswell, (New York: Harper & Row, 1960).

choice seems, at first sight, to be Bultmann's and C. H. Dodd's concept of the "eschatological event" in the present. To avoid this one may work toward a modification of Pannenberg's view, as does Moltmann[15] by elaborating further a modified Barthian eschatology. In any case, it is clear that the *Christus praesens* concept demands an eschatological corrective, lest Christology become historicizing science concerning a man of the past, Jesus of Nazareth, or a theory, a de-historicized form of wisdom. We will have to keep in mind this problem as we come back to the question of eschatology in later chapters.

We may observe that in fact there seems to be a strong interest, in traditional and contemporary theology, in saying that the Jesus Christ we are talking about *is* the *Christus praesens*, or the *Christus praedicatus*, the proclaimed Christ, or the "Jesus Christ who proclaims himself" (Hermann Diem). At first sight, this concern includes the Reformation confessional statements, and modern systematic theology related to this tradition, as well as New Testament scholarship in the Bultmannian tradition and also such an author as Paul van Buren. In fact, classical conciliar Christology operated with the same conviction without having made that fact expressly clear.

But why, we ask, has this apparent consensus led to such extremely different and contradictory theologies? Obviously, one and the same concern or statement (in this case *"Christus praesens"*), made by different theologians and at different times, may not necessarily reflect the same theological thought. As far as the content is concerned, the various advocates of "Easter theology" have not at all intended to say the same thing. *"Christus praesens"* can mean sacramental "representation," or presence of the Spirit as the Word is preached, or worshipful "reenactment" of the Christ-event of the past, or "encounter" with the kerygma (Bultmann), or even the statement that "Jesus' freedom is contagious" (van Buren). And all of those approaches can actually utilize and accept as historical information the exegetical results just outlined. This is to say that a consensus concerning the interpretation of the earliest Easter witnesses' statements does not automatically lead to a consensus concerning the mode of the presence of Christ today. If, theoretically

---

[15] Jürgen Moltmann, *Theologie der Hoffnung*, some of which is already contained in "Exegese und Eschatologie der Geschichte," in *EvTh*, No. ½ (Jan.–Feb. 1962), pp. 31 ff.

speaking, New Testament scholarship should reach a total consensus regarding the interpretation of all resurrection passages, the question of the relation between Jesus and the Church today would not at all be settled.

The traditional Western understanding of the technical term *Christus praesens* and of its more recent paraphrases, such as "Jesus Christ who proclaims himself," is merely a prolongation of the Christ of the past into the present. The radical implications of faith in the resurrected Christ, i.e. the consequences of the *Christus praesens* for Church and world have seldom been taken seriously. For most of Western theology, and Protestant theology in particular, these implications were unpleasant, for they indeed lead to an understanding of the Church and of Scripture and tradition which is considered unfortunate, if not unacceptable, by traditional Protestant theology (to which Bultmann and Ebeling still adhere with their ultimately undefined respect for the Biblical canon). Most quarters of Protestant scholarship, when dealing with the "post-Easter kerygma," think in fact of what we called "the historical-resurrected Christ." There is a way of dealing historically with the Easter kerygma of the earliest congregations as if this had nothing to contribute to our present existence as the Church, although it is only *as* those who *are* the Church that we can deal with the Easter kerygma at all.[16] Protestant theology's substitute for the true understanding of the *Christus praesens* has become the doctrine of justification, irrespective of whether it appears in the dress of classical Reformation concepts or in the form of a theology of existence. Thus it was actually the doctrine of justification which shaped Protestant ecclesiology; because of this, it would be understandable if the charge of having neglected the connection between Christology and ecclesiology were not accepted. Bultmann, and even more so Ebeling, would insist that they have kept the Church in mind when speaking of Easter. Here is a source of basic misunderstanding and confusion. Their starting point is not the presence of Christ in the Church, but the historical accounts of the early witnesses to the resurrection.

We must maintain, however, that Jesus Christ is *recognized only*

---

[16] Besides John Knox (*vide* Introduction, FN 11), Richard R. Niebuhr, *Resurrection and Historical Reason* (New York: Charles Scribner's Sons, 1957), has been disturbed by this observation; cf. the chapters "The Solitary Exister" (pp. 51 ff.) and "The Remembering Church" (pp. 62 ff.); but he does not unfold his critical insight.

in the Church. ("No one can say 'Jesus is Lord' except by the Holy Spirit," I Cor. 12:3b, RSV.) A subthesis of this statement would be the affirmation that according to the New Testament the "upbuilding of the Church" and the service of the Church is more important than the justification of the individual. This need not be expounded here, since Karl Barth has made this a main emphasis in his *Church Dogmatics*, expecially in IV, 1, where the doctrine of justification is part of the doctrine of reconciliation and, more generally, of the "obedience of the Son of God." Our interest in this chapter is more narrowly confined to the question of how Jesus Christ, past and present, is recognized in the Church. By saying that Jesus Christ is recognized only in the Church, we point to a state of affairs which is of cardinal importance. Inasmuch as the earliest Easter witnesses were able to speak of the risen Christ as Israel's fulfillment and as the Jews' and the Gentiles' hope only because of the "appearances" of the risen Christ, the believers of any generation in later centuries are able to recognize him (as the present One in whatever appropriate definitions and designations) *only because of his presence.* Whatever the Early Church's consciousness was, it was shaped by her memory of Israel's expectations in the light of the appearances of Christ as the fulfillment of these expectations. And this "shaping" is the work of the *Christus praesens.* In other words, the Church is the *locus* of the "intentionality" of perceiving in an appropriate way the presence of Christ. The Church is the matrix within which the understanding of Israel's Bible and of the New Testament is possible. The "corporate consciousness" if this term may be used here without further definition—of the Church is the climate within which is uttered the creed which says that the understanding of Jesus Christ is caused by Jesus Christ's presence. The peculiar logic of what Yahweh has done with Israel, and in Jesus with both Jews and Gentiles, is only accessible to the intentionality which is characteristic of the Church, and of which the Church confesses that it is the very work of the *Christus praesens.* In short, the "effect" of the presence of Christ in the Church is not merely the believers' interest in the Bible and in Israel (or worse: in their own justification), but it is the establishment of the climate within which, or intentionality with which, Yahweh's present and future work can be perceived, expected and praised.

Classical Christology, however, was not primarily interested in the present function of the risen Christ, although the Greek Fathers cer-

tainly presupposed this interest implicitly. But on the whole, especially in the West, classical Christology focused upon the task of
defining who the God-man Jesus might have been when compared
with the supposedly non-controversial entities "God" or divinity and
"man" or humanity. And their interest was primarily in the *divinity*
of Jesus Christ (which they initially thought was less problematical
than his humanity), perhaps because of the predominant interest in
God's *revelation* in Christ, so typical of Christian theology since (at
the latest) its contact with Gnosticism. Jesus' humanity was stressed
only in order to guarantee the reality of his death, i.e. in an anti-
docetic manner. Despite this intent, a docetic tendency has been
characteristic of almost all theology since the time of the Cappadocians. It was at that time, if not before, that a superhuman or
"sacred" concept of humanity began to mold the definition of the
"true humanity" of Jesus. Peter Lombard as well as Thomas
Aquinas deepened this docetic tendency, which was not fully overcome by the Reformers either. Today we must search for a Christology which takes Jesus Christ's humanity as seriously as it does his
resurrection, to avoid the expression "divinity." But the term
"humanity" is also complicated. The two corresponding notions,
when Jesus Christ is recognized in the Church, should not be "humanity" and "divinity," or "human nature" and "divine nature," but
rather the "obedience" of Jesus and the "rule" or "claim" of Christ.
The former terms are static in nature and it is well known that
classical Christology tended toward static thinking despite the attempts of later Reformation theology to give some flesh and blood to
this static picture.[17]

The old nature-Christology was expressed in "objectifying language." As soon, however, as one tries to escape from the realm of
the objectivity of these definitions, in order to do justice to Christ's
work *for us* (*Christus pro me*, or *pro nobis*), it is almost unavoidable
that one emphasizes one "nature" at the expense of the other. This is
precisely what happened to medieval soteriology and also to the
soteriological Christology of the Reformers. The divine nature was
stressed at the expense of the human nature.

[17] Martin Chemnitz, in *De duabus naturis in Christo*, 1570, introduced the
time concept into classical Christology which became, in Johann Gerhard's
Loci theologici, 1610–1622 (IV, 14), the *status* doctrine: to the Chalcedonian concept is added the importance of the exalted and the humiliated *status*
of Christ.

It is understandable that the various forms of contemporary theology of existence have attempted to depart radically from this form of thinking. An early stage of the development toward this end can be detected in Albrecht Ritschl's criticism of classical nature-Christology,[18] then in Wilhelm Herrmann, until—interrupted by Barth's Christology—Bultmann and Ebeling have ventured to elaborate what they consider a really appropriate and understandable Christology (although they do not call it this).[19] Their approach, however, is not as radically new as it may appear. It is indebted to the traditional Western concept of God, which found its first, and at the same time most perfect, expression in Augustine's theology. Jesus Christ recognized in the Church becomes in Bultmann's and Ebeling's theology "Jesus Christ recognized by faith," and "faith" is initiated by Jesus.[20] The historical Jesus becomes the initiator of the faith, which recognizes him as the "risen Christ," which is to say that *Jesus has risen into the kerygma.* This conclusion circumvents the understanding of the resurrection "as such" (which, of course, is not the interest of this theology), but it seems to solve the question of the *Christus praesens.* He is present in the proclamation of the kerygma. Is this not in line with Luther and Calvin, who insisted that when the Word is preached Jesus Christ's own voice is heard? The answer to this question is indeed complicated. Part of it will have to be affirmative; the other part will necessitate the critical question: Is this Jesus (who has risen into the kerygma) unique, or is he exchangeable in his function as initiator of my faith? Why could not Paul perform the same function? Or even Gandhi? While certainly not Bultmann, and perhaps not even Ebeling, are open to this charge, it is clear that Schubert Ogden[21] has drawn the consequences from their theology by actually having reached this problematical openness. Paul van

---

[18] Albrecht Ritschl, A *Critical History of the Doctrine of Christian Justification and Reconciliation,* Engl. transl. by J. S. Black (Edinburgh: Edmonston and Douglas, 1872).

[19] Except for chap. IV of Gerhard Ebeling's book, *Theologie und Verkündigung* (Tübingen: J. C. B. Mohr, 1962), now in English translation by John Riches as *Theology and Proclamation* (Philadelphia: Fortress Press, 1966).

[20] Cf. Gerhard Ebeling, *The Nature of Faith,* translated by Ronald Gregor Smith (Philadelphia: Muhlenberg Press, 1961), chap. IV and *passim.* Cf. also *Word and Faith,* translated by James W. Leitch (Philadelphia: Fortress Press, 1963), chap. VII, "Jesus and Faith" (pp. 201 ff.).

[21] Schubert M. Ogden, *Christ Without Myth* (New York: Harper & Row, 1961); cf. also the recent collection of essays *The Reality of God* (New York: Harper & Row, 1966), *passim.*

Buren takes issue with Ogden with admirable clarity,[22] though van Buren himself has not made it crystal clear why his Jesus is not exchangeable for someone else.

But even if Jesus is not exchangeable, is the affirmation helpful which describes the presence of Christ today in the form of an extension of the historical result of the resurrection, of which, in turn, it is rightly said that it cannot be grasped historically? To proceed in this way is to affirm a docetism in reverse: the humanity of Jesus before Easter was necessary in order to make possible the belief in his presence after Easter. This, however, remains an utterly theoretical assertion which does not make credible his presence today, nor does it in any way make meaningful an invitation to *hope*. A demonstration of this can be found in Ebeling's *The Nature of Faith*, which, in its last chapter, "The Future of Faith," is totally void of any indication of future activities of God and, consequently, of hope on the part of the Christians. Faith, according to Ebeling, only liberates man to face the present world-reality and to expect that he will be able to continue with this in the future. Who, then, is the Jesus Christ who is said to be present in the proclamation of the Word in the Church? The *act of recognition*, faith itself, becomes the *content* of what is to be said of Jesus Christ. But if this is so, can we then still speak of the Church as the realm in which Jesus Christ is recognized? This would hardly be necessary, and the fact is that neither Bultmann nor Ebeling see any reasons for doing so. Their intent is to elaborate, in modern form, individual justification, which they consider the cardinal doctrine of the Christian faith. This emphasis, we must maintain, is indeed the fundamental interest of Western theology in its traditional form. The interest in the believer is by far overshadowing the interest in Christ.

Early Western theology received from the Greek Church fixed christological formulae which did not fit into Western ecclesiology; the doctrine of justification had to provide the link between the two. This is a seemingly simple historical observation, although it is of great importance for the whole development of Western theology from Augustine to Bultmann. The Western Church, beginning with Tertullian and Cyprian, was primarily interested in the systematization of the understanding of the empirical Church. This was never the interest of the Greek Fathers. But it was from them that Christology received its dogmatically balanced and scholastically detailed

[22] *Op. cit.*, pp. 57 ff.

shape. The Western Church, including the Middle Ages and the Reformation, added little to classical Greek Christology.[23] The Eastern results were merely accepted by the West. But the Nicene and Chalcedonian formulations obviously did not fit smoothly into a theology which was preoccupied with such questions as repentance, dealing with the "lapsed," the sacraments, the definition of the episcopate and the like. Thus Augustine (if he had a Christology at all) and the later Fathers, including Luther, Calvin and especially Melanchthon, concentrated on the question: How does this Jesus Christ, so defined in conciliar theology, effect my salvation, or my status in the Church or my relation to God? And it was Augustine who first embraced this whole complex of questions by starting with an anthropological notion of faith: Faith is a noetic-cognitive notion which is in competition—and that means parallel—with other forms of cognition.

Justification has become the test-question of all Reformation theology and, as we learn today, partly also of Roman Catholic dogmatics. This has its merits and to deny them would be very unwise. Nevertheless, the time has come for asking the critical question whether the Old and New Testaments invite us to emphasize justification at the expense of a much broader and less individualistic view. Such an emphasis leads almost irresistibly to the interest in an *ordo salutis*, a systematized description of the "steps" leading to salvation.[24] After all, other interpretations are entirely possible. Irenaeus, for instance, who rediscovered for the Church the Pauline epistles, interpreted Paul from his Spirit passages, not from the concept of justification. Today we await eagerly Ernst Käsemann's new findings in the realm of these questions.[25] Existential analysis in contemporary theology, however, still finds itself completely impris-

---

[23] Cf. Jan Koopmans, *Das altkirchliche Dogma in der Reformation* (Munich: Chr. Kaiser, 1955). The Reformers' actual contribution to theology consists of their unfolding of the doctrine of justification. The early council decisions remained as unchallenged to them as they had to Augustine's mind.

[24] This is typical of Protestant scholasticism and popular piety and also of Roman Catholic dogmatics; cf. the *Decretum* and the *Canones de iustificatione*, Council of Trent, *Sessio VI, Denz.* 792a–843.

[25] *Op. cit.*, Vol. II, the essays "*Neutestamentliche Fragen von heute*," pp. 11 ff., and "*Gottesgerechtigkeit bei Paulus*," pp. 181 ff. We may also refer to the publications by Johannes Munck, W. D. Davies and, especially, Kurt Stalder, "*Das Werk des Geistes in der Heiligung bei Paulus*" (Zurich: EVZ-Verlag, 1962). An important step in a new direction is indicated in K. Stendahl's article "The Apostle Paul and the Introspective Conscience of the West," *HThR, LVI* (July 1963), 199 ff.

oned by the main structures of Western theology's interest in justification. This permits the somewhat exaggerated statement that there is
ultimately little dogmatical difference between the theologies of
Augustine, Billy Graham and Rudolf Bultmann. They all ask: How
can I hear from these ancient texts that God's work in Jesus Christ
now calls *me* to a decision which will *mean freedom* and *salvation* for
me in the future?

It is most important that whatever procedure of christological
thinking one decides upon one must not lose sight of the "history-
embracing" dimension of God in Jesus Christ about which we as the
Church can think and speak only as those who are in history. But our
approach must not be "historical" in the sense of merely investigating the past events of Jesus' crucifixion and resurrection and their
"relevance" to our time; rather, it must be "historical" in the sense of
looking in faith forward and backward at the same time, for it is only
then that we grasp the present. And it is in the so-defined present, i.e.
in our existence in and as the Church, that we can speak of the
Christus praesens at all. If we were not there, we would indeed do
better to look for the wisdom of Socrates or of Gandhi.

b) Continuity and Contingency in History

What is the "history-embracing" dimension of God in Jesus
Christ? Our christological thoughts have compelled us to move close
to the border of the contemporary discussion of the "meaning of
history." This discussion has produced an enormous amount of literature.[26] It is, of course, not our task here to review this literature or
to take issue with the various theories advocated in it. But we must
examine some of those aspects of the contemporary discussion which
have a direct bearing on Christology, although only within the limita-

---

[26] A substantial part of the recent and current publications is surveyed and partly
evaluated by Alan Richardson, *History Sacred and Profane* (Philadelphia:
Westminster Press, 1964); cf. also my essay *The Theological Significance of
History* (Vol. LXXV, No. 6 [Apr. 1960] *Austin Seminary Bulletin*). Cf. also
Hendrikus Berkhof, *Christ the Meaning of History* (Richmond: John Knox
Press, 1966), transl. from the 4th Dutch edition by Lambertus Buurman. Berkhof makes Jesus' own history appear as a key to the understanding of all history. This approach is still past-centered, for all that is to be expected for the
future is confined to the direct or indirect impact of the "missionary en-
deavour" (see pp. 81 ff. and 180 ff.). This is, in essence, a version of the
Christus prolongatus theory, as one may call it.

tions of our specific interest in Christology as crystallized in the question concerning Christ's presence today in relation to the principle "No revelation after Ezra" as applied to the apostolic era.

We can safely presuppose a consensus among contemporary theologians on both sides of the Atlantic regarding the inadequacy or even the impossibility of nineteenth-century "historicism" or historical positivism. None of the present authors who is of interest to us seriously advocates that we must continue with the method of asking exclusively "what really happened in the past" in order to find the clue to theological problems. But what are the alternatives that seem open today? The various attempts to overcome the last century's historicism seem to have led to two approaches to the "meaning of history": (1) to a renewal of the concept of "redemptive history" and (2) to existentialist theology. The former operates with a distinction between (divine) suprahistory and ordinary world history, while the latter focuses upon the "meaningfulness" (*Bedeutsamkeit*) of past events, thus concentrating on the historicity of the individual existence. It must be noted that these two approaches are not mutually exclusive.

The first type, the idea of *Heilsgeschichte*,[27] i.e. the idea of an inner kernel or hidden meaning of world history, distinct from it but giving meaning to it, is, of course, not new in the history of theology. Theophilus of Antioch and Irenaeus were its first advocates. But the modification and application of it, presented by Tillich's old teacher Martin Kähler,[28] are what interest us today. Its advantage over nineteenth-century historicism was and still is obvious: faith does not rest upon the historical-critical findings about the "historical Jesus" but rather is concerned with and caused by the Christ preached by the post-Easter witnesses. Thus Kähler operates with two concepts of history. They reappear in Bultmann's distinction between *Historie* and *Geschichte*, although Bultmann did not adopt Kähler's interest in redemptive history. One must judge, in fact, that Bultmann's double

---

[27] Cf. Karl Gerhard Steck, *Die Idee der Heilsgeschichte* (Zollikon: EVZ-Verlag, 1959), for an analysis of Hofmann, Schlatter and Cullmann; and Cullmann's own exposition of his concept of redemptive history in his recent book *Heil als Geschichte* (Tübingen: J. C. B. Mohr, 1965), especially Part 5, pp. 268–313.

[28] Martin Kähler, *Der sogenannte historische Jesus und der geschichtliche biblische Christus*, 1892 (new edition, Munich: Chr. Kaiser Verlag, 1953); Engl. transl., *The So-Called Historical Jesus and the Historic, Biblical Christ* (Philadelphia: Fortress Press, 1964).

concept is not thoroughly clear.[29] The reason for this may be the fact that Bultmann was not able to share Kähler's view of redemptive history,[30] although it is only this particular view which necessitates a double concept of history. The chief criticism of the concept of redemptive history, as distinct from "ordinary history," however, also applies to Bultmann's, Gogarten's and the so-called post-Bultmannian theologies, irrespective of their affinity with a concept of redemptive history. Both approaches, redemptive history and existentialist theology, depreciate "ordinary world history." In either case Jesus Christ is disconnected in one way or another from world history. What for one group is suprahistory is for the other group an "eschatological event" of meaningfulness to the "solitary exister" (a term of R. R. Niebuhr). The similarity between the two groups should not be surprising; both the theology of *Heilsgeschichte* and existentialist theology, different as they indeed are, have one and the same source, namely, the reaction against the historicism of the last century.

The second type of interpretation of the "meaning of history," existentialist theology, is very much at the center of current theological discussions. A brief review[31] of its main points and some critical remarks are necessary and inevitable steps toward the further development of our thesis concerning the *Christus praesens*.

Existentialist theology is concerned with "hermeneutics" only in a secondary way. Its primary interest is the question of how past events, and the records related to them, are relevant to the present. Today a broader usage of the term "hermeneutics" includes the various aspects of this primary interest. But the question of the relation of past events to the present is not limited to events recorded in the Bible.[32] The new approach to history, utilized by existentialist

29 So, e.g. Heinrich Ott, *Die Frage nach dem historischen Jesus und die Ontologie der Geschichte* (Zurich, EVZ–Verlag, 1960), p. 7.

30 Cf. Heinrich Ott, *Geschichte und Heilsgeschichte in der Theologie Rudolf Bultmanns* (Tübingen: J. C. B. Mohr, 1955), and recently "Rudolf Bultmann's Philosophy of History," in *The Theology of Rudolf Bultmann*, ed. Charles W. Kegley (New York: Harper & Row, 1966), pp. 51 ff.

31 For part of the following analysis and for the location of some illustrative quotations in English translations of German books, I am indebted to a seminar paper by the Rev. Robert N. Van Wyk, a former student at Pittsburgh Theological Seminary.

32 For an excellent history of the term "hermeneutic," and for the inquiry itself, see James M. Robinson, *The New Hermeneutic*, pp. 1–77.

theology, is said to have been advocated by Wilhelm Dilthey, Benedetto Croce, R. G. Collingwood and some others. While these philosophers and historians concerned themselves with the relation between past events and the present, it was a part of Martin Heidegger's philosophy which was utilized to analyze *the existence, or the self-understanding, of the individual who finds himself related to past events* in the manner allegedly described by Collingwood and others. Thus existentialist theology has accepted from various philosophers and historians a new concept of the relation between past and present, and from Heidegger a new concept of the analysis of existence itself. This summary statement, however, does not reflect the true complexity of what has happened to theology during the last few decades. The sequence of events was confusing; Heidegger's thoughts were utilized by theology long before Collingwood's approach to history began to appear on the theological scene. While Bultmann himself started with Heidegger's analysis of existence and paid attention to Collingwood only later, the so-called post-Bultmannians started with Collingwood's stimulating thinking about history, or with Bultmann's summarizing conclusions, and only then began to ask the extent to which Heidegger's analysis could be utilized. This difference is the reason for the partial disagreement between Bultmann and his younger pupils. Our main concern at this point is Collingwood's thinking about history and its influence upon recent theology.

The historian, according to Collingwood, has no events which he can study. The events as such are gone. The historian can deal only with evidence of past events, with documents which are in themselves interpretations of the events. But the documents do not bring back the events. The events "have finished happening before he begins thinking about them. He has to re-create them inside his own mind, re-enacting for himself so much of the experience of the men who took part in them as he wishes to understand."[33] What he understands, then, is neither the event as such nor any general law of the development of history but the inside of the events, that is, the thoughts or the self-knowledge of men. "History is thus the self-knowledge of the living mind. For even when the events which the historian studies are events that happened in the distant past, the condition of their being

---

[33] R. G. Collingwood, *The Idea of History* (New York: Oxford University Press, 1956; first English edition, 1946), p. 97.

historically known is that they should 'vibrate in the historian's mind,' that is to say, that the evidence for them should be here and now before him and intelligible to him."[34] Collingwood maintains that while the process of nature can be properly described as sequences of mere events, events of history cannot. They are not processes of "mere events" but "processes of actions, which have an inner side, consisting of processes of thought; and what the historian is looking for is these processes of thought. All history is the history of thought."[35] There is "only one way" in which the historian can discern the thoughts which he is trying to study: "by re-thinking them in his own mind."[36] Collingwood calls this thinking process "reenactment." The historian reenacts past thoughts in the context of his own situation and knowledge. This is a "labor of active and therefore critical thinking"[37] which shapes the historian's own self-understanding.

It is obvious that this approach to history leaves no room for general philosophical or theological laws or principles under which the multiplicity of human life could be subsumed. No general principle causes or guides the development of history. Rather, throwing off the yoke of such principles, the new approach to history reverses the process and subsumes everything under the categories of history of human thought, thereby turning a methodological principle into a philosophical assertion (formulation by Van Wyk). The basic reality is reality of human thought.[38] This conclusion will be of great interest when compared with Bultmann's concept of the kerygma.

Bultmann agrees with Collingwood that the understanding of history is guided by a "pre-understanding."[39] Collingwood had formu-

[34] *Ibid.*, p. 202.
[35] *Ibid.*, p. 215.
[36] *Ibid.*
[37] *Ibid.*
[38] Cf. the statement by Ortega y Gasset, in *Toward a Philosophy of History* (New York: W. W. Norton & Co., 1941), pp. 212 ff.: "Let us say, then, not that man *is*, but that he *lives* . . . Man is what has happened to him, what he has done . . . Man, in a word, has not nature; what he has is . . . history . . . Man finds that he has no nature other than what he himself has done."
[39] Rudolf Bultmann, *History and Eschatology*, The Gifford Lectures, 1955 (Edinburgh: University Press, 1957), p. 113, *passim.* Yet, Bultmann may not have done full justice to Collingwood. This point is elaborated by Jasper Hopkins in "Bultmann on Collingwood's Philosophy of History," *HThR*, LVIII (Apr. 1955), pp. 227 ff. Hopkins attempts to show that Bultmann has tendentiously interpreted Collingwood with terms of kerygma theology and

lated it like this: "What particular parts and aspects of the past we now recall by historical thought depends on our present interest and attitude towards life."[40] This, in itself, is not a controversial statement. Historians have always known that one cannot avoid applying a selective principle in historiography. What is new and controversial, however, is the evaluation of the need of selectivity. Since history is the "self-knowledge of the living mind,"[41] or, in the words of Bultmann, "existential knowledge,"[42] history is reduced to the historicity (*Geschichtlichkeit*) of the individual who is concerned with history. What really matters happens in the present.

History is of interest only insofar as it allows or perfects self-knowledge. Self-knowledge is necessary because it is the nature of man to live in confrontation with decisions, and these, in turn, are conditioned by the past. Bultmann, therefore, qualifies the term "self-knowledge" by saying that "self-knowledge is consciousness of responsibility over against the future."[43] He claims that the historicity of the human being is completely understood when seen in the light of responsibility over against the future. This responsibility *is* decision. Bultmann seems to feel that this aspect is neglected in Collingwood, whose whole concept appears to him not deep enough, or, may we say, not pessimistic enough? Man's decisions are conditioned by his own past. Man is not free to decide, but he must decide, lest he be irresponsible.

It is at this point that Bultmann suddenly speaks "theologically." Not unlike Augustine, Bultmann makes *sin or the human predicament the starting point of theology.* Man needs a new self-understanding. He cannot speak to himself the word of liberation. He must receive it. It is the kerygma. The encounter with the kerygma calls for a decision which will free man from his own past and liberate him to a new self-knowledge. This liberation, i.e. faith, takes the believer

---

Heidegger's philosophy in order to support his own position. Hopkins' points are convincing, except for the statement (p. 230) that "Bultmann would not be likely to subscribe to the doctrine of eternal thoughts and repetition of acts of thinking." I believe that Bultmann's structural understanding of the kerygma is indeed similar to Collingwood's metaphysical concept of eternal thoughts, i.e. thoughts which are outside time and which therefore can be repeated.

[40] Collingwood, *op. cit.* p. 203.
[41] *Ibid.*, p. 202, *passim.*
[42] Bultmann, *op. cit.*, pp. 119–122, 133.
[43] *Ibid.*, p. 136.

out of the world into an unworldly existence, although he remains within the world, within his historicity. "The paradox of Christ as the historical Jesus and the ever-present Lord" makes this possible. In faith, the believer "is already above time and history. For although the advent of Christ is an historical event which happened 'once' in the past, it is, at the same time, an eternal event which occurs again and again in the soul of any Christian in whose soul Christ is born, suffers, dies and is raised up to eternal life.[44] Thus the Christian becomes a "contemporary of Christ" and "time and the world's history are overcome."[45] This paradoxical existence of the Christian is compared by Bultmann with "the Lutheran statement *simul iustus, simul peccator*"[46] (at the same time righteous and a sinner). Bultmann concludes his book by stating that the meaning of history always lies in the present: when the present is understood as the eschatological present, then the meaning of history is realized. "In every moment slumbers the possibility of being the eschatological moment. You must awaken it."[47]

One must really marvel at Bultmann's courage in uttering such sentences. He knows as well as do his critics that he has reached conclusions typical of eighteenth-century pietism and of other forms of utterly subjective theology. But he knows that he has reached these by coming from a totally different presupposition. Nevertheless, the conclusions are what matter.

Bultmann's concept of the "eschatological event" as being present in the believer's life fits in well with Collingwood's concept of history. The kerygma of the Early Church now "vibrates in the mind" of the historian, that is, theologically speaking, of the believer. Past events are important to the believer only insofar as they stimulate the "vibration" in the believer's mind which leads to a new self-understanding. Collingwood's "vibrating mind" becomes in Bultmann "faith" caused by the kerygma. The original appearing of Jesus Christ has no significance in itself apart from the believer's present interest and desire (shaped by his predicament), except perhaps for the one fact that it itself was the initial proclamation of the kerygma which permits it to be repeatedly proclaimed. What may remain important about the original appearing of Jesus Christ is, conse-

[44] *Ibid.*, p. 153.
[45] *Ibid.*
[46] *Ibid.*, p. 154.
[47] *Ibid.*, p. 155.

quently, the crucifixion and the resurrection. But the resurrection is already interpreted as the raising of Jesus into the kerygma, which thus leaves the crucifixion. But even the latter's significance has little to do with the original event but rather with the believer's being crucified with Christ, and therefore with its being an ever-present reality. This is the concept of the *Christus praesens* according to Bultmann.

A number of critical remarks would be in order here; e.g. history is replaced by an existentialist interest in soteriology; the form of the believer's predicament will shape his understanding of the kerygma; this theology has no place for the Church except in the sense that there are to be some people who proclaim to others the kerygma: the Church, then, is the contemporary form of Cyprian's and Augustine's institution for salvation. At this point, however, we only want to register such critical observations. We must first proceed with our brief review of existentialist theology's approach to history.

Today's existentialist theology, largely based upon or at least initially sympathetic to Bultmann, shows two more or less distinctly profiled shapes. One group of writers, e.g. the early Fritz Buri[48] and especially Schubert Ogden, have loosened Bultmann's connection between the past and the eschatological present. The other group, e.g. represented by James M. Robinson and most impressively by Gerhard Ebeling, have tightened the connection between the eschatological present and the past; the "past" is, according to their thinking, anchored in the historical Jesus.

Ogden makes his point quite clear by summarizing Bultmann's position, as he understands it, as being inconsistent with regard to the historical importance of the historical event of Jesus of Nazareth.[49] Ogden himself provides, as an alternative to Bultmann, the thesis that "Christian faith is to be interpreted exhaustively and without remainder as man's original possibility of authentic existence as this is clarified and conceptualized by an appropriate philosophical analysis."[50] Although Ogden wants to understand faith on the basis of the "unconditioned gift and demand of God's love," decisively manifest

---

[48] Buri's more recent publications, e.g. *Das dreifache Heilswerk Christi und seine Aneignung im Glauben* (Hamburg: Evangelischer Verlag, 1962) and collections of sermons, as well as stimulating personal conversations, have convinced me that Buri no longer belongs exclusively to the group here mentioned.

[49] Ogden, *op. cit.*, p. 112.

[50] *Ibid.*, p. 146.

in the event of Jesus of Nazareth, he interprets this gift as the "ever-present ground and end of all created things."[51] Van Buren, there-fore, judges that "the particular, historical prerequisite for faith, which is the event of Jesus of Nazareth, has been replaced by a universal and omnipresent prerequisite or cause." And he concludes that "in presenting 'Christ without myth,' Ogden has also made room for faith without Christ, or at least without a 'Christ' bound up with the historical man Jesus of Nazareth."[52] We will see later that this position is not far removed from extreme Augustinianism. Theology, and more particularly Christology, has thus been transformed into "pistology," that is to say, into an "appropriate philosophical analy-sis" of *faith*, leading to "authentic existence," as the sole center of theology. Again we briefly register critically the result: In addition to Bultmann's depreciation of history and neglect of the Church, Ogden relativizes Jesus of Nazareth by pushing Bultmann's concepts to the utmost extreme so that the new self-understanding becomes a prin-ciple inherent in human nature. It is only consistent that Ogden has recently joined those who seek, aided by Whitehead's metaphysics, new avenues toward an understanding of God in his relation to na-ture.

It is precisely at this point that Robinson and Ebeling see the danger. Whatever our discontent with their views may be, they are beyond the suspicion of having reached their conclusions by neglect-ing exegetical and historical work. Robinson states that the kerygma is located in the saving event of a historical person. "The kerygma is not the objectification of a new, 'Christian' religious principle, but rather the objectification of a historical encounter with God."[53] Referring favorably to Bornkamm and Fuchs, Robinson asserts that what is seen in and through the kerygma is Jesus himself, in whom "transcendence becomes possible."[54] Ebeling goes even further, "for faith is manifestly not Christian faith if it does not have a basis

---

[51] *Ibid.*, p. 153.
[52] Van Buren, *op. cit.*, p. 63.
[53] Robinson, *A New Quest of the Historical Jesus*, "Studies in Biblical Theology," No. 25 (London: SCM Press, 1959), p. 84.
[54] *Ibid.*, p. 50. I quote this in order to show that Robinson takes great pains to anchor the kerygma in history. It is interesting to compare this basically Continental approach with the method typical of the Scandinavian interest in transmission of tradition, e.g. in Birger Gerhardsson, *Tradition and Trans-mission in Early Christianity* (Lund: C. W. K. Gleerup, 1964, No. XX of *Coniectanea Neotestamentica*), esp. pp. 13 ff., and 40 ff.

in the historical Jesus himself."[55] Jesus "as he comes to be known by strictly historical methods,"[56] is again the starting point and basis of theology, because "if it were to be shown that Christology had no basis in the historical Jesus but was a misinterpretation of Jesus, then that would put an end to Christology."[57] This is also the view of Bornkamm, Fuchs and Käsemann, the last of whom actually had reopened the whole discussion on the "historical Jesus" in 1953.

This new concern with history is not in any way, however, a repudiation of the Dilthey-Croce-Collingwood approach, but rather remains truer to those men than did Bultmann. As with Bultmann, the new concern with history is a concern with the historicity (*Geschichtlichkeit*) of the individual man, but also with the historicity of the man Jesus. Bultmann knew of only one access to Jesus Christ, the encounter with the post-Easter kerygma. The so-called post-Bultmannians know of "two avenues of encounter with Jesus."[58] In the traditional language of theology we could say that Bultmann had reduced faith to *fides salvifica*, while the "new quest" approach reintroduces the concept of *fides historica* in addition to *fides salvifica*. The aim is, however, to relate the two (historically!) in such fashion that the unfortunate split between them, typical of traditional theology, is avoided. But the price for this is high: what *fides historica* knows about the historical Jesus is shaped by our present concern for authentic existence. We learn from Jesus' intentions, commitments, from his faith and self-understanding, that he accepted his death and living "out of transcendence."[59] The kerygma is not an interpretation put upon the history of Jesus after Easter, "but is already the meaning residing in it for Jesus himself."[60] In Collingwood's terminology, this is the "inside" of the historical event. It must "vibrate" in the historian's (believer's) mind if it is to have any *meaning* (*Bedeutsamkeit*) at all. We are back at the point where Collingwood started: Concern with past events begins with a concern for the

[55] Gerhard Ebeling, *Word and Faith*, p. 204.
[56] *Ibid.*, p. 290
[57] *Ibid.*, p. 289.
[58] Robinson, *op. cit.*, pp. 85–86.
[59] *Ibid.*, pp. 93 ff., *passim*.
[60] *Ibid.*, p. 106. This is the basic assertion of those who advocate the "new quest." The reasons for this decision to make Jesus the model and example of genuine belief is quite understandable. If compelled to choose between Bultmann and traditional "objectifying language" about Christ and the "benefits" that came from him, we would have to take sides with Robinson.

similarities and correspondences between the past and the present. Thus Ebeling writes: "The task of Christology, then, is to give an account of the statement, 'I believe in Jesus.' "[61] And he summarizes: "The proper question regarding the past is not: What happened? What are the facts? How are they to be explained? or something of that kind, but: What comes to expression? . . . *it was faith that came to expression in Jesus.*"[62] Thus Jesus is the witness to faith and the ground of faith who awakens faith in us—who gives us courage to believe.[63] Faith is faith in God's love, which frees us from the past and enables us to face the future. The kerygma points to Jesus' faith. For us to believe, then, is to share in his faith, i.e. to allow the faith which came to expression in him to come to expression in us.[64] Jesus is a model of individual faith in God.

This summary of existentialist theology's approach to the meaning of history should provide sufficient basis for the judgment that the *difference between "redemptive history" and Bultmann's and Ebeling's concept of history is only relative.* Both approaches operate with a notion of suprahistory, the former directly and the latter indirectly. The former stresses *continuity* in history as something which is open to review and to "objectified statements," the latter stresses *contingency* in history in the form of ever-new reenactments of the interpretation of authentic existence through the kerygma (post-Easter, according to Bultmann, and "residing in Jesus," according to Ebeling). We could also say that the latter is the more careful and skeptical, i.e. largely non-metaphysical, version of the former. Both approaches presuppose a static, unmoved and, so to speak, photographic notion of God or of Being which is set as the "norm" over against sin or "inauthentic existence."[65] This means, most noticeably in existentialist theology, that history is depreciated

[61] Ebeling, *op. cit.*, p. 202.

[62] *Ibid.*, pp. 295–297 (italics mine).

[63] *Ibid.*, pp. 238, 243, 244, 302, and *The Nature of Faith*, p. 55.

[64] Ebeling, *Word and Faith*, p. 295, *passim*.

[65] Cf. the systematization of Bultmann's theology, highly praised in the foreword by Bultmann himself, by John Macquarrie, *An Existentialist Theology* (Harper Torchbook, New York and Evanston: Harper & Row, 1965; 1st ed., London: SCM Press, 1955), esp. pp. 29 ff., and recently his *Principles of Christian Theology* (New York: Charles Scribner's Sons, 1966), esp. chaps. III, XII, and XIV, truly the first "Systematic Theology" grown on Bultmannian soil and indeed a remarkable reinterpretation of all the classical *loci* of theology.

as something essentially bad and unfortunate which is to be "over-come." No wonder that the Old Testament has no place of impor-tance in existentialist theology,[66] while in "redemptive history" it is pressed into the strait jacket of preconceived dogmatical ideas.

The underlying promise of Augustine's statement that "our hearts are restless" until they rest in God seems to be taken care of in a theological concept of history which operates with a notion of God who "rests" in himself, i.e. who is timeless and motionless. This is the God of much of Western theology. He has no history himself, but can only make himself manifest in history. Such manifestations or "interventions" by God in history suggest implicitly the existence of periods during which God is absent. This unfortunate view is the alternative to the still more unhappy idea that history is "caused" by God, i.e. to pantheism. History itself is a mishap, as it were, and the true believer must either "overcome" it or, as in a theology of *Heils-geschichte*, subsume it under the dogmatical categories of God's plans. I would call this a basically docetic and utterly individualistic approach to theology and to Christology. This approach necessitates the unfortunate striving to make "relevant" the significance (*Bedeut-samkeit*, "meaningfulness") of events of the past or of texts which give an account of such events. God's decisive interference in history is a matter of the past and his actions since that time are restricted to acts of individual verification and confirmation of what he has once done or said. This is fundamentally the concept of deism, for the hidden existence of which in Western theology we should like to make Augustine responsible. A timeless God (or "ground of being"

[66] E.g. R. Bultmann, "Prophecy and Fulfillment," in *Essays on Old Testament Hermeneutics*, ed. Claus Westermann (Richmond: John Knox Press, 1963), pp. 50–75. The absence of any attention to the Old Testament is also typical of much of today's "process theology," e.g. Schubert Ogden's new book *The Reality of God*. This is to be regretted, for "process theology," stimulated by Hartshorne's helpful concept of the interrelation between "relativism" and "absolutism," is a serious attempt to free theology from the unfortunate concept of a timeless and static God, an attempt parallel to our own thesis. Unfortunately, however, "process theology" has advocated the idea of a history of God, which still hovers above Israel's election and history and, consequently, also above Jesus of Nazareth. An approach which might be of more substantial help is presented by Klaus Schwarzwäller, *Theologie oder Phänomenologie* (Munich: Chr. Kaiser Verlag, 1966), esp. pp. 90 ff., 122 ff., 212 ff., where the results of Old Testament research are finally taken seri-ously by a systematician. (Because of its recent appearance I was not able to utilize Schwarzwäller's views in the writing of this chapter).

or "being") whose main desire is to turn "restless hearts" into hearts
who rest in him, or inauthentic existences into authentic existences, is,
however, a resting and retired God himself.

In the process of unfolding the thesis of the present book, we will
have to try to speak of history in such terms as conceive of God
himself as having a history. We shall do this by keeping in mind the
suggestions of "process theology," but at the same time carefully
attempting to speak of "God's history" only to the extent to which
the election of Israel and the implementation of God's righteousness
in the resurrection of Jesus necessitates such speech. His history in
Jesus Christ, who is God's own "restless heart," is the sole reason
for our not being compelled to choose between "continuity" and
"contingency" in history. For it is only on the basis of the concept of
a static being of God that this distinction has become necessary. But
history which hastens from promise to fulfillment, whereby fulfillments are again turned into promises,[67] is *God's own way with his
people* toward the "new creation" of which only "his people" know,
although they know of it vicariously for the rest of mankind. We will
have later to substantiate the thesis that the *presence of Christ* means
nothing short of an understanding of one's own involvement in the
mission of the Church, of Jews and Gentiles, i.e. in the ever-new

[67] This insight is substantiated by Old Testament research of the last two
decades; cf. the article by Walther Zimmerli, "Promise and Fulfillment," in
Essays on Old Testament Hermeneutics, pp. 89–122 (from the German in
EvTh, No. 12 [July–Aug. 1952], Heft ½, pp. 6 ff.) Cf. also Jürgen Moltmann,
Theologie der Hoffnung, esp. pp. 85 ff. I find myself in basic sympathy with
his main thesis, though not always with his conclusions and applications.
Moltmann's stress on hope is, it seems to me, detrimental to the *memory*
of the Church, almost as though God's promises had no contact with the
historical realities of the past but were merely proleptic announcements of
the future. This tendency may be a result of Moltmann's indebtedness to
Ernst Bloch's philosophy of hope, a philosophy which constructs the content
of hope out of an analysis of the lack of perfection of the present rather
than out of promises of the past, a point of which Moltmann is aware, of
course. Before Moltmann, Walter Kreck had published a theological treatment of eschatology, containing a helpful survey of recent concepts in the
first chapter, and unfolding his own position in two subsequent chapters, *Die
Zukunft des Gekommenen, Grundprobleme der Eschatologie* (Munich:
Chr. Kaiser Verlag, 1961). After Moltmann's book, though written simultaneously, there appeared a major analysis of theological eschatology and of
various philosophical concepts of hope by Gerhard Sauter, *Zukunft und
Verheissung, Das Problem der Zukunft in der gegenwärtigen theologischen und
philosophischen Diskussion* (Zurich/Stuttgart: Zwingli Verlag, 1965). Moreover, numerous smaller publications reflect the increasing interest in the
understanding of "hope" and "future" on the Continent in recent times.
(See Chap. IV, FN 17, for additional titles.)

forms of accepting the invitation to see in Jesus both our true human-ity and our true worship. Our being in the Church or, more precisely, our *being the Church* enables us to see continuity in the contingent events of the past and to hope toward unprecedented events to come, an expectation without which our reception of past events and texts, e.g. the Bible, would become arbitrary or meaningless. It is only through this theological understanding that Christology is linked with ecclesiology, or better still, ethics. And it is only on this basis that an alternative to the impasse in present hermeneutics becomes possible.

c) *The Dilemma in Present Hermeneutics*

The question concerning the relation between Jesus and the Church is answered by existentialist theology in a very definite way. Instead of expounding the classical Roman Catholic or Reformation concept that the Holy Spirit *represents* the resurrected and exalted Christ, this theology, with its antipathy for metaphysics of the real-istic type and against objectified statements, advocates the reenact-ment of the essence of the Christ-event in and by the faith of the individual. It is obvious, however, that this approach is not free of "metaphysics" either; in fact it is highly indebted to nineteenth-century philosophical idealism, which had its roots in Plato. The metaphysics, which were necessary for traditional theology's under-standing of the representation of the exalted Christ by the Spirit, has simply been transplanted, in a modified and more hidden form, into the realm of the believer's appropriation of the kerygma's thrust toward new self-understanding. Also, apparent intellectualism is rooted in the idealistic origin of this theology: Jesus, in the era after his death, reaches the *thoughts* of the believers. Their *thoughts*, shaped and liberated by justifying faith, can now face world-reality; but world reality itself no longer speaks the language of Jesus; he is essentially a foreigner to reality.

It is understandable that existentialist theology has experienced modifications and received criticism in its appropriation by Anglo-Saxon theology. And it is noteworthy that, at the time of this trans-plantation, it has become more obvious than before that it deeply respects the Biblical word and, in fact, the Biblical canon.[68] It is for this reason that some of its original adherents or sympathizers in

---

[68] Professor Ebeling, whom I had told of my plans to discuss critically aspects of his theology, warned me "not to pin him down on Heidegger but on the Bible and on Luther."

America now begin to feel that it is outdated or, at least, that it
demands a radical reinterpretation. It would be an exaggeration to
say that the European form of post-Bultmannian theology is explor-
ing the relation between the *Bible* and "modern man," and the Anglo-
Saxon form of it, the relation between the *Christian* and "modern
man," but some indications point in this direction. Our interest at
this point is limited to the theological presuppositions of contemporary "hermeneutics," as it concerns the theologians on both sides of
the Atlantic. We must admit from the outset that the participants of
this discussion are fundamentally concerned with our own question,
namely, the contemporaneity of Jesus Christ with us today. Of
course, our survey and evaluation of their concept of history does not
exhaust the theme of hermeneutics. But the understanding of history
is part of hermeneutics, since the interpreter is at least in part concerned with the question: Which categories sufficiently and adequately describe what happens between us and an event (text) of the
past? It is in this sense that "theology is hermeneutics," for there is
no denying that theology deals with the interpretation of past events.
The question is only whether this is a broad enough definition of
hermeneutics, or, what is the same thing, too narrow a definition of
theology. The formulation is obviously an abstract one and it may be
asked whether the employment of an abstract (philosophical) question is meaningful for the definition of the task of theology. Could it
perhaps be that this deliberately abstract and seemingly neutral
(philosophical) question shapes the theology which it is intended to
serve? With this question we are in the midst of the controversy over
contemporary hermeneutics.

Coming from various backgrounds, a great number of authors
have advanced critical arguments against the hermeneutical approach
of Bultmann and his "school." Some critics have argued on the basis
of a concept of the authority of Scripture; some on the basis of
confessional tradition; others on dogmatical grounds; still others on
philosophical grounds (e.g. Karl Jaspers). Historical arguments have
been brought forth[69] against the concept of myth as defined by
Bultmann, and critical publications by exegetes have reached such
a quantity that only a few have found it possible to follow them.[70]

---

[69] Cf. Eduard Buess, *Die Geschichte des mythischen Erkennens* (Zurich: EVZ-
Verlag, 1953).

[70] Günther Bornkamm has provided a summary report, "Die Theologie Rudolf
Bultmanns in der neueren Diskussion," *ThRu*, Neue Folge, 29/1963, pp. 33 ff.
Much information is also contained in Robert W. Funk's recent attempt to

The key concepts of the new hermeneutical approach, such as *Bedeutsamkeit* ("meaningfulness"), "objectifying language," etc., have become the themes of countless publications and conferences.

No careful observer will deny that the whole controversy has also its comical aspects. Many advocates of the new hermeneutical approach (despite their declared purpose of speaking understandably to "modern man") have indeed uttered incomprehensible sentences which look even stranger when translated from German into English or vice versa. Yet many convinced opponents of this school have added little to their academic glory by operating with a heavy emotional investment which has often resulted in the misunderstanding and misrepresentation of the views of the other side. Much unpleasant hostility has also been shown by some of the discussion partners and there is a tendency of the adherents of each group to read and quote primarily the works of those with whom they already basically agree. This is especially typical of some of the advocates of the new hermeneutical approach, who judge harshly and label readily theological positions different from their own which they have nevertheless not studied with sufficient patience. They are convinced that a revolution has taken place in theology and that henceforth all concentration must be focused upon the new task rather than upon the interpretation of what they consider to belong to the past. A comparison may even be drawn with the situation of modern music, in which many composers of the period after Arnold Schönberg label all earlier works as "new baroque."

Let us parenthesize, as it were, these comical and sad aspects of the present controversy over hermeneutics, and try rather to penetrate to a more fundamental problem. Our question is whether the complexity of arguments for and against the new hermeneutical approach can be reduced to a clearly definable basic theological difference. The answer to this question must be prepared by four partly historical observations:

1) Historical-critical exegesis originated on the Continent in the eighteenth century[71] and bears the marks of the spirit of that century

---

connect Continental European language philosophy and Anglo-Saxon linguistic analysis with the current problems in New Testament hermeneutics: *Language, Hermeneutics and the Word of God* (New York: Harper & Row, 1966).

[71] See my essay "Johann Salomo Semler: The Rise of the Historical-Critical Method in Eighteenth-Century Theology on the Continent," in *Introduction to Modernity: A Symposium on Eighteenth-Century Thought,* ed. Robert Mollenauer (Austin: University of Texas Press, 1965), pp. 109 ff.

even today. The history of exegesis since the rise of the historical-critical method is of course a very complicated one. Staying within the limits of our systematic-christological interest, let us be content to say that the origin and further development of this method is characterized by the strong intention to abolish the traditional twofold or threefold meaning of Scripture. Origen's concept of the threefold and Thomas Aquinas' concept of the fourfold meaning of Scripture were, systematically speaking, amplifications of the basic concept of a double meaning of Scripture. And it was this concept of a deeper, higher or fuller meaning, the concept of the *sensus plenior*, that was denied by the pioneers of historical-critical exegesis. These scholars conceived of their work as a legitimate continuation of the exegetical intent of the Reformers, and in this they were right. But the result of eighteenth-century exegetical work was the separation of exegesis from systematic theology. Some exegetes of that period were not even alarmed by this outcome, but rather defended expressly a theological double-mindedness. J. S. Semler, for example, supported the conservative ecclesiastical policy of his government while at the same time producing contradicting results on an exegetical basis. In the light of this dichotomy, Schleiermacher's theological work may be defined as a grandiose attempt to put together what the eighteenth century had allowed to fall apart. Critical exegesis *and* systematic theology received the same honor, and were tied to each other in such fashion that each needed and supported the other. But the price was high: Schleiermacher had only one way of accomplishing this balanced correlation, namely the declaration of *faith* as the foundation, criterion and content of theology. Nineteenth-century exegetical work, therefore, accepted readily and with untroubled conscience Schleiermacher's permission to read Biblical texts as expressions of faith. The exegete felt free to concentrate on merely historical exegesis in the secure hope that the systematician would stick to his own task of systematizing the Christian faith. It was only at the turn of the century, with the raise of the history-of-religions school, and more radically, after the First World War, that both exegetes and systematicians became aware of the fearful possibility that perhaps they had been dealing with texts which were totally irrelevant to modern man and which had been of interest and influence only as long as Western Christian culture had not been called into question.

Now G. E. Lessing's skeptical question[72] as to how "accidental historical truth" can be become the foundation of eternal truth, again moved into the center of attention. The question has stayed with us ever since, and Lessing's name seems forever connected with theological hermeneutics. The simple form of the question is: What do these texts have to do with me and what do I have to do with them? It is again, though in different expression, the question of the *sensus plenior* which is disturbing the mind of the interpreter. In a delightful article[73] Rudolf Bohren describes with humor, and yet with deep sorrow over the situation of contemporary preaching, the current attitude toward exegesis: "After he [sc.] the preacher, has buried the text historically-critically, he is now supposed to resurrect it existentially." And he continues by asking whether post-Bultmannian exegesis does not reveal its own inner schizophrenia by doing precisely what it does not want to do, i.e. by trying to gain a "mystical" sense of Scripture through existentialist interpretation on the basis of the "literal," sense which was gained through historical-critical interpretation, thus again operating with a *twofold meaning of Scripture*. Without discussing Bohren's statement at this point, let us merely raise a question which seems to point in the same direction: Is it not obvious that contemporary exegetes in their hermeneutical considerations have already entered into the center of systematic theology, if only with the assertion that traditional systematic theology no longer exists? It is quite apparent that they are wrestling with the ancient problem of the *sensus plenior:* the deeper, more lasting, more timeless, more personal meaning of that which the text, historically-critically examined, has said.

2) A second observation will help prepare the answer to our question as to whether the complexity of the contemporary discussion can be reduced to one basic alternative in theology: Why is it that *Anglo-Saxon theology* has given no signs of interest in herme-

---

[72] Two early discussions of this question were presented by Friedrich Traub, "Geschichtswahrheiten und Vernunftwahrheiten bei Lessing," in *ZThK* (1920), pp. 193 ff., and by Heinrich Scholz, "Zufällige Geschichts und notwendige Vernunft-Wahrheiten," in *Harnack-Ehrung* (for Harnack's seventieth birthday; Leipzig: J. C. Hinrich'sche Buchhandlung, 1921), pp. 377 ff.

[73] Rudolf Bohren, "Die Krise der Predigt als Frage an die Exegese," in *EvTh*, ½ (Jan.–Feb. 1962), pp. 66 ff., the quotation is found on p. 73; see also his book *Predigt und Gemeinde* (Zurich/Stuttgart: Zwingli Verlag, 1963), Engl. transl., *Preaching and Community*, tr. by David E. Green (Richmond: John Knox Press, 1965), esp. pp. 79 ff.

neutics until, very recently, Bultmann's and Ebeling's books have begun to conquer the theological scene, especially in America? Anglo-Saxon theology has not participated in the fundamental theological crisis which is typical of post-Schleiermacher Continental theology. Leaving aside ecclesiastical and political reasons, we can judge that Anglo-Saxon theology was shaped in its questions and thought-forms by a philosophy totally different from that on the Continent. A historical description of this shaping would have to begin with Francis Bacon, whose sharp distinction between science and religion has become typical of the Anglo-Saxon situation. Irrespective of the question whether Bacon succeeded in his intent, it is of interest to us that he placed much weight upon experience and the empirical findings of experiments. In his *De dignitate et augmentis scientiarium* (1605, completed 1623) he distinguished between a *theologia inspirata* and a *theologia naturalis*, whereby he confined the former to the realm of faith. The latter he discussed philosophically, although he was aware that only the former is really theology. Thus he stated that the truth of the Christian faith is not accessible to "reason," which meant to him "science." Thomas Hobbes, continuing with Bacon's emphasis upon experience, systematically unfolded the view that theology (to him, "metaphysics") and philosophy of experience had no common ground. His interest was focused upon man in his various realms of existence. Matters of faith are unrelated to scientific thinking. While philosophy is concerned with the practical questions of man and society, theology is given the invitation to pursue its own business without being forced to defend its conclusions and its modes of operation before the forum of the sciences. (It is interesting in this connection to remember that the German-speaking Continent knows no equivalent to the English word "science"; theology on the Continent is a *Wissenschaft*, as is shown by the existence of theological faculties in Continental universities, a tradition not even challenged in East Germany today.) John Locke and the classical philosophers of empiricism of the eighteenth and nineteenth centuries manifested the victory of positivism and empiricism. Only George Berkeley seemed to be an exception, with his spiritualism and epistemological idealism, which permitted him to believe that theological truth can be defended rationally. But despite his rehabilitation of earlier English Platonism, Berkeley agreed with Locke that only empirical perception provides certainty. Later stages of British philosophy show that the main trend followed the development marked by the names of Bacon, Hobbes and David Hume. And it was at this time that theology established itself over against philosophy, whose themes had little in common with theological subjects. It is noteworthy, however, that a strong dose of theism or deism has remained typical of Anglo-Saxon philosophy, and British and American thought in general. The relation between theology and philosophy has always seemed to be a rather peaceful one, although, or perhaps because, they had so little in common. Many quarters of Anglo-Saxon theology have not yet entered into the fundamental crisis so characteristic of early twentieth-century theology on the Continent. Could this be the reason for the late advent of hermeneutical questions in Anglo-Saxon theology? Or should we direct the question more pointedly to Continental theology, and ask: Is the strong interest in hermeneutics on the Continent a late fruit of (or attack on) Platonism or German idealism, i.e. of the Continental and especially German interest in metaphysics? If one stresses the first question, the conclusion would be that Anglo-Saxon theology, with good reasons, is now entering into the crisis which Continental theology has already experienced. If one prefers the second question, the conclusion would be that the recent American publications on hermeneutics are an unnecessary attempt to import German theology into America.

3) The third observation concerns the simple fact that *very few commentaries* have grown out of the hermeneutical discussion of the past twenty years. While American exegetes have produced practically no scholarly commentaries at all, New Testament exegetes on the Continent have been preoccupied with hermeneutical controversies which have not led to commentary work either. Those who seem to have devoted their lives to hermeneutics have yet to prove their exegetical abilities in form of expositions of whole books of the Bible.[74] The Continental situation regarding hermeneutics is not unlike the American preoccupation with archaeology, in that neither has yet led to the real testing ground, the commentary. Commentaries have had their great time in the period of late-nineteenth-century historicism, both on the Continent and in Britain and America, and again on the Continent during the period of the twenties and thirties

---

[74] Bultmann's commentary on John's Gospel is, of course, an important exception, and we can soon expect a commentary on Matthew by Günther Bornkamm.

of this century. The first period is marked by the absence of a strong systematic theology on the part of the exegetes, while the second period is, on the contrary, characterized by an amazing interest of exegetes in systematic theology. Could it perhaps be that commentaries cannot be written by an exegete who is disturbed by unsolved systematic-theological questions? If this were so, it would be understandable why last century's historicism, with its low opinion of systematic theology, and the exegetes of the second quarter of this century, with their strong involvement in the political and confessional struggles of the Church, were so able and willing to write commentaries. The great Old Testament commentaries which have been produced by German-speaking theologians during the past few years still seem to be fed theologically by the impulses of the latter period. And the fact cannot be overlooked that the contemporary Old Testament exegetes are participating only indirectly in the hermeneutical controversy. This fact can be explained either by accusing the Old Testament exegetes of theological-hermeneutical naiveté, or by blaming the New Testament exegetes for having wasted their time with speculative-hermeneutical discussions which have hindered them from doing what they should be doing, according to their own program, i.e. interpreting Scripture. One could, of course, go a step further and propose that the commentary is an outdated form of theological literature and that it has had its time. This proposition is, within limits, an understandable opinion, although if it should mean that exegetes might feel excused from the task of intepreting Scripture for the benefit of preachers and Church members, it would certainly be a most dangerous view. It is a fact that Continental preachers today put their confidence in Old Testament scholars who have really provided helpful and scholarly tools for the weekly task of preaching, while they have not been helped by many New Testament exegetes; many former students of the well-known advocates of a new hermeneutics are reported to preach overly simple and almost old-fashioned pietistic sermons. The situation of the American preacher is certainly no better, for he lacks the help even of Old Testament commentaries, and must be content with layman's commentaries, which have appeared in great number, or with scholarly historical and archaeological publications. With the exception of German Old Testament scholarship (often heavily criticized by American scholars) we may safely judge that today's academic-theological exegetes are leaving the preacher on his own, an observation which is connected with our present theological helplessness. Yet we must be open to the possibility that these exegetes, upon whom falls today's criticism and blame, are thinking through certain questions vicariously on behalf of all those others whose task involves the study of Scripture. Honesty may demand that we be ready to enter again into a commentary-less period of Church history similar to those of centuries past.

4) Finally, let us ask what today is embraced by the term *hermeneutics*. Hermeneutics was at one time a kind of preconsideration to exegesis. But already with Schleiermacher[75] the use of the word and the meaning indicated by it took new shape. Hermeneutics was no longer concerned merely with technical recipes for interpretation or with theological assertions concerning the place and authority of the text, but hermeneutics now embraced both the text and its reader. Not only does the reader interpret the text but the text also interprets the reader, and this, in turn, determines his hermeneutics. Understanding is, according to Schleiermacher (and later Dilthey), the opposite of production, and, in going back behind the product of an author to the author's mind, the interpreter can understand an author better than he understood himself. Thus Schleiermacher developed his concept of hermeneutics from an analysis of understanding; it was this step in the history of theology which has connected hermeneutics with epistemology in the broad sense of the term, a connection which has not been dissolved up to the present day. If epistemology embraces questions of perception, recognition, understanding, understandability, relevance and "meaningfulness," if all this is connected with the phenomenon of language, and if it is agreed upon that this whole complex adequately circumscribes at least the structural elements of what was traditionally called theology, then the conclusion presents itself that *hermeneutics has taken the place of* (systematic) *theology*. This is indeed what has happened among those who advocate the new hermeneutical approach. Philosophical thoughts about history and the individual, the understanding of the past in the present, the analysis of man's existence and the analysis of language and what it constitutes have taken the place of systematic theology, and the traditional *loci* of theology only reappear

---

[75] Friedrich Schleiermacher, *Hermeneutik und Kritik,* ed. F. Lücke, 1838; now available in a new critical edition by H. Kimmerle (Heidelberg: Abhandlungen der Heidelberger Akademie der Wissenschaften, 1959).

insofar as they have bearing on the central hermeneutical questions. If one adds to this our observation 3, that hardly any commentaries are being produced, one may reach the conclusion that today systematic theology *and* exegesis are swallowed up by hermeneutics. But lamentation over this fact is useless, since traditional theology obviously had not succeeded in answering the questions of those who now advocate an entirely new approach.

These four observations permit us to return to the main question: Can the many arguments and criticisms concerning the contemporary problem of hermeneutics be reduced to one fundamental difference of positions? The answer to this question is indeed affirmative. And the awareness of the basic difference between two approaches to the task of theology is shared by all serious participants in the controversy. This awareness is precisely the "impasse in present hermeneutics." If this impasse were not noticed by theologians on either side, the discussion would come to a standstill. This has not yet happened, although there is some indication of a hardening of the fronts. But just this is what must not be permitted to happen.

The fundamental difference between the two approaches is constituted by two different evaluations of *reality* or, underneath this, possibly even by two different *concepts* of reality. The evalutions are of interest to us in this context because the assignment of the place and function of world reality within theology is at stake.[76] Where does theological thinking begin: with an analysis of (part of) world reality or with—to put it vaguely—revelation? It follows that this dilemma also raises the dilemma of the verification of theological statements. Thus the understanding of the place and function of *reality*, i.e. the *beginning* of theology, and of *verification*, hang together and circumscribe the realm within which two fundamentally different approaches to the task of theology seem to be rooted. At the risk of overstating the case, let us use the terms *"world-verification type"* and *"revelation-verification type"* to indicate what is typical of the two different approaches. These two types of theology already constitute a more important alternative in theology today than the confessional and denominational differences of the past. The two types may be illustrated by the names of Bultmann and Barth, although this is no more than an illustration. It would be superficial to judge that Bult-

---

[76] Cf. Ebeling "Theology and Reality," in *Word and Faith*, pp. 191 ff., and "Faith and Unbelief in Conflict about Reality," *ibid.*, pp. 374 ff.

mann's theology is oriented on world reality and neglects revelation reality and that Barth proceeds the other way around. In any case, it no longer even makes sense to speak of Barthian and Bultmannian "schools."

Having drawn attention to the limitations of this illustration, we can nevertheless say that the *world-verification* type is an important aspect of Bultmann's theology and also of the theological works of those who are or were his pupils. They try to examine the texts and to verify their own statements in the light of the reality of this (human) world. Anthropological relevance is always an important, though not always the only, criterion of their theological thinking and speaking. What the ancient text says and what the theologian today says must meet the reality of the reader and hearer. Bultmann himself finds the theological reason for this demand in the historical *"dass"* ("that") of the breaking-in of the eschatological event into history, i.e. into (the "that" of) Jesus of Nazareth. The identity of the historical "that" of the coming of Jesus of Nazareth with the coming of the eschatological event in world-historical dimension is, according to Bultmann, a "paradoxical identity"[77] but an identity nevertheless. And it is at the point of the historicity of this "that" that theological thinking is anchored; and it is because of this that theology is guarded against docetism, so much at least is intended. (We have already mentioned that Käsemann, Bornkamm, Ebeling and Robinson have been discontented with the "mere that" and have tried to say "more" about the historical Jesus; see Chapter I, b).

The *revelation-verification type*, however, while not in the least intending to neglect anthropological relevance, attempts to preserve in all theological statements the freedom of the subject of revelation, i.e. God in the trinitarian understanding. The revelation of the triune God, by all means having come into the "that" of the manhood of Jesus, but also remaining with the Church in the Holy Spirit, creates, constitutes and preserves reality. He is prior to the "reality" into which he has entered; he conquers and uses it. The reality of the triune God is a "primary reality" over against the "secondary reality" of world reality, which is called into being in order to provide a

[77] Cf. Dorothee Sölle, "Paradoxe Identität," in *Pastoraltheologie*, Sept. 1964, pp. 366 ff., a review article on the Catholic book on Bultmann by G. Hasenhüttl, *Der Glaubensvollzug* (Essen: Ludgerus-Verlag, 1963).

platform, stage or framework for the occurring of revelation. But it "can" happen only because of God's reality in his Lordship in which he is already "our" God before we have registered his revelation within world reality. This is, in general terms, the teaching of Barth as he has unfolded it in the Church Dogmatics, II, 1.[78] There is every reason to say that this approach continues the line of development from Athanasius through Anselm and the Reformers. The verification of theological statements is primarily connected with the reception of revelation reality. Understanding is obedient reception and acceptance, and the category of the relation between God and the world is analogy[79] rather than identity or "paradoxical identity" in the historical "dass."

It should surprise no one that the world-verification type is disappointed with the position advocated by the revelation-verification type. The reason for this is that the first type asks "philosophical" questions and is disappointed in the second type's theological answers, which, however, were not meant to be relevant to "philosophical" questions. "Philosophical" questions means in this context questions which are lifted from an analysis of world reality. Here again we are confronted with the problem of the "starting point" of theology.

Could it be that this alternative is perhaps a transposition of the ancient philosophical alternative between (Plato's) metaphysics and anamnesis on the one hand and empiricism on the other? But the two types of theology do not clearly represent these two philosophi-

[78] Barth's doctrine of the Trinity is examined in an important new book by a pupil of Ernst Fuchs: Eberhard Jüngel, Gottes Sein ist im Werden (Tübingen: J. C. B. Mohr, 1965). Jüngel attempts to show that Barth's doctrine of God is by no means as epistemologically naive as some Bultmannians had been inclined to think. Jüngel's book outdates many recent suggestions toward a "process theology," and cannot be bypassed by anyone concerned with these questions.

[79] Cf. to Barth's concept of analogy Walter Kreck, "Analogia fidei oder analogia entis?" in Antwort (for Barth's seventieth birthday; Zollikon-Zurich, EVZ-Verlag, 1956), pp. 272 ff., which presents a discussion with Hans Urs v. Balthasar's interpretation of Barth. To the problem of analogy itself, cf. Wolfhart Pannenberg, "Analogie und Doxologie," in Dogma und Denkstrukturen (for E. Schlink's sixtieth birthday; Göttingen: Vandenhoeck & Ruprecht, 1963), pp. 96 ff., and John McIntyre, "Analogy," in SJT, Vol. XII, No. 1 (Mar. 1959), pp. 1 ff., and Hampus Lyttkens, The Analogy Between God and the World: An Investigation of its Background and Interpretation of its Use by Thomas of Aquino (Uppsala: Almquist & Wiksells, AB, 1952).

cal avenues of thought, as can be seen in Bultmann's and Ebeling's theology. These theologians are not ready to go all the way with the world-verification approach. It is not only that their concept of faith has a non-empirical aspect, and not only that the kerygma, according to their thinking, breaks into world reality from the "outside," as it were, but both of them maintain a strongly theistic (or deistic?) complex of thoughts. This is even more true in J. A. T. Robinson's book *Honest to God*, which starts with a pompous program of world verification and ends with a highly religious and metaphysical assertion about "transcendence" and the *numinosum*.[80] The advocates of the world-verification type of theology obviously do not want to sacrifice their integrity as theologians and Christians on the altar of philosophical empiricism. But they refuse to move with traditional theology and with Barth to systematic thoughts about God's inner-trinitarian being. Is this merely an expression of epistemological humility or is it the consequence of their decision to begin theology with an understanding of world reality?

The revelation-verification type, on the other hand, does not represent a distinct philosophical pattern either. The Reformers and Barth made it expressly clear that they had taken great pains to avoid falling victim to any one particular philosophy. And it is certainly true that Barth, for example, has tried hard to guard himself against Dietrich Bonhoeffer's accusation[81] that his theology has moved toward "revelation positivism." "The world" is taken seriously in Barth's theology. Those who doubt this could with the same right, or with even better reasons, also deny that the other type of theology takes "the world" seriously. Nevertheless there is a grain of truth in Bonhoeffer's statement concerning Barth's understanding of revelation, for it is indeed true that Barth does not pay much attention to general epistemological questions. The *Deus dixit* is indeed the source from which all parts of the *Church Dogmatics* are fed.

It seems strange that the disadvantage of the world-verification type lies in its close connection with philosophical questions, and that the shortcoming of the revelation-verification type is related to the absence of philosophical questions. This confusing situation illustrates the dilemma in present hermeneutics. It could well be that

---

[80] See the further discussion of these questions in Chap. IV.
[81] *Prisoner for God* (New York: The Macmillan Co., 1953), letters of the 30th of April 1944 and later the following month.

Ernst Fuchs' and Gerhard Ebeling's interest in language and "language event" is not as useless as is often thought in circles of revelation-verification type theology. Fuchs[82] was not the only one to know of the "language event." Barth knew of it long before him (already in CD I, 1).[83] But the problem of the evaluation of the understanding of world reality for theology still remains unsolved even if an agreement could be reached concerning the function of language. It would require very artificial manipulation of biblical texts to show that the Bible knows of an isolated, abstract world reality or human reality which is only later "confronted" with the Gospel. Reality is seen only through the Gospel; the first Adam is understood only through the Second Adam, Jesus of Nazareth. Should this be labeled and critized as "metaphysical" or "idealistic"? Such is the criticism advanced by some Anglo-Saxon theologians, although they cannot challenge this statement on exegetical grounds any more than can Bultmann, nor have they yet made clear what they really mean by "metaphysical," which term is often used by theologians in an extremely vague if not dilettantish manner. But it is obvious that Bultmann and Ebeling are received on the American theological scene with enthusiasm, especially in those quarters which have always been particularly concerned with the analysis of the human situation and with a rationale for conversion theology. To put it bluntly: Those who have maintained that it is the task of theology *first* to analyze the human situation and *then* to preach the Gospel in appropriate and understandable form are now particularly fond of Bultmann's and Ebeling's books. Whether this means that the two authors are correctly interpreted is another question, but the corresponding ele-

---

[82] E.g., *Zun hermeneutischen Problem in der Theologie* and *Zur frage nach dem historischen Jesus* (Vols. I & II of Fuchs' collection of essays; Tübingen: J. C. B. Mohr, 1959 & 1960), partly contained in *Studies of the Historical Jesus*, "Studies in Biblical Theology," No. 42 (Naperville, Ill.: Alec R. Allenson, Inc., 1964). On Ernst Fuchs, cf. now Jürgen Fangmeier, *Ernst Fuchs*, (Zurich: EVZ-Verlag, 1964).

Despite my contention that much of Fuchs' writing is not understandable and indeed irrational, I must admit that the Continental theologians' utilization of Heidegger's "language philosophy" has so far been more fruitful for theological work than has the appropriation of linguistic analysis by Anglo-Saxon theologians. However philosophically speaking, the latter is of much greater stringency than the cryptically "mystical" language philosophy of Heidegger. I was interested to hear that Professor Paul Ricoeur supported the same evaluation in recent conversations in Pittsburgh.

[83] Cf. E. Jüngel, *op. cit.*, pp. 16–26, 33 ff.

ments of their theology and traditionally empirical Anglo-Saxon thought have been noticed not without reason. There is no doubt that a world-verification type theology will be greatly concerned with Lessing's question and much disturbed by the problem of "how to make relevant" the truth of the ancient texts. But because it does not want to convert itself into philosophy, the world-verification type of theology is forced to live with this problem and therefore has given it a central importance, as is indicated by the fact that hermeneutics has taken the place of theology. A certain concept of God is indispensable for answering the question: What does the ancient text say to me? The advocates of this type of question react negatively to theologies that say "too much" about God (Barth) and also to those that say "too little" (van Buren). For undisturbed operation, the world-verification type of theology seems to require a *fixed concept of God*, though not elaborated in detail, and a very *complex concept of man* and the conditions of his existence. *It begins with the latter and presupposes the former.* It requires a strong concept of the present, as related to the past, but neither present nor past are in any necessary way related to the future. The message of this theology is "confirmation" and "confidence," also regarding *my* future, but it is *not forgiveness* concerning the past and *expectation* of things to come.

The further development of our thesis concerning the *Christus praesens* will lead us away from this type of theology. We will refuse to accept the dilemma of a choice between these two types of theology as a basis for further theological inquiry. Regarding hermeneutics, we will seek to avoid concentration on the one-sided question: What do the ancient texts say to me? We will rather begin with the opposite question: Why am I reading the ancient texts and what am I saying now? Or, to put it positively, we will try to replace the question of how to make biblical texts relevant to modern situations, with the opposite question of how to make the modern situation relevant to the biblical texts. The first (and traditional) question has grown out of the philosophical, Augustinian notion of time and eternity; and it is only consistent that it has led modern scholars back into philosophical considerations which are the modern version of the *sensus plenior* discussion. But these scholars, unwilling to sacrifice their theological integrity, face an impasse which cannot be debated away by the employment of still more differentiated forms of philosophical analysis of existence. The hermeneutical conference at Drew University in April 1964 has certainly shown this, and Hans Jonas has summarized it well.[84] In order to substantiate the thesis that it is theologically legitimate to ask the hermeneutical question in the opposite direction (i.e. how to make the modern situation relevant to the biblical texts) we will have to discuss the impossibility of the modified principle "No revelation after Ezra" under the point of view of the reception of tradition.

d) The Formation and Reception of Tradition in Research and Worship

We are now approaching the center of this chapter's question. In the midst of conflicting theological opinions, we have noted a relatively wide consensus that the Church is to speak not merely of the "historical Jesus" but of the risen Christ. Christ, who is not the product of time and history, has entered into history, become subject to time and is confessed, by his having been raised, to rule over history. This confession is made by the Church, which is subject to time and open to historical investigation. Indeed, the Church is under the same subjection to time which Jesus took upon himself before the resurrection. But, because of his resurrection, the Church comes to grips with her own past and looks upon her own present with hope. The union between the Church and her Lord constitutes for the Church a mode of existence in time which is different from Jesus' mode of existence in time during his earthly life, for the Church does not repeat the loneliness of Jesus, nor do her individual members relive his solitary-vicarious existence. *The presence of Christ* and the union between Christ and the Church are an inalienable part of any statements about the Church. But recognizing the presence of Christ means recognizing the presence of the *risen* Christ. The risen Christ is the *future* of the Church, "each in his own order: Christ the first fruits, then at his coming those who belong to Christ" (I Cor. 15:23). Therefore, when remembering the resurrection the Church *hopes. Memory and hope are the dimensions of the presence of Christ.*

In agreement with tradition and also with parts of contemporary theology, we have reiterated the thesis that Jesus Christ is recognized

[84] See Introduction, FN 2.

only in the Church. If the Church is understood only in relation to the *Christus praesens*, it follows that any statements about Jesus Christ himself (who is recognized only in the Church) are necessarily related to the recognition of the *Christus praesens*. Statements about the Church (ecclesiology) and statements about Jesus Christ (Christology) are inseparably connected *because* of the *Christus praesens*, i.e. because these statements can only be made in the recognition of the *Christus praesens*. His presence constitutes the Church ever anew. Worship, theology and the various services of the Church are the expression of the Church's recognition of the presence of Christ.

But the trend of the thoughts just outlined seems to be disrupted by the following problem: Is it not true that the Church knows of the pneumatic presence of the risen Christ only because of her knowledge of his appearance in history? And is it not also true that the Church can understand his appearance in history only because he is also present in the Church, constituting her ever anew? At first sight this impasse is disturbing. Premature attempts to break the antinomy lead either to historicism, which stresses the "historical Jesus" or the "historical risen Christ" and understands the Church merely by referring to her memory, i.e. her ability and willingness to remember these past events; or else to spiritualism, which stresses the presence of Christ in the Spirit at the expense of his appearance in history. In either case Jesus Christ is not conceived as the history-embracing Christ, and the Church, consequently, is not understood as being in union with the *Christus praesens*.

There is only one way to break what appears to be a vicious circle: *viz.* by the insight expressed in theological thought *and* prayer, that the *Christus praesens* opens for the Church the dimensions of the past and present in such fashion that history becomes transparent for the work and Lordship of Christ. History, by itself incapable of having "produced" Jesus Christ but nevertheless having "contained" him before the resurrection, is now revealed to the Church in its proper place, function and meaning, i.e. as the realm, platform and instrument of the *witness to and glorification of Christ*. Jean-Louis Leuba, whose study on tradition is very helpful in this connection, says: "By this roundabout way of history the Spirit glorifies Christ himself without adding anything to him by this glorification. And it is just this glorification which is the '*traditio*,' the joining in (*Einreihung*) of the Christ into linear time and space. This *traditio* does not add to Christ anything that he was not already or did not already possess. But Christ, by taking upon himself subjection to the dimensions of history, reveals the reality and the truth of this history."[85]

The presence of Jesus Christ, therefore, opens up the understanding of his having been the *Christus praesens* in the *past*, i.e. of his having used history for his own witness and glorification. At the same time, this recognition of the *Christus praesens* in the past opens up the meaning of the periods of history which Christ claimed for the purpose of his witness and glorification. The *Christus praesens invites the Church to see how history is relevant to Christ.* What the Church can see concerning the past, she can also see in relation to the present and she can prepare herself for the future, so that past, present and future appear in their relevance to Christ. The *Christus praesens* invites the Church to reverse the often-heard demand "to make Christ relevant to the present situation." The situation, past, present or future, is to be made relevant to him.

The various expressions of the Church's attempts to see her own past and present in the light of the presence of Christ, manifest in writings, liturgies and indirectly in forms of art, are the *tradition* of the Church. The tradition is the record of the "joining in of Christ into linear time and space," to use Leuba's formulation. It is the record of the recognition of the *Christus praesens* in the Church in times past. The theological evaluation of tradition is directly linked with the understanding of the Church, in that the formation as well as the reception of tradition are theological questions concerning the Church and her relation to the presence of Christ. This emphasis on the Church does not invalidate Bultmann's and other theologians' interest in the "personal encounter" between the individual and (the kerygma of) Jesus Christ. But it is certainly true that Protestant theology has dealt with the question of tradition without paying sufficient attention to the fact that the problem of tradition is a subcategory of ecclesiology. The Protestant tendency toward the use of individualistic categories is merely an expression of this basic neglect. The proper understanding of the Church in the light of her union

---

[85] Jean-Louis Leuba, "Tradition und Traditionen," in *Schrift und Tradition*, ed. Kristen E. Skydsgaard and Lukas Vischer (Zurich: EVZ-Verlag, 1963), being the report of the European section of the theological commission of "Faith and Order" (Montreal, 1963); p. 20 (my translation).

with the risen Christ[86] will, however, not belittle the importance of the individual and of his personal encounter with Christ. But theological reflection must not begin with the believing individual and proceed from there to the Church, as if the Church were an aggregation of individuals, each of whom has contributed his gifts and experience in order to create one whole, the Church. The christological understanding of the Church proceeds rather in the opposite direction.

We have defined tradition as the record of the recognition of the presence of Christ in the Church in times past. The risen Christ has made known his reality by using a multitude of forms of expression, all of which constitute the tradition of the Church. Contemporary theologians[87] have frequently used the formulation "tradition and traditions" to indicate that Christ, the tradition himself, is witnessed to and glorified within the many traditions with which he is not identical, but without which his presence would not be manifest. What now is the criterion for discerning the tradition within the traditions? There is no other and no better answer to this question than the ancient biblical and early trinitarian reference to the work of the Holy Spirit whose *proprium* it is to create the awareness and certainty in the congregation of believers that they have recognized the true Jesus Christ. But the Holy Spirit *is* the mode of the presence of the risen Christ and thus we return to our basic thesis concerning the *Christus praesens*. Utilizing this traditional concept we can now approach the problem of Scripture and tradition and then conclude this chapter with some propositions concerning hermeneutics. The appropriateness of the traditional language concerning Christ and the Holy Spirit will have to be reexamined in the systematic part of our study.

We are now prepared to penetrate into the main question of this chapter, pointedly formulated thus: Why and how must and can the Church today verify her thoughts and statements concerning God

---

[86] These questions will be discussed in Chap. VI after a criticism of Protestant individualism has been presented in Chap. III. At this point our interest is limited to a demonstration of the dimensions of the *Christus praesens* and we will have to operate with a still undefined notion of the Church.

[87] E.g. Yves M.-J. Congar, *La Tradition et les traditions*, I. *Essai historique*, II. *Essai théologique* (Paris: Fayard, 1960 & 1963); and *Tradition und Kirche* (Aschaffenburg: Paul Pattloch Verlag, 1965); see also reports of the two study commissions of "Faith and Order," Montreal, 1963, and an extensive bibliography on the subject "tradition," 1930–1962, by G. Pedersen in *Schrift und Tradition*, pp. 157–169.

and man by referring to ancient texts? And in what way can the biblical texts be said to occupy a special place among the ancient texts? The reception and interpretation of tradition and of the biblical texts in particular must occur in the light of the *Christus praesens* so that God's activity in Jesus is not limited to a certain period of the past, nor his deeds and promises of the past invalidated. God's ever-new activity and presence in the risen Christ is to be seen as part of his ongoing faithfulness to his people. Thus the Church, when reading texts of the past, is hoping into the future; and when hoping into the future, the Church is remembering the promises of the past. This statement is no more than a phenomenological observation. It is tantamount to the seemingly trivial observation that no one would be interested in the Bible and in ancient creeds if he did not find himself in the "stream of creeds and confessions" which affirm God's ongoing faithfulness. But this is indeed more than a trivial observation. Subjectively speaking, the beginning of the recognition of "the things of God" is that we are *captured by the faithfulness of God,* expressed in the form of statements, sermons, recited creeds, hymns, deeds and promises, the validity and authority of which the thinking Christian feels compelled to examine. The examination of these phenomena and the testing of the thought processes related to them are indeed the only avenues to the perception and understanding of what we may call the peculiar logic of God's doings with Israel and with all of mankind. While we will reserve the examination of the phenomena and thought structures for the systematic part of the present study, we must enter into the Scripture-and-tradition question not without the awareness of the cardinal importance of this seemingly trivial observation.

The so-called Scripture-and-tradition problem is burdened by the traditional Protestant interest in making a sharp distinction between the first part of tradition, the canonical Scripture, and the second part, the subsequent material; this distinction is the Christian theologians' version of the principle "No revelation after Ezra." The classical Protestant fear was that Roman Catholic theology's approach to tradition would result in a "world-verification" type of theology, to take up the expression used in Chapter I, c. Scripture was conceived as qualitatively different from later tradition, which was understood as a "more worldly" expression of the Church's awareness of the *Christus praesens.* The trend in recent publications, however, is quite different, and an interesting shift of concern can be observed in both Protestant and Roman Catholic studies on tradition. While noted Roman Catholic scholars[88] are trying hard to show that the mainstream of Catholic theology, especially since the Council of Trent, has not advocated an equation of Scripture and tradition but has ultimately been interested in only one "source" of revelation, recent World Council of Churches studies, as well as private publications by Protestants, have attempted to do more justice to the theological importance of tradition. This is a healthy development, and one which could have begun much sooner if only the theologians had been aware of the striking similarities between the theological evaluation of tradition by the Tridentine theologians and their Protestant contemporaries. The issue of "Scripture and tradition" no longer constitutes the main point of difference between Protestant and Catholic theology. Rather it is the understanding of the Church, of her union with Christ and her task in the world, which remains as an unsolved problem.

The classical and somewhat outdated Protestant-Catholic controversy on Scripture and tradition has obscured the understanding of the positions of the Early Church Fathers, in that the post-Reformation problem has been superimposed upon the early Fathers' theology. Although some of them, notably Irenaeus and Tertullian, dealt with the problem of tradition, we must judge that their main interest was in the establishment of the biblical canon for the sake of fixing a core of tradition as a whole; the modern version of the problem was not their concern. The same can be said about the ecumenical councils. The later councils all referred to the unchallenged authority of Nicaea, which was considered inspired, but Scripture was not seen as being in competition with the authority of the councils or of important Fathers. Only toward the end of the classical period of Early Church theology did Church tradition gain the upper hand over Scripture. The well-known statement of Vincent of Lerins[89] and corresponding definitions within the later Greek Church, especially

---

[88] Besides the works of Congar, see especially George Tavard, "Scripture and Tradition: Sources or Source?" in *JES*, Vol. I, No. 3 (1964), pp. 445 ff; and "Tradition in the Early Post-Tridentine Theology" in *ThSt*, Vol. 23 (1962), pp. 377 ff., and *Scripture and Ecumenism*, ed. by Leonard J. Swidler (Pittsburgh: Duquesne University Press, 1965).

[89] *Commonitorium* 2,5 (Migne, *PL* 50, 639): "*quod ubique, quod semper, quod ab omnibus creditum est, hoc est . . . vere proprieque catholicum.*" The tradition does not tolerate any *profectus* (progress) or any *permutatio* (change). The fixation of tradition is guaranteed by the *universitas*, the *antiquitas* and the *consensio omnium*.

by John of Damascus,[90] produced an evaluation of tradition which
de facto challenged the importance of the Bible. Tradition became a
depositum and theology was left with the task of merely making
distinctions. The time of writing commentaries was over, and the law-
yers of the Church began treating the *depositum* in legal and no
longer in theological terms. This development culminated in the decisions of Toulouse (1229) and Tarracon (1234) prohibiting the use
of the Bible. Even the Council of Trent (*Sessio* IV)[91] treated the
Bible as if it were a basic lawbook which contained in principle what
later dogmatical explications would bring to fuller light. This evaluation is, of course, only possible on the basis of a principle of
"growth" or "unfolding" of something which exists without change;
or better: what "grows" or "unfolds" merely belongs to the epistemological realm. The authority of tradition is an indispensable
tool for those who desire to *understand* what is, in any case, true. In
this understanding, truth does not change; what changes is the manner and degree of clarification.

It is obvious that tradition understood in this way no longer serves
as a living expression of the Church's awareness of the *Christus
praesens*. The presence of Christ in the Spirit, if mentioned at all, is
merely invoked and claimed as the guarantor of the authority of the
teaching office of the Church. Tradition without critical and living
reception, without selection and reexamination, is a sign of death.
A theology which has lost its criterion of reception produces histor-
ical-theological experts, but not living and responsible theologians.
Theologians, however, are not keepers of archives but interpreters of
the present in the light of God's history with his people in the past.
Not only is the Catholic Church guilty of having prohibited this free
and responsible functioning of her theologians, but the Protestant
Church has fallen victim to precisely the same temptation by having
absolutized the authority of the Reformers and the confession books
of the various denominations. What *criterion* can be found and used
to avoid the lifeless repetition of the statements of the Fathers, as
well as to avoid the opposite extreme, the faithless and individualistic
disconnection from the witness of the Church in generations past?

[90] *De fide orthodoxa* IV, 12 and 42: the unwritten and written *paradosis* is, as
distinct from Western theology, meant to be a help for Orthodox worship
(*proskynein Christon*): it is not "saving knowledge" in the Western
(Catholic *and* Protestant) sense.
[91] *Denz.* 783–786.

In order to answer this question, we cannot avoid making a distinction between the *form* or place and the *content* of tradition. This distinction is implied in the work of the Reformers; but it was first formulated in concrete terms by August Twesten in 1826.[92] Twesten distinguished the *sole authority of Scripture* as the "formal principle" from *justification by faith alone* as the "material principle" of Protestantism. A modification of this distinction will be useful in our connection here, although Twesten's reference to justification is problematical. But the questions concerning the form and place of tradition as over against the Bible, on the one hand, and of the content of tradition as compared with the content of the Bible, on the other hand, ought not to be separated from each other, nor should one of them be overstressed at the expense of the other.

The question concerning the *form* and place of tradition focuses upon the concept of canon. We may take Oscar Cullmann's position as representative of those authors who seem to base their view of Scripture and tradition primarily upon this "formal principle." Cullmann intends to provide a historico-theological proof for what can hardly be proved (merely) historically, namely, the qualitative difference between the eyewitness *paradosis* and the later human explication, the *paradosis tōn anthrōpōn*. The former is "by a direct *apokalypsis* from the Lord,"[93] while the latter is only indirectly the work of the risen Lord and is exposed to the criticism which Jesus himself used of "human traditions" (Mark 7:8). The sum (statistically?) of all the traditions from each eyewitness "constitutes the *paradosis* of Christ.[94] The witness of the Apostles is unique in a qualitative and normative, not only in a chronological way. Cullmann's concept of time serves here as a proof.[95] Thus the content of I Cor. 11:23 ff. is *apo tou kyriou*, from the Lord, while Justin Martyr's words are only indirectly a witness, as are also sometimes Paul's words if expressly qualified by him as merely human words (e.g. I Cor. 7:25, "But I give my opinion as one who by the Lord's mercy is trustworthy"). One can readily agree with Cullmann[96] that Tertullian and Irenaeus,

---

[92] Following M. L. de Wette, Twesten unfolded this concept in his *Vorlesungen über die Dogmatik der evangelisch lutherischen Kirche*, Vol. I (Hamburg: F. Perth, 1826; 4th ed., 1838).

[93] Oscar Cullmann, "The Tradition," in his *The Early Church* (Philadelphia: Westminster Press, 1956), p. 66; cf. now *Heil als Geschichte*, pp. 269 ff.

[94] "The Tradition," p. 73.

[95] *Ibid.*, pp. 75 ff.

[96] *Ibid.*, p. 96.

though chronologically more remote from the New Testament than Barnabas and the Shepherd of Hermas, can be much closer to the content of the apostolic witness than earlier witnesses. But Cullmann's whole argument is based upon a distinction between "apostolic" and "post-apostolic," a distinction which would be fatal to the Church in our time if Cullmann did not use his elaborate concept of the sacraments in order to safeguard the continuing activity of the risen Christ. Moreover, it cannot really be determined historically what difference there is between Paul's "direct *apokalypsis*" ("not a vision"[97]) from the risen Christ and the claims of later Fathers also to have had such revelations! One cannot avoid the suspicion that Cullmann wants to cast into historical form what can only be *believed in actu*. His concept of canon depends upon the theological evaluation that "it was at that very time that God granted to the Church the grace of recognizing the difference between the period of the incarnation and the period of the Church."[98] But why, we ask, was it not at another time that God granted such insights? Cullmann's answer is[99] that the early Christians understood that they were living at "the mid-point of time, the mid-point of the history of salvation"; and this is also why "the Old Testament was received into the canon . . .": it "was admitted only because" of this understanding. This reference to the Old Testament is obviously subject to challenge. Moreover, it must be asked whether Cullmann's theological statement is compatible with the historical question he has raised. J. Daniélou's criticism of Cullmann[100] is quite meaningful: "He [Daniélou] says that I speak of apostolic tradition as a theologian, and of ecclesiastical tradition as a historian." While we would not criticize Cullmann's conclusions concerning the canon, we cannot admit that he has done more than merely unfold the assertions with which he began. The formal principle of *sola Scriptura* was a theological axiom to begin with and it has remained so throughout the course of the argument.

Another group of scholars is primarily concerned with the *content*

---

[97] *Ibid.*, p. 61. Karl Rahner, "Visions and Prophecies," in *Studies in Modern Theology* (Freiburg: Herder; London: Burns & Oates, 1965), pp. 88 ff., explores in an original way the "possibility and theological significance of private revelations and visions" (pp. 89 ff.).

[98] Cullmann, *ibid.*, p. 92.

[99] *Ibid.*, p. 93.

[100] Quoted by Cullmann, *ibid.*, p. 80.

of the later tradition as compared with the content of the Bible. Their question is: What are the additions, omissions, distortions and changes which occurred in the Early Church and already in the later books of the New Testament? Ernst Käsemann,[101] for instance, applies the same freedom of making distinctions and of accepting a great variety of streams of traditions to the New Testament itself, as other scholars did to the interpretation of the works of the Fathers. The canon of the New Testament is disregarded as a factor within the actual operation of theological-exegetical work. This approach is of course nothing new in itself. F. C. Baur, at the latest, marks the beginning of this method. But Käsemann is more courageous and consistent in the application of this principle of operation than were others before him, especially because he tries not to slip into the temptation of judging the earlier by the later stages of development (as did the great scholars of the nineteenth century, e.g. Cardinal Newman). He calls into question the *sola Scriptura* principle, though he uses it himself, fully realizing the risk he is taking.

So much for the summary of the two basic approaches to the distinction between Scripture and later tradition. But we have not yet received a criterion for the reception of tradition, i.e. for selecting from the tradition those voices that make transparent *the* tradition among the traditions. We can only agree with Albert Outler[102] when he says that "*Solus Christus* is . . . the measure of the permissible boundaries of Christian teaching . . ." and that "Jesus Christ is the Christian dogma." The "*traditum*" from God and the "*actus tradendi*" as worked by the Spirit are certainly the center of theology, as Outler says. Who will deny this? But if this and only this is said without further qualification, one may either agree with Käsemann's method or else take refuge in Cullmann's safe distinctions. Both could agree with Outler that "the Holy Spirit . . . recreates the original act of tradition (*traditum*) by an act of 'traditioning' (*actus tradendi*), so that the tradition of Jesus Christ becomes a living force in later lives. . . ."[103]

It seems that one reaches ultimately the same result whether one operates with or without a fixed canon-concept. And, contrary to

[101] Ernst Käsemann, *Exegetische Versuche und Besinnungen*, I and II, partly contained in *Essays in New Testament Themes* (cf. FN 9, above).

[102] Albert C. Outler, *The Christian Tradition and the Unity We Seek* (New York: Oxford University Press, 1957), p. 128.

[103] *Ibid.*, p. 111.

one's first reaction or impression, it appears that it is *less* risky to work *without* than *with* a fixed canon-concept. *The true canon-concept is manifest in the seriousness with which one works with the text* and not in the theological or historical affirmations which one makes about the canon. The investigation of the content and appropriateness of tradition runs parallel with the daring undertaking of New Testament content criticism. We may ask whether there is really a *theological* difference between Luther's criticism of the Epistle of James, Käsemann's criticism of II Peter, Harnack's criticism of Ignatius and Barth's criticism of Schleiermacher. A *theological* criterion is necessary in every instance. It is of little use to determine this criterion in advance, for if it is to be correct (e.g. Luther's "*Was Christum treibet*," What brings forth Christ) it is too broad; and if it is specific enough (e.g. "personal encounter" or "Kerygma as liberating my existence") it is no longer correct. General hermeneutical preconsiderations are of little use in bridging the gap between exegesis and systematic theology. Exegetical work inevitably leads to dogmatical decisions. The same respect for the text and the same willingness to listen is required whether we read biblical texts or texts of the later tradition. The "canon" will be "discovered" *in actu* and this discovery will be part of dogmatical thinking itself.

But it will be permissible and useful to apply a modification of Twesten's distinction between a formal and a material principle. *The formal principle will be that the "earlier" will have to explain the "later," and not vice versa.* To be sure, this is not a material principle, otherwise Ignatius would really be closer to the content of the New Testament than Athanasius, and Thomas closer than Calvin. There is no "progress" in theology which can be measured chronologically. It is undoubtedly true that we modern Christians find it more difficult to "hear the Gospel" in Justin's Apologies than in Chrysostom's sermons. But this does not mean that the authors themselves *heard* the Gospel in proportion to the degree to which we think we can hear it when reading their writings. By the same token, we can say that modern theological writings speak more concretely to contemporary man than many passages of the Bible, but this does not imply that the former have more authority than the latter. *Formally* speaking, the "earlier" has priority over the "later" and the "later" must be interpreted in the light of the "earlier." The application of this formal principle suggests that the study of the Fathers and the whole tradition of the Church be carried out in the form of history of *biblical interpretation.*[104] It should be repeated that this cannot be a "material principle," but it certainly is the only meaningful and historically honest method of taking the Fathers as seriously as they deserve to be taken. The material that is worth our time and study, our respect and willingness to listen, must be concerned with the explication and application of biblical material. And this can be said of many of the Fathers and of the councils. Origen the heretic, Tertullian the schismatic and the Antiochians who lost the game rank equally with Augustine, Luther and Calvin according to this formal principle, insofar as their works are part of the "stream of tradition," i.e. of discussing, debating, unfolding, criticizing and clarifying earlier material which deals with, or is identical with, the *earliest* tradition, Scripture. The canon, therefore, is the concept that brings to expression this formal principle. The examination of the relation between the canonical material and later tradition is the *scholarly quest* of the faithfulness of the "later" to the "earlier" within tradition, and ultimately of the "later" to the "earliest," to Scripture.

The *content* question, however, can only be decided *in actu*, that is to say, in the worshipful and prayerful reception of the *Christus praesens* who opens up to the Church and its individual members and scholars the dimensions of the past, the present and the future. The different "degrees of urgency" of the Church's and theology's task will be seen in the present and will determine the principle of selection of tradition, that is, of thankful reception and of critical elimination. What holds true regarding the earliest tradition, Scripture, is quantitatively even more obvious with respect to later tradition, i.e. that certain books of the Bible do not "speak" at certain times,[105] and that certain Fathers and council decisions of the Church are

---

[104] Gerhard Ebeling's theological program is based upon his thesis that the history of the Church is to be seen from the point of view of history of biblical interpretation; cf. *Kirchengeschichte als Geschichte der Auslegung der Heiligen Schrift*, and *Die Geschichtlichkeit der Kirche und ihrer Verkündigung als theologisches Problem* (Tübingen: J. C. B. Mohr, 1947 & 1954); see also his " 'Sola Scriptura' und das Problem der Tradition," in *Schrift und Tradition* (FN 85), pp. 95 ff., and the article "Tradition" in *RGG*, 3rd ed., Vol. VI, pp. 976–984.

[105] The classical example is Luther's low opinion of the Epistle of James. We may also think of the Epistle to the Hebrews, which for a long time has not received much attention but which today is preferred by many preachers over other epistles.

recognized as most meaningful in one period and as quite irrelevant or even dangerous in another. The Church at present must not look for a "fuller meaning" *in* the texts written by the Church of the past (e.g., the Bible) but the Church at present must understand *herself as* the *sensus plenior* of the ancient texts, if it is really true that her history is constituted by promise and fulfillment. *There is no other material principle for receiving the content of tradition than the recognition of the Christus praesens.* This, however, is a reception of tradition within the context of prayer and worship, an insight which the Western Church should learn again from the Early Church and perhaps from today's Eastern Orthodoxy. No final commentary can ever be written and no final word can ever be spoken about the theological value of the content of biblical and ecclesiastical tradition *for today.* What, for example, the first epistle of John said about and against the world may have been necessary at his time and may again become necessary; what Ignatius said about the function of the bishop may have been necessary in a time of persecution; Hippolytus' understanding of the Church may have been useful against his "Moral Rearmament" colleagues in Rome; and Augustine's concept of world and man was needed to combat Pelagius, and his notion of the Church to fight the Donatists. But who would judge that these conclusions are to be of perennial authority in the Church, except a theologian who treats Scripture and tradition as a legal codex because of his unawareness of the ever-new presence of Jesus Christ?

By way of summary we can say that the problem of Scripture and tradition is a question of the relation between the Church and the presence of Jesus Christ, who was also present to the Church in times past. The competition between Scripture and later tradition was not recognized by the Early Church, but became a fact toward the end of the classical period of Early Church theology. The Reformation discovered this and operated with the *sola Scriptura* principle in theory, although Protestant Orthodoxy evaluated Reformation tradition as positively as did Catholic theology with regard to all of tradition. Later scholarship either emphasized anew the *sola Scriptura* principle (e.g. Cullmann) or else disregarded the canon and paid attention only to the faithfulness with which later tradition represented the "content" of the biblical books (e.g. Käsemann). But the difference between these approaches is not a fundamental one. Both of them are in basic agreement with the Reformers and, in fact, with the whole of Western tradition that God has *ceased* to perform *new* acts which are qualitatively of the same order as those witnessed to in the Bible. All of these approaches, therefore, look for a "basic message" or kerygma and examine later tradition as to its faithfulness to it. We are not able, however, to crystallize an eternal "content" out of the biblical books, such as "justification," for instance. Thus we suggested that we should distinguish between a formal principle of interpreting the "later" by the "earlier" (which constitutes formally the canon and the *sola Scriptura* principle) and a material principle of the reception of tradition in the light of the *Christus praesens*. The two approaches are distinct from each other because the former is based upon scholarly research and the latter upon prayer and worship. But the two must not be separated as though research and worship should be allowed to exist in isolation from one another.[106]

Our inquiry so far has shown that not only the understanding of the Church and its task but also the distinction between Scripture and tradition are clearly dependent upon the understanding of the union between Christ and the Church. One can scarcely say that contemporary theology does more than pay lip service to this fundamental affirmation. Western theology is still imprisoned by the idea that God's contact with mankind, and especially man's understanding of this contact, is limited to a certain era in which God made known what later generations would have to repeat and apply. Western theology's concentration on such concepts as "justification," understood as the timeless essence of the Bible, demonstrates our observation. A confrontation between early Eastern Orthodoxy and the Western Augustinian understanding of the Church's union with Christ will give further evidence to our thesis. It is only then that we can deal with the systematic question of what significance the terms "God" and "*Christus praesens*" have for the theology of the Church in our time.

Before continuing with our historical reflections, it may be useful to list some propositions concerning tradition[107] and hermeneutics, in order partly to summarize the findings of the chapter and to set the tone for the second and third chapters.

---

[106] Cf. Markus Barth, "Sola Scriptura," in *Scripture and Ecumenism* (see above, FN 88), pp. 75–94.

[107] We must leave undiscussed some important questions which would spring from the above discussion, for example: (a) To what extent can we speak of an "action of God in the formation of tradition," as does James Barr (*SJT*, Vol. X, No. 1 [Mar. 1957] and *SJT*, Vol. XI, No. 1 [Mar. 1958]. Cf. my dis-

PROPOSITIONS REGARDING TRADITION AND HERMENEUTICS

1) The task of theology is the interpretation of events, present and past, and of interpretation of interpretations. But (and this is neglected by Bultmann, though perhaps contrary to his intent) the one who interprets is *not only man* (out of his self-understanding) but God in his ever-new acts. He shapes the "corporate consciousness" of the Church.

2) It follows that if this were not so, man could only pronounce himself guilty or forgiven, and without this "speech event" there would be neither guilt nor forgiveness, neither prayer nor divine preservation. This would lead to ontological idealism.

3) But God declares *in his history* with his people what history is. He interprets the events by always being ahead of his people, pressing toward fulfillment, for he is the God of the Exodus and not the God of Plato. "Promise" and "fulfillment" are the noetical categories of the "progress of history."

4) God causes the history of tradition in the Old and New Testaments and in the Church, making manifest *the* tradition among the traditions by being present in Jesus Christ through the Spirit. It is because of the *Christus praesens* that the Church can understand history as God's history of promise and fulfillment, expressed in human words related to events.

5) The texts of the Old and New Testaments have been recognized by the later Church to have *sufficient momentum* to have taken later believers into the movement from promise to fulfillment. Reviewing all of tradition, the Church can today repeat the judgment of the Early Church concerning the earliest tradition, Scripture, by saying: This record of God's movement suffices for our purposes of formally examining the later records.

6) For exegesis this means that the Bible can be recognized only in and by the Church (as can Jesus Christ himself). We read the Bible

---

cussion in A *Theology of Proclamation* [Richmond: John Knox Press, 1960], pp. 41 ff.), without falling into the spiritualistic hope "that God in his providence watched over and guided the molding of the tradition." Barr has recently pursued this further (*Old and New in Interpretation*, cf. FN 2, above) and moved close to the concept of tradition being the force that provides the matrix within which general intellectual history is possible. Noteworthy is the forward thrust of his understanding of tradition. (b) How can the entirely non-dualistic concept of history in the circle around W. Pannenberg (*Offenbarung als Geschichte*, cf. the criticism in EvTh, ½ [Jan.–Feb. 1962], devoted to this theme) be utilized without ending up with a relativistic concept of revelation? (c) To what extent can one speak of "typology" regarding the Old Testament without reversing this retrospect-typology to a prospect-typology leading into the period of Church history?

because we are the Church; we go back consciously to the *magna charta* of men's words expressing God's promises and fulfillments—whereby the first decisive fulfillment, the advent of Jesus Christ, is seen as the climax of this collection of human witnesses—pointing again in promise form to the future, to the "new creation" of which Christ is the firstborn and the Spirit the down payment.

7) The interpreter of the Bible is to relate his own situation, i.e. the "raw material" of his own uninterpreted situation, to the *magna charta*, the Bible, in order to see how he is to interpret (anew) his own situation. Thus he makes his own situation relevant to the text in order to have it interpreted by the text. The task of exegesis is done when this circle is closed, i.e. when both have happened: my making relevant the situation to the text and my receiving a new interpretation of my situation from the text.

8) But the majority of individual texts will not lend themselves directly to this interpretation of the interpreter. They will have to be seen in a larger context, and the particular exegesis will be of no other benefit than to shed light on later (or earlier) exegeses which he will carry out. Piece after piece of the mosaic is studied so that the Bible itself will become more and more powerful in the Church's understanding of history as the movement from promise to fulfillment.[108]

9) The forcible attempt to "make relevant" texts which do not lend themselves at a certain time to the closing of the circle must presuppose a timeless God who has no history with his people; the same is to be said about the attempt to discard such texts because of their having disappointed the personal interest of the interpreter.

10) The individual interpreter should be aware of his own place within the tradition of the Church and the course of his own life:

a) he is not the only person to interpret this text;
b) he is not the first one to have interpreted it;
c) this is not the first text (nor the last) he will interpret;
d) he is not to look for a *sensus plenior* in the text, but he is to recognize the Church to which he belongs as the *sensus plenior* of the biblical texts.

[108] The implications for "Christian Education" are far reaching. Teaching and preaching are by no means parallel (running) activities of the Church. Teaching is the utilization of the memory of the Church and the building up of new material for later memory, i.e. teaching is the carrying together of pieces to enlarge the "mosaic"; and the purpose of teaching is not to aim at a "direct encounter" with Jesus Christ. Bible texts, historical material and ethical questions can be studied in a teaching session without asking prematurely "what relevance" this material has for the present situation of the participants. If our Church teachers continue asking this question they should not be surprised at the disappointing outcome, *viz.* that their teaching sessions are a kind of watered-down worship service.

II

***

Union with Christ in
Greek Patristic Thought

THE FIRST CHAPTER has dealt with the question of Christology in such fashion that the complexity of the problem and its connection with ecclesiology, history and hermeneutics have been at the center of attention. The purpose of that discussion was to show the dimensions of the problem and to prepare a critical evaluation of the Augustinian heritage in contemporary Western theology. To continue this preparation, we must now focus our attention upon Christology itself. Classical Christology originated in Greek patristic theology, and the following brief chapter will therefore deal with aspects of the Greek Fathers' Christology. Our discussion will be guided by the questions: Has Greek patristic thought produced any insights concerning the *Christus praesens* which were neglected in later Western theology? And: Are the Greek Fathers, the architects of classical Christology, responsible for any of the unfortunate developments in Western theology?

a) The So-called Gnostic Framework of Christology

Western theology has frequently accused the Greek Fathers of having unfolded their theological topics within the framework of

Gnosticism or, more specifically, within the thought world of Platonism or Neo-Platonism. This criticism originated in the nineteenth century[1] and has dominated most of patristic research ever since. The systematic fruits of this historical criticism are still noticeable in recent attempts to rid theology of a "two-story" world view. Dietrich Bonhoeffer's *Ethics*, Bultmann's program of demythologization and Pannenberg's recent criticism of Barth's "Platonism"[2] can serve as examples of three quite different attempts to free theology from the bondage of the Gnostic or Neo-Platonic framework. Justifiable as these theological programs may be, we will have to address ourselves here to the more specific question of the intent of the Greek Fathers. Even if it should be agreed that no remnants of Gnostic concepts can be tolerated in modern theology, one cannot therefore devaluate the contribution of the early Fathers as a matter of course.

The "Neo-Platonic" is that world view which operates with a hierarchy of beings, beginning with the highest and reaching down to the lowest matter, which is *eo ipso* devaluated. Even if complicated and differentiated, the Neo-Platonic world view basically represents a "two-story" concept of the universe. "Gnosticism," however, prior and related to Neo-Platonism, is to be defined from the standpoint of theology as the concept of a *movement* of the savior, the *Logos* or the *heavenly man* from the highest God down into the region of human perception and back to its place of origin. This is of course no exhaustive definition of Gnosticism, but it describes sufficiently that aspect of Gnosticism which lends itself to a christological formulation. The movement of the savior is a *circle*, the journey of the redeemer from God down to earth and home to God. We can leave aside the question whether this concept necessarily implies a docetic understanding of the redeemer, and we also bypass the problem of human knowledge, of *gnosis* itself.

Our interest is limited to the Gnostic framework, i.e. to the circle, the "journey of the redeemer." The obvious theological advantage of the circular journey concept of Gnosticism is the possibility, if not the necessity, of speaking simultaneously of the redeemer and of the

[1] See FN, 18 Chap. I. Continuing with the anti-Greek trend in Protestant theology, Harnack's *History of Dogma* has had much influence on later patristic scholarship.

[2] *Offenbarung als Geischichte*; cf. also Otto Weber's criticism of Barth's "Platonism" in *Grundlagen der Dogmatik* (Neukirchen: Buchhandlung des Erziehungsvereins, 1962), Vol. II, pp. 172, 184.

redeemed, for the homeward journey of the "heavenly man" is for the purpose of leading (the souls of) the redeemed home to the place of the origin of the redeemer himself. Translated into Christology, this would mean that statements about Jesus Christ are at the same time statements about salvation. The Gnostic framework lends itself to a theology in which Christology and soteriology coincide. A further step in the utilization of this concept can lead directly to the (more biblical) view of redemptive history (*Heilsgeschichte*). In other words, the Gnostic circle is, structurally speaking, the "condensed form" of *Heilsgeschichte*; for if one "breaks open" the circle and bends its ends apart, one can speak of God's *initial* contact with his people, leading *eventually* (at the "middle of time") to the incarnation and *finally* (at the "end of time") to the consummation. Thus the circle has become a curve, describing God's self-disclosure in history. What served originally as a description of the movement of the *Logos* from the Father to men and back to the Father, now provides the framework for the understanding of the whole of redemptive history: God's movement with his people from creation, fall and covenant through the history of Israel to the climax of God's self-disclosure in Jesus of Nazareth and leading man home to God in the *apokatastasis panton* at the end of time. The original, primitive Gnostic circle was more directly concerned with the movement and fate of the redeemer, though the participation of the redeemed was spoken of simultaneously; but the later and more elaborate view of redemptive history was directly concerned with the movement and fate of mankind, seen as the product of the redeemer's movement.

This shift of emphasis can be observed in the development from Ignatius to Irenaeus. Ignatius, without being a Gnostic, but certainly utilizing the "Gnostic framework," is primarily concerned with the redeemer's journey out "of the silence of God"[3] into human flesh and back to the Father.[4] His journey is truly God's journey, for it is God who suffers[5] and whose blood is shed.[6] He is to be spoken of "as God," as Clement II continues to teach a few decades later. Prayers can be directed to him.[7] The purpose of his coming was to establish the *henosis*, the oneness between God and man, which oneness is reflected in the relation between the bishop and his congrega-

[3] Magn. 8:3
[4] Rom. 3:3
[5] Rom. 6:3
[6] Eph. 1:1
[7] Eph. 20:1

tion. *Henosis*, union, is the key to Ignatius' theology. The believer can enter into union with God through the redeemer either by suffering the death of a martyr (physical *martyrium*) or by partaking of the eucharist (spiritual *martyrium*). But union with Christ is the goal of the believer's life in any case, and it is a martyr's union.[8] Those who celebrate the eucharist "do not live like men but like Jesus Christ."[9] They are imitators of the sufferings of God[10] and thus "reach God,"[11] or, as Ignatius can say, they even "become Word of God"[12] and "pure bread of Christ."[13] The advent and departure of the redeemer is the basis of the believer's *henosis* with the exalted Lord and the physical or spiritual *martyrium* is the cause for the participation, or better, the guarantee for remaining in this union. Ignatius only seemingly neglects the importance of history in his concentration upon the Christ-event itself; he believed that the coming of the Logos in the flesh, the epiphany of the redeemer, happened at the end of time.[14]

The Apologists maintained theoretically this strong christological basis for soteriology; at least they did not deny the tradition that had come down to them. But their interest focused upon a more moralistic understanding of the imitation concept of the earlier Fathers. This emphasis molded their understanding of Jesus Christ as the model and pattern for obedient behavior before God. The usual criticism leveled against the Apologists stresses this point and accuses them of having moralized and thereby belittled the main points of early Christian tradition. This criticism has been overdone, for it has done injustice to the Apologists' courageous atttempt to discuss theology with unbelievers. We must admit, however, that the Apologists have not added anything valuable to early Christology. But their chief shortcoming is not in the realm of Christology but rather in their most unfortunate way of dealing with the Old Testament, i.e. in hermeneutics, where they opened wide the doors to Stoic concepts, which also influenced negatively Tertullian and through him Western theology.

Leaving aside Marcion, whose soteriological thoughts are far more

[8] Rom. 8:1
[9] Trall. 2:1
[10] Rom. 6:3
[11] Rom. 1:2; 2:1
[12] Rom. 2:1
[13] Rom. 4:1
[14] Magn. 6:1

radical than his obviously traditional-Gnostic christological notions,
we can safely judge that Christology was formulated in a decisively
new way by Theophilus of Antioch and especially by Irenaeus, who
was influenced by Theophilus.[15] Theophilus seems to be the first to
have "broken" the Gnostic circle and to have transformed it into the
"curve" of redemptive history. Irenaeus[16] continued and systematized this approach in controversy with Gnosticism, of which, however, he had no systematic understanding. But his painfully elaborate
enumeration of Gnostic systems shows at least his interest in isolating
his own theology from Gnostic influence. In Irenaeus' theology, Jesus
Christ now embraces all of history, but yet he enters into history.
He reveals the Father, but the Father also reveals him, for "the Word
is God himself,"[17] inasmuch as the Son is in the Father and bears in
himself the Father.[18] But the incarnate Son is *substantialiter* identical with us, although in such fashion that one cannot separate the
works and the words of Jesus, which (separation) is possible regarding ordinary men. Irenaeus combined the "historical Jesus" and the
"*geschichtliche* Christ" in greater depth and more cogently than does
contemporary New Testament scholarship. At the same time, he
unfolded a truly eschatological understanding of the incarnation by
making it quite clear that the believer has not reached his final destiny by partaking in the benefits of the life, death and resurrection of
Jesus. The final consummation is still to be expected and as such it
sheds light on the understanding of the Christ-event as well as on the
present existence of the believer. Nevertheless, we must admit that
Irenaeus operated within the framework of Gnosticism;[19] and his
theology bears all the positive and negative marks of the concept of

[15] Friedrich Loofs, *Theophilus von Antiochien adversus Marcionem* (*TU*, No.
   46, 2, 1930; now Berlin: Akademie Verlag), advanced the thesis that Theophilus influenced Irenaeus so strongly that almost all the credit of originality
   should be given to Theophilus. But Loofs' thesis has not remained unchallenged.
[16] Helpful introductions to Irenaeus' theology are John Lawson, *The Biblical
   Theology of St. Irenaeus* (London: Epworth Press, 1946), and Gustaf Win-
   gren, *Man and the Incarnation* (Philadelphia: Muhlenberg Press, 1959; Swed-
   ish ed., 1947).
[17] *Adv. Haer.* II, 13.
[18] *Adv. Haer.* III, 6, 2. Irenaeus also stressed the importance of the "obedience
   of Jesus" (III, 21, 10; III, 22, 4), a most important insight that was almost
   lost after the time of Athanasius.
[19] Cf. R. M. Grant, *Gnosticism and Early Christianity* (New York: Columbia
   University Press, 1959), *passim*.

Heilsgeschichte: the (biblical) emphasis on history, understood backward from its expected end, but also the (unbiblical) attempts to outline the history of the plan of God within the realm of "evil" world history. But despite this disadvantage, one most decisive gain goes to the credit of Irenaeus: his historical understanding enabled the later Church to express in a legitimate theological way the fact that the Church has a past and a future and that its task in the *present* lies in the adoration of the present, risen Christ.

Later Greek theology made full use of this theological avenue. It was especially Athanasius[20] who combined the Irenaean heritage with a deep understanding of the impossibility of calculating objectively how man stands over against God. He was fully aware of the "Johannine" corrective to an objectified theology of *Heilsgeschichte*. The Cappadocians partly continued with this emphasis on adoration as a starting point of theology, as is manifest in their involvement in monastic movements. But the Cappadocians also took up the other part of Irenaeus' theology and of later tradition, namely, the question concerning the "natures" of Jesus Christ. Greatly stimulated by the premature formulation of the problem by Apollinaris of Laodicea, this lead to the long debate about nature Christology which is characteristic of the christological councils. Irenaeus' and Athanasius' strongest point, *viz.* the stress on the oneness of Christology and soteriology, gave way to a certainly more philosophical discussion about the relation between the two natures of Jesus Christ. But even then the Greek theologians maintained fully the best part of their tradition: the intimate connection between the adoration of the present, risen Christ and the intellectual formulation of theological thoughts. The question is only the extent to which the adoration continued to mold the formulation as it had done in earlier Greek theology. But the intent was certainly not to separate dogmatical thought from practical adoration. A proof of the strength of this tradition is the work of Gregory Palamas centuries later.

It may be justifiable to say that the "Gnostic framework" was less harmful to the theology of the Greek Fathers than the strong influence of Neo-Platonism, which began to dominate the theological scene with and after Origen, at the latest at the time of the great christological councils. It was at that time that the "two-story" world view was no longer seen as a framework for the description of a

[20] See my study *Athanasius*, esp. pp. 20 ff. and 71 ff.

movement but became part of the content of the theological question itself. Early Eastern theology in its best parts accepted the Gnostic framework as a *form of language* but did not make it an "object of belief." The Gnostic language *enabled* the early Fathers to express their chief concern, the vicarious function of Jesus Christ for the universe. We will have to face the question[21] whether the same concern can be expressed today in language totally different from that of the early Greek Fathers.

It is undoubtedly true that our positive evaluation of the contribution of this early period ought not to include the rather vague concept of *faith* and the obvious neglect of the biblical understanding of *grace.* Nor should we overlook its evidently unfortunate devaluation of history and of earthly human life, of such great influence in later Eastern and Western theology. Nevertheless, we must disagree with the usual Western criticism of the Greek Fathers which has declared them *de facto* unimportant and irrelevant to modern Western theology. The Gnostic language dress as such is not sufficient reason to dismiss a whole complex of theology which has emphasized the very insight which is lacking in Western theology: the doing of theology in the awareness of the *Christus praesens.*

The Western criticism, however, is not incomprehensible. Later Greek theology indeed lent itself to philosophical speculations and presented the West with a series of complicated questions for the handling of which Western theologians were not adequately equipped by tradition or intent. Plato and Aristotle would not have become so influential in Western medieval theology had the Fathers of the Greek councils been able and willing to abstain from raising philosophical questions, to which they gave theological answers. Conciliar Greek theology handed to the West (philosophical) problems which had not originally been part of the Eastern tradition, or which had at least not occupied a central place in it. This is another way of saying that *Greek theology was "more orthodox" before the Orthodox councils* than after. But it was conciliar theology which reached ecumenical recognition, partly because earlier theologians, and individual theologians on the whole, were suspected of Origenism.

We conclude then that the gnostic framework in Greek patristic thought appeared originally in the primitive form of a circle; that it was transformed into the curve of redemptive history which forms

[21] See Chapter VI.

the best part of preconciliar theology; that the disadvantages of this concept were the price paid for the great contribution of the Greek Fathers to the later Church, *viz.* the theological legitimation of the intimate relation between theology and adoration; and that this contribution was not utilized in the West because it was overshadowed by the Neo-Platonic thought structures of conciliar theology.

b) *The Dilemma Regarding Ontology and Epistemology*

Western theologians have devaluated the importance of Greek patristic thought not only by referring to its Gnostic framework but also by criticizing the alleged "ontology" of early Greek theology. Many quarters in modern Protestant theology are suspicious of ontology, especially since the influence of Kant (on the Continent) and of Anglo-Saxon pragmatism began to dominate theological thinking. Dietrich Bonhoeffer,[22] however, reopened the discussion in 1931; and the recent debates concerning the later work of Heidegger,[23] in connection with a new approach to the phenomenon of language, have again drawn attention to ontological questions. But the recent philosophical approaches to ontology are quite different from classical ontology as it was presented by Parmenides and later by Plato and Aristotle. Thus Kant's criticism[24] and the influence of Neo-Kantianism have prevailed regarding the theological evaluation of Greek patristic thought. The inherent difficulty was, however, that Western theologians expected to find in the Greek Fathers that type of ontology which the Western tradition had formed and continuously used and defended in Western scholastic theology. But this expectation was hardly correct. At least it was incorrect with regard to what we have called "the best part" of early Eastern tradition, and it is only partly right with respect to Greek conciliar and later Byzantine theology.

Concerning the use of ontology in Greek patristic thought, we can

---

[22] Dietrich Bonhoeffer, *Akt und Sein, Transzendentalphilosophie und Ontologie in der systematischen Theologie*, 1931 (reprint with introd. by Ernst Wolf; Munich: Chr. Kaiser Verlag, 1956); Engl. transl. by Bernard Noble, *Act and Being* (Harper & Row, 1961).

[23] E.g., Heinrich Ott, *Denken und Sein* (Zollikon: EVZ-Verlag, 1959).

[24] Kant substituted his *"Transzendentalphilosophie"* for the old ontology which received its name from and found its classical exposition in Christian Wolff's *Philosophia prima sive Ontologia* in 1729/30.

repeat, on the whole, what we said about its Gnostic framework. The early Fathers *made use* of traditional ontological concepts without intentionally turning them into theological content questions. In this they differ from the later medieval realists who were inclined to believe that what is *said "in intellectu fidei"* also is *"in re,"* in reality. *Statements of faith,* e.g. that God is a person or is in heaven or that the risen *Christ is in the flesh with the Father,* etc., were not equated by the early Fathers with *descriptions* of the mode of being of the trans-intelligible. The notion of an ontic description of trans-intelligible realities outside of faith, i.e. outside the framework of *worship,* had no legitimate place in the thinking of the Greek Fathers, nor in later Eastern Orthodoxy.[25] A fine example of this can be found in Athanasius' exposition of John 17:21: "Even as thou, Father, art in me, and I in thee, that they also may be in us."[26] And Eastern ecclesiastical art, such as the Ravenna mosaics, shows clearly the early Eastern believers' awareness that deliberately anthropomorphic pictures of the trans-intelligible "contents of faith" are permissible just *because* of their use in adoration and worship, their only legitimate use. Icons as well as creedal formulations undergo a *transfiguration* in worship. They are not meant to be *de facto* descriptions of ontic realities to which "pure reason" or the natural mind has access outside of faith. The Early Church (in East *and* West) was not aware of a tension or competition between theology and philosophy. The Fathers used philosophical language without any reflected suspicion or awareness of the inherent problems. But they did not doubt that philosophical wisdom is superseded by the mysteries of the Christian faith. Otherwise they would not have mentioned with admiration the "conversion" of philosophers like Justin, Clement of Alexandria and Augustine. Only later did Western theology begin to distinguish between the philosophical and the theological activities of the human mind.

Nevertheless, the fact that the Greek Fathers were not aware of the problem does not of course mean that it did not exist. And the willingly received influence of such outspoken Platonists as Metho-

---

[25] Cf. Vladimir Lossky, *The Vision of God* (London: Faith Press; and Clayton: American Orthodox Press, 1963), a historical investigation of the problem of the recognition of God from the early days of Eastern theology to Gregory Palamas.

[26] Athanasius, *Contra Arianos,* III, 17–25; in chap. 24 he makes it expressly clear that the analogy of the oneness is only seen in our creedal confession.

dius and Pseudo-Dionysius indicates clearly the readiness to change *means* and *instruments* of worship into *objects* of adoration. *Creeds* were originally meant to be the doxological results of prayerful theological reflection; but because of the many complicating factors during the period of the first four councils and because of the creeds' unfortunately *static* terminology, they became starting points for new reflection as though they were descriptions of heavenly realities. The concept of "nature" is a good example: the longer it was used in the christological controversy, the more static it became. And the West was, and still is, left with the impression that the employment of the *physis* concept in Greek theology is the clearest indication of the static way of thinking of early Greek Orthodox "ontology." But the history of the early use of this term shows that this judgment is inadequate. Yet, the victory of the Alexandrian thought structure over Antiochian theology seems to support it. And we must admit that with regard to Chalcedon the judgment is justified that ontological concepts gained the upper hand over the doxological use of traditional ontological language, although the Byzantine Church has continued to look at the results of the councils entirely within the framework of worship.

Only a powerful and living theology can stand the tension between subjective human recognition and divine reality. Irenaeus, in many ways Origen, and certainly Athanasius operated with *two orders of recognition* just because of their awareness of this tension. They realized that the books of the Bible and later Church tradition affirmed, in the dress of retrospective human recognition and language, the preeminent reality of God's doings. Athanasius, for instance, clearly distinguished between the view "from God's side," as we may call it, and the view "from man's side." What is true from God's side has preeminent reality over against human recognition and can only be adored, not rationally analyzed. But the human recognition within space and time can be unfolded logically. The statement, for example, that the *Logos* is co-eternal with the Father is derived from and *risked* on the basis of the recognition of the presence of Christ in worship, as it is also recognized in earlier witnesses. The *art of theology* consists in unfolding the divine reality in terms of human language in the full realization that human recognition must be imbedded in adoration. Theology unfolds in retrospect what has been recognized in faith and tested against biblical and other witnesses.

Thus Athanasius carefully balances statements concerning subjective human cognition against statements concerning objective divine reality. Most of Athanasius's writings reflect in their architecture this double order of recognition: what is first recognized and accepted is artfully placed as that which is to be unfolded and proven, and that which is seemingly presupposed in this operation is dependent upon that which is recognized first. Theological thinking is a circle which has no distinct and definable beginning, such as the preexistent Christ, a definition of the invisible world, or the "historical Jesus." The unfortunate one-sidedness of some Greek theology is a distortion of the true Greek theological tradition; and the beginnings of this deviation can be observed in the extreme positions of the two opposing parties, Alexandrian and Antiochian theology. While the former one-sidedly begins with a fixed concept of the pre-existent *Logos* and moves from there to the question of how the *Logos* became *flesh*, the latter proceeds in the opposite direction by starting with the cognition of Jesus Christ as man. But both theologies have sacrificed the double order of recognition. When this happens, the strongest point of early Eastern theology is weakened: the *theological* importance of the realization of the *Christus praesens* in worship. Worship, then, merely serves as the realm within which fixed dogmatical formulations are preserved, respected and handed down to the next generation. It is sad to observe that the greatest strength of the early Greek Church thus turned out to be its greatest weakness.

We can summarize by saying that the Protestant suspicion of the ontological element in Greek patristic thought is only partly justified. The best part of the classical Eastern tradition merely made use of traditional ontological language whereby the cognitive aspect was realized in worship. But later developments, partly beginning with the Cappadocians and obviously manifest in conciliar theology, no longer endured the tension between subjective recognition and objective realities and tended to turn creedal statements into objects of faith and adoration. The traditional importance of worship is maintained up to the present form of Eastern Orthodoxy; but theological thinking and formulation is no longer kept alive and fed by the activity of worship; rather, the ancient formulations are sanctioned and preserved within the framework of worship. Thus the Western criticism is partly justified, although it must be kept in mind that the Western Church has little enough on which to pride itself on this account. Early and medieval Western theology fell victim to Aristotelian and Neo-Platonic ontological thought structures more readily than did early Eastern theology. The problem is indeed one of language; and it is surprising that despite Augustine's insights into this complex matter the relation between ontological questions and language has not been dealt with until very recently, when the influence of Dilthey and Heidegger (on the Continent) and of linguistic analysis (mainly within English-speaking theology) has become effective.

While these recent discussions do not belong directly to our question concerning the contribution of early Greek theology, a more general statement will help avoid misunderstandings. With regard to both the interpretation of early Greek theology and the formulation of our present task in Church and theology, we should not agree with those who fear that any kind of ontological statement in theology necessarily implies a "theological ontology." It will hardly be possible to find and use an adequate language and thought structure for the expression of the interpretation of the present and the past (including the Bible) which succeeds in entirely avoiding ontological sentences. Granted that Plato's and Aristotle's concepts of the relation between ideas and phenomena, between essence and existence, and all the terms which belong to this thought world are no longer useful for the task of theology; we must also see that a historico-political thought structure, which we prefer today, will likewise imply ontological statements. This insight will at least restrain us in our criticism of early Eastern theology, although the task of critically reinterpreting the conciliar Christology is undoubtedly unavoidable.[27]

c) *Deification and Doxology*

A third criticism of the early Greek Fathers advanced by Western theologians, especially Protestant scholars, concerns the content itself of early Eastern theology. This criticism is more severe than the

[27] Private conversations with Greek Orthodox theologians in the Soviet Union, as well as some of their recent semi-official statements and publications, have confirmed the hope that Orthodox theologians today also share the view that the theology of the ecumenical councils needs critical reexamination. We only honor the Fathers of the Church by receiving critically what they have handed down to us.

understandable reservations regarding the Gnostic and ontological thought forms. Of especially grave consequence was Albrecht Ritschl's[28] critical evaluation of the "specifically Greek idea of piety," which he thought to have recognized in the theology of the Greek Christians. This judgment became typical of European and Anglo-Saxon theological liberalism; and found its historical exposition in the second volume of Harnack's *History of Dogma*, which influenced most of the standard works on the subject, such as those by Loofs, Seeberg, Bonwetsch, McGiffert, as well as those of M. Werner, W. Köhler and H. Lietzmann. The influence of this critical concept upon two or three generations of scholars and ministers can hardly be overestimated. Harnack's condemning verdict is best expressed by the simple label "deification." Redemption for the Eastern Fathers equals "deification," which is[29] "sub-Christian" because it lacks moral elements, is "unacceptable" because its formulation does not fit the Gospels, and demands the impossible because it is the Christian expression of the "egotistical desire for immortal duration." After Harnack it became fashionable to conceive the whole of early Eastern theology as centering around the poles of mortality and immortality (*aphtharsia, incorruptibilitas*).

Besides some Roman Catholic defenses and early Protestant attempts to rehabilitate the Greek Fathers,[30] it was the work of Karl Barth and also of Emil Brunner which began the shift within Protestant historical scholarship. Brunner, in his desire to reestablish the authority of Irenaeus and Athanasius, says of the latter in almost enthusiastic reaction against the famous historians: "The *Logos* doctrine of Athanasius is the finest of all in its systematic, and at the same time non-speculative existential character. Athanasius above all has clearly worked out the idea that man, created in the Word of God, has in it his life-principle—granted by grace—and since he has fallen away from the Word can only be restored by the Word coming to him again. 'God's Word had to come Himself.' Only the Logos could

---

[28] A. Ritschl, *A Critical History of the Doctrine of Justification and Reconciliation* (see FN 18, Chap. I), pp. 1–21, etc.

[29] A. von Harnack, *Das Wesen des Christentums* (Leipzig: Hinrichs'sche Buchhandlung, 1900), pp. 145–147; Engl. transl., *What Is Christianity?* (New York: G. P. Putnam's Sons, 1901).

[30] The first attack on Harnack in this matter was risked, so far as I know, by K. Bornhäuser, *Die Vergottungslehre des Athanasius und Joh. Damascenus* (Gütersloh, 1903); cf. Harnack's review in *ThLZ*, No. 17 (1903), pp. 476 ff.

make good, since He alone reveals God and in this revelation brings back the life which had been lost."[31] More solid, however, is the rehabilitation advanced by Arnold Gilg,[32] who has carefully examined the so-called deification passages of some of the Fathers. Roman Catholic studies[33] have strengthened the new approach, and we can hope that the recent ecumenical contact with Eastern Orthodoxy will stimulate further interest in the examination of the *content* of early Greek theology.

Is it really true that the Greek Fathers were concerned primarily with *redemption*, and that redemption meant to them *deification?* The first part of this question would require a detailed study, one which has not yet been undertaken. The number of those theologians is still limited to whom it might occur that the Christian faith is not adequately described by the term "religion of redemption." And among this small number we would expect to find few historians who devote their time to the Greek Fathers, especially because of the generally accepted opinion that the Greek Fathers do represent a theology of redemption. Special studies on the subject[34] have concentrated on the form and development of the doctrine of redemption, rather than on the question as to whether the doctrine of redemption actually occupies a central place in the theology of the Greek Fathers. The term "redemption" demands, of course, further precision. If it refers to man's separation from the world, the world being considered evil and opposed to God, it would have a Gnostic flavor and could claim only partial biblical foundation. If it should refer, however, to man's liberation from himself, from his past and present, from his involvement in attempts of self-liberation, from selfishness, death, and fear of death, it could claim with greater right to summarize a central aspect of the biblical books. It does not seem

---

[31] Emil Brunner, *Der Mittler* (Tübingen: J. C. B. Mohr, 1947, 1930); Engl. transl. by Olive Wyon, *The Mediator* (Philadelphia: Westminster Press, 1947), p. 624.

[32] Arnold Gilg, *Weg und Bedeutung der altkirchlichen Christologie* (1936; now Munich: Chr. Kaiser Verlag, 1955); cf. also *ThZ*, 1954, pp. 113 ff., and J. Gross, *La divinisation du chrétien d'après les Pères grecs* (Paris, 1938). Cf. also Jaroslav Pelikan, *The Finality of Jesus Christ in an Age of Universal History* (Richmond: John Knox Press, 1966).

[33] E.g. Jean Daniélou, *Platonism et Théologie Mystique* (Aubier, 1944), and various contributions to the collection *Das Konzil von Chalcedon*, ed. A. Grillmeier and H. Bacht, Vol. I–III (Würzburg: Echter Verlag, 1951 *et seq.*).

[34] E.g. H. E. W. Turner, *The Patristic Doctrine of Redemption* (New York: Morehouse-Gorham Co., 1952).

fair to categorize all of Greek patristic thought as representing the first type of understanding of redemption. But this is done even by modern scholars who have recognized the shortcomings of Harnack's view.[35] Pelikan, for instance, sees "the chief content of the Christian message as Athanasius interpreted it" as *"rescue."*[36] It is certainly true that the notions of corruptibility (*phthora*) and incorruptibility (*aphtharsia*) are much more important in early Eastern than in early Western theology. The West substituted the notions of "sin" and "forgiveness" for the corresponding Greek terms. And it is also true that the Greek terms seem to be more directly rooted in Platonic and Stoic thinking than in biblical passages. Yet, we must recognize the relative advantage of these Greek terms over the later Latin concepts, for it is obvious that the former do not lend themselves as readily to an individualistic interpretation as do the latter. The subjective-individualistic understanding of the traditional Greek theological terminology belongs already to the later period of Greek patristic thought, the beginnings of which can be seen in certain passages of the Cappadocians, notably Gregory of Nyssa. But whether the use of these terms proves that "the chief content" was the interest in "rescue" is another question. Why was it, we may ask, that the Eastern hierarchs, for example, Athanasius and Cyril of Alexandria, had such great interest in "Church politics," often to the point of taking very questionable actions, if their chief interest was in fleeing the world? Even the founders and advocates of monasticism (Basil) and of a certain asceticism (John Chrysostom) cannot fairly be accused of world-denying tendencies. Their interest in the "world" and their concern for the worshipers' vicarious function for the rest of mankind cannot very well be denied. John Chrysostom's famous twenty-one sermons, which he delivered in Antioch in 387 in times of political crisis, are an excellent example of a preacher's awareness of his and the whole congregation's responsibility for the community.

Nevertheless, it is true that a certain stream within early Greek Orthodoxy preserved the negative Gnostic and Neo-Platonic world view which found its expression in an exaggerated emphasis upon the concept of redemption as "rescue from the world." The later Byzan-

---

[35] E.g. by J. Pelikan in his excellent meditation on Athanasius, *The Light of the World* (New York: Harper & Row, 1962), and by W. Pannenberg, *RGG*, 3rd ed., Vol. I, p. 1767, and *Grundzüge der Christologie, passim.*

[36] Pelikan, *op. cit.*, p. 77.

tine Church was thus able to accept the political domination of Islam without decisive inner shifts in her theology. The world-denying stream of tradition thus obviously gained the victory over better traditions. But this does not mean that all of early Greek theology should fall under a verdict which may justifiably be passed on later Byzantine theology. Moreover, if the West had not had the chance to cast its theological insights in the form of ecclesiastical and political power structures at the time when the Church took possession of the Germanic territories, it could have fallen victim to exactly the same introspective and world-denying theology which became typical of the Byzantine Church. Western mysticism, rooted in Augustine and further advanced by Erigena, also shows the readiness of Western theology to go in that direction.

We have asked whether the Greek Fathers were really centrally concerned with redemption, and whether redemption was identical with deification, as Harnack had maintained. The above remarks concerning the first part of this question were intended at least to indicate that the Greek Fathers cannot be accused of having only one concept of redemption, i.e., the idea that the Christian faith is the answer to the question of how to escape the (evil) world. The second part of the question, the evaluation of the deification passages, is a detailed historical problem.[37] We can here only summarize some of the main aspects of the history of "deification." It will be helpful to remember that the concept of deification itself comes from Plato and that it was further developed by Plotinus on the one hand and by the many facets of the mystery religions on the other. But the original idea of deification is spiritual and not physical. Plato says in the *Sophists*, and also in the *Timaeus*, that the soul that can perceive the ideas walks among men "as God." Those who *know* God are united with God, for it is only in the *ideas* that this recognition is possible, and God belongs to the realm of ideas. True virtue is manifest in the three forms of love, truth and faith, and it is with the help of true virtue that the soul can become "like God."[38] The soul raises above the material world and reaches communication with the original ideas. Clement of Alexandria and, influenced by him, Gregory

---

[37] Cf. besides the literature mentioned in FNS 32 and 33, my studies on Hippolytus's concept of deification and chap. 2 of my *Athanasius*, pp. 36 ff. (See above, Preface, FN 3.)

[38] Plato, *Laws* I, 643D, and *Theaetetus* 176B; cf. also *Republic* VII, 525B, and *Timaeus, passim.*

Nazianzen[39] seem to have followed this concept of deification. There was, however, also a more directly ontic and almost physical concept of deification, also stemming from Plato.[40] The same Gregory Nazianzen and many other later Fathers accepted at least the terminology related to this concept. The term "mixture" (*mixis* or *krasis* and their *composita*), which had occurred already in Plato, began to play an important role in Christian soteriology. It most often referred to the unfortunate thought of the "flowing-into-each-other" of divine and human substances. This is the classical concept of deification which Harnack and others had in mind when they accused the Greek Fathers of a "physical" or "pharmacological" understanding of redemption. We are interested here only in this judgment, and not in a detailed investigation of the Greek roots of the concept of deification.

We must admit that one trend in Greek patristic thought accepted uncritically the "physical" notion of deification. Methodius in his *Convivium* (or Symposium), the two Gregories and later Pseudo-Dionysius seem indeed to transgress the border between the Creator and the creatures, although scholarship has not yet spoken the final word on the delicate question of what the Greek mind really envisioned when it spoke of "physical" union. But regarding the mainstream of what we have called "the best part" of the tradition, such a theologically irresponsible neglect of the qualitative difference between the Creator and the creatures does not ever enter the question. Athanasius more than once makes it clear that an identification of God and man is far from his mind.[41] Rather, his understanding of redemption culminates in the proclamation of the *adoption* of men into sonship. It is not understandable why reputed Protestant scholars felt capable of interpreting Athanasius as having proposed an identification between God and men, since the whole of the Arian controversy centers upon the claim that only one man, namely, Jesus Christ, has the honor and office of being one with the Father for the sake of the rest of mankind.

But why, we must ask, did Athanasius, and with him the liturgies

[39] Gregory Nazianzen, *Oration* 38, 7 is based upon Clement Alex.
[40] E.g. *Phaedrus* 279A; cf. *Plutarch*, Numa 3.
[41] E.g. *Ad Serapion*, I, 25; also 19, 22, 24, 30; and III, 5; *Ad Epictetum*, 6; *Contra Arianos* III, 19–20. All these passages refer to the work of the Spirit which leads to adoption, though "deification" may be the term to express this miracle.

and later tradition, speak of deification at all? The "best part of the tradition" saw in the work of God in Jesus Christ something infinitely stronger than and qualitatively different from the little more than moralistic understanding of the fruits of the incarnation as presented by Justin Martyr and Clement of Alexandria. Irenaeus and Athanasius knew that the fruits of Christ's coming exceed the realm of mere doctrine and ethical instruction. In him, God's own rights were given to men through their adoption as sons. And this center of the Good News is, in their opinion and practice, to be adored and to be received in worship. No expression could possibly be strong enough to describe in one formula the matter in question. Thus Irenaeus already[42] uses the term "deification" as the *doxological climax* of everything he has to say about the fruits of Christ's work. While Irenaeus' theology is somewhat limited to the idea of the *restoration* of fallen man to his original destiny, Athanasius more daringly tries to say that man's final salvation will be even *more* than "restoration" to his original state. Thus Athanasius makes more liberal use of the deification concept. But as always when he speaks eschatologically, he does not separate his thoughts from the context of worship. *The deification concept of the "best part" of the Greek theological tradition is a doxological and not an ontological concept.*

We can safely disregard the judgment of nineteenth-century liberal Protestantism concerning the use of the deification concept by the Greek Fathers. Those Fathers who were inclined to understand deification physically, i.e. as an ontic description, are of no great importance to our modern problems anyway. Those, however, who used the term in full awareness that the limit between Creator and creatures cannot be done away with may contribute much to our contemporary discussions. A new look at the doxologically received concept of deification may suggest the following helpful theological thoughts concerning God's dealing with man: (1) "deification" guarantees that the initiative is on God's side; (2) it also suggests a non-individualistic understanding of salvation because of its imbeddedness in the

---

[42] The classical passages are: *Adv. Haereses* III, 19, 1; IV 19,1 and 3; IV 20, 5 and 38, 4: and the *praefatio* to book V. None of them ought to be read out of context. The passages are always the final part of a chain of thoughts concerning man's participation in the newness of Jesus Christ. Athanasius in *De Incarnatione*, chap. 54, is obviously dependent upon Irenaeus, and no more than Irenaeus does he take the deification concept as a separate theological topic.

worship of the whole Church; (3) it is declared to be a "mystery," a secret, and yet something which causes joy in advance; (4) it indicates that the "present Christian existence" is not the end of the dealings of God with man; something greater and final is to be expected!

These remarks are not to suggest that the term "deification" is to be considered as especially fortunate. It lends itself indeed to grave misunderstandings. And this is precisely what has happened whenever this "fruit of worship" has slipped into rational thinking and become a separate theological topic describing an ontic reality. Nevertheless, it is amazing that Eastern Orthodoxy, when speaking of deification, was seldom in danger of sliding into mysticism,[43] while Western theology soon became aware of its proximity to mysticism and therefore tried hard to avoid using the deification concept.[44]

d) The Vicarious Work of Jesus Christ

Having considered three typically Western criticisms of Greek patristic thought, we can now point out some aspects of the central intent of the "best part" of Eastern theological tradition. The justification for speaking of the "best part" is based upon a categorization of the various streams of Greek theological tradition. Three theologically distinct groups can be recognized and named without undue systematization: (1) the Christocentric-pneumatic theology which begins with Ignatius in primitive form and is continued in the theology of redemptive history of Irenaeus, finding its mature expression in Athanasius, Basil, partly in the two Gregories and (within limits) in Cyril; (2) the liturgical–non-dogmatic theology reflected in the rich development of the liturgies, in forms of monastic piety, partly in Hippolytus' ecclesiology, in sermons and in church art; (3) the apologetic-ethical theology, represented in early forms by some of the Apostolic Fathers, more clearly by the Apologists, unfolded by

---

[43] Cf. D. Tschizewskij, Gab es im alten Russland echte Mystiker? EvTh, No. 6 (June 1962), pp. 304 ff.; and Vladimir Lossky, op. cit. (see FN 25); also Andreas Theodorou "Die Mystik in der orthodoxen Ostkirche" in Panagiotis (ed.), Die orthodoxe Kirche in Griechischer Sicht, I, pp. 175 ff. (Stuttgart: Evangl. Verlagswerk, 1959).

[44] I owe this insight to a remark by Professor Outler of Perkins School of Theology, in a conversation on the evaluation of deification.

Clement of Alexandria, maintained in part of Origen's system, and of continuing influence in monasticism and Byzantine practical piety as well as in philosophical speculation.

A combination of the first and second groups of theology is what we have called "the best part" of tradition. It is the unfolding of Ignatius's concept of *henosis*, the union between the Father and the Son and, consequently, between man and God in the Son. If it were not for the second group, the first group would lack the framework of worship and prayer. And indeed, Protestant scholars have been inclined to read the Fathers of the first group as if their thoughts were disconnected from worship. But this view is, with few exceptions, not correct historically. The "best part" of Eastern theological tradition is not interested merely in the "how" and "why" of redemption but in the "that" of union with Christ. Christology and soteriology were not separated from each other, nor was Christology reconstructed from an analysis of the benefits of the incarnation. Rather, the adoration of the risen Christ in worship enables the believer to recognize earlier witnesses as pointing to the same risen Christ, and opens the believer's eyes to the hope of the future restoration and even "deification," i.e. to the final acts of God with man. This historical perspective is reflected in the structure of the liturgy as it is still celebrated today in Eastern Orthodoxy. Admittedly, the architecture of the divine service represents too directly the notion of *Heilsgeschichte*, as though the believers were able to reproduce or reenact before the eyes of faith the whole of God's history with his people. The liturgy, therefore, lacks connection with the present, and has rather a heavenly taste. But this neglect of the present did not have to follow necessarily from the adoration of the risen Christ. The fact that it did is rooted in the unsolved christological formulations[45] which tended toward docetism. Leaving aside this problem for the moment, we focus our attention upon the *theological intent*, the expression of the core of theology according to the Greek Fathers of the "best tradition," the union with Christ. It is just at this point that we can learn today from the Greek Fathers, our justifiable criticism notwithstanding.

The best part of Eastern tradition surprises us because of its lack of a concept of justification and because of its neglect of detailed theological statements about grace. But it cannot be denied that the

[45] See our discussion of the "dilemma of classical Christology" in Chap. VI, a.

Christocentric view of the New Testament books is strongly maintained and that Christology itself is strictly based upon the resurrection. The emphasis on the *Christus praesens* in dogmatics as well as
in the liturgies makes this unmistakably clear. And the fact that the
incarnation of the God-man and his continuing presence in worship
is *adored* as a miracle and a *divine gift* should warn us against the
statement that the understanding of grace is absent. The absence of a
formulated doctrine of grace does not at all imply the neglect of the
factual awareness of grace. But the situation is different regarding
justification: here indeed we can observe a trend in Eastern theology
from which the Western Church has departed.[46] The Eastern tradition has not taken up the Pauline speech of justification but has,
beginning with Irenaeus, interpreted the Pauline epistles in the light
of the Spirit passages. If we had to choose among various Western
terms in order to label the intent of the Eastern tradition, we could
say that the term *sanctification* would well describe the general theological atmosphere. The great shift of emphasis after the time of the
Apologists to a strictly christological understanding of theology and
of the Church (taking up the thoughts of Ignatius) produced a concept of the work of Christ which culminates in the affirmation that
God in Christ has taken man into his possession. If it helps our
Western understanding we can call this "sanctification." Calvin of all
Western theologians seems to come closest to this approach. The
Eastern Fathers' stress on God's *taking possession* of his people is
well in line with the Old Testament, and we will have to ask quite
seriously whether this concept is today perhaps to be preferred over
the classical Western speech of "justification." Jesus Christ, the
Pantokrator, the "Artificer of all," prepared a dwelling place for
himself and entered into a human body, like a king who enters into a
city and dwells in one of its houses. *Because* of his dwelling in *one*
house, Athanasius says in this famous parable,[47] "the whole city is
honored," and no enemy would dare to take possession of it. Because of the *relationship* (*kata ten syggeneian*)[48] between his flesh
and that of the rest of mankind, man is taken into his possession.
The One stands good for the rest of mankind and it *now* becomes

---

[46] Cf. the instructive article by K. Stendahl, "The Apostle Paul and the Introspective Conscience of the West" (already referred to above, Chap. I, FN 25).
[47] *De Incarnatione,* 9.
[48] *Contra Arianos,* II, 69.

clear that man could not have redeemed himself. The knowledge of man's inability to save himself is *not* the presupposition of theology and worship, but rather *follows* from worship theologically. This is a deep insight which Augustine did not have.

The work of Jesus Christ, or, as traditional Western theology had it, the *office* (*munus*) of Christ, is his having come in the flesh for the sake of uniting men with himself, the only whole man. His resurrection is adored as the establishment of his rule over all men who lived after and before his incarnation. The *newness* and *wholeness* of this One man, directly based on the relevant New Testament passages, is understood to be representative for all of mankind, which is taken into possession by his very coming. We can say, of course, that this thought is only possible on the basis of a reality concept which permits logically (and ontologically) the affirmation that the New Man is united with men who lived after his time and even before. And it is indeed true that even the best part of the Eastern tradition did not know a satisfactory answer to this problem. The more it operated with a "nature" and "reality" concept in order to solve this problem, the less important became the *work* of Christ. During and after the christological councils, theology began to pay more attention to this problem than to the question of Christology itself, a development which we have already observed. The Christology of the Greek Fathers can be of use to our present theological situation only when we succeed in translating their static concepts into the functional terms which were originally intended.

The pre-conciliar exposition of Christology came closer to a functional understanding of the person and work of Christ than the later dogmatical formulations. In defense of the Antiochians we can say that they, despite their quickly recognizable errors, tried harder than the Alexandrians to preserve the historical-functional categories of earlier tradition. "Functional" would be a Christology which pays equal attention to what the West later called the "kingly office" (*munus regium*) and the "priestly office" (*munus sacerdotale*) of Jesus Christ. Any separation of these two aspects, for other than didactic purposes, results in a split between Christology "as such" and soteriology. But this was not the intent of the earlier Fathers. They tried to speak of man's participation in the newness of Jesus Christ in such terms that: (1) the risen Jesus Christ is understood as continuing his priestly task, and (2) the Church takes part in Jesus

Christ's vicarious function for the rest of mankind. But this insight was lost in the christological controversies, despite the rather impressive formulations of Athanasius. He tried to be faithful to his Christocentric starting point by projecting all statements about the believers, the new men, onto Jesus Christ himself, the New Man. The New Man alone was obedient to the Father and the new men participate in his obedience. He alone responded to the Father; he alone is priest. But, seen from the opposite direction, he alone is God's love, will, call and demand to me. Thus Athanasius prepared the ground for a theology which could combine the emphases of Anselm and Abelard into one. We will later (Chapter VI) come back to this inviting possibility of showing ways of understanding the vicarious work of Jesus Christ without employing the problematical notion of "imputation." Moreover, it can help unfold a theology in which Christology, soteriology and pneumatology are not separated from each other, because they are recognized as three aspects of the same theme, held together by the *Christus praesens* in worship.

In accordance with our deliberations on Scripture and tradition, we have, in this chapter, tried to advocate an understanding of the Greek Fathers which evaluates them in relation to their own past and their present situation, and which takes their intent seriously even if their thoughts have caused unfortunate developments. Thus, we have briefly examined three typically Western criticisms, the first related to the Gnostic framework, the second to the problem of ontology and the third to redemption and deification. We have admitted that severe criticisms and reservations will be justifiable and necessary. But we have suggested that the theology of the Greek Fathers was "more orthodox" before than after the Orthodox councils. Moreover, a grouping of the Fathers into three categories seemed legitimate, and it has enabled us to speak of the "best part" of Greek theological tradition as over against the main bulk of its theological productivity. Within this "best part" we thought to have observed theological insights which were not generally accepted by the Western Church in later times, and which could be of great service in our contemporary theological discussions. They are:

> 1) the emphasis on worship and prayer in which theology is embedded, so that statements about Jesus Christ, salvation and the Church are held together;

2) the insight that Jesus Christ embraces all of history, so that a separation between the "historical Jesus" and the risen Christ is not possible (nor a separation between "nature" and "grace," to use Western terminology);

3) the affirmation (with the unfortunate term "deification") that the present Christian existence of the believer is not the end of the story, but that the Church looks forward in hope to God's final acts;

4) the absence of individualistic categories;

5) the emphasis on union with Christ in such fashion that the believers participate in the continuing priesthood of Christ.

III

Concentration on Justification
in Western Theology

WE HOPE THAT we have sufficiently prepared ourselves to undertake now a critical evaluation of the Augustinian heritage in contemporary Western theology. Our discussion will be limited and guided by the question of the connection between Christ and the Church or between Christology and ecclesiology. This concentration and limitation corresponds to our counter-thesis to the individualistic trend in contemporary theology, *viz.* our interest in emphasizing the *Christus praesens.* But for technical reasons as well it is mandatory to limit the scope of our discussion, for it would be impossible to deal here with all aspects of the influence of Augustinianism; the history of Western theology itself is to a great extent the history of the understanding and reception of Augustine. Our special concern will justify the division of this chapter into four parts: Following a survey of such of Augustine's thoughts as were of constitutive importance in later Augustinianism, we will focus our attention first on the relative absence of Christology from Augustine's concept of the Church, secondly on the influence of his "vision of God" concept on his understanding of reality, and thirdly on his personalistic thought structure which resulted from his eschatology. This thematic division enables us best to indicate the parallels between Augustine and certain aspects of contemporary Western theology. Of the latter the Lutheran stream of tradition is more relevant to our thesis, for it is not by accident that Bultmann, Tillich and Ebeling are rooted in this tradition. The Calvinistic tradition, and even more so Anglican theology, are more heterogeneous than Lutheranism, although their indebtedness to Augustinianism can easily be shown too, and there is no denying that existentialist theology has begun to establish itself in these quarters as well as in Lutheranism. Nevertheless, our primary interest is in the inner connection between Augustinianism and the concern of existentialist theology for justification, a concern which is rooted in Lutheranism.

a) Western Reception of Eastern Shortcomings

Latin theology in the time before Augustine cannot measure up to the height and depth of the Greek patristic thought of the first four centuries. The early Western Church lived from the richness of Greek theology, liturgy and pious experience. Greek was the language of the Septuagint, of the New Testament and of theological treatises. It was not until the end of the second century, and, more widely, at the beginning of the third, that in the West the Greek language gave way to Latin. This change was more than a mere change of language; although many Greek works were translated into Latin, the influence of the Greek Fathers decreased, and the Latin-Roman mind began to determine the shape of Western theology. This was already the case at a time when the Greek and Oriental churches still maintained their theological and ecclesiastico-political superiority. The Western Christians developed their own thought forms and practices without being able or willing to fill these forms with theological content, their mentality being practical and directed toward concrete church life. This fact explains the moralistic and often legalistic atmosphere which we notice when reading the earliest Latin Christians, an impression still presented by the works of the famous pre-Augustinian Western Fathers. It is Tertullian to whom the West owes its theological vocabulary; it is Cyprian who can be called the architect of the Western institutionalized Church; and it is Ambrose who was the first to take advantage of the Constantinian privileges for the Church. All of them exercised a strong influence upon Augustine, but none of them had more than a general familiarity with Greek theology.

It is the mind of Augustine which has been compared to a lens in which earlier Latin *and* Greek theology converged and from which later Western theology received almost everything which was contained in the theological traditions before Augustine. Augustine is said to have been the last Church Father who embraced in his mind both Eastern and Western theology, and he certainly was the first whose typically Western theology influenced almost exclusively only the Western Church. But is it really true that he embraced both Western and Eastern traditions? Was this theology not rather a combination of Latin *ecclesiology* and Greek *philosophy?* This is the question which we will here attempt to deal with, bearing in mind the importance of the answer; for it was Western (Protestant) theological liberalism which tried to persuade the last three generations of Western theologians that the Greek Fathers had fallen victim to Neo-Platonic *philosophy* while Augustine had rediscovered the Pauline *Gospel!* It would be an irony of history if a new generation of historically critical theologians, prompted by ecumenical contact with Eastern Orthodoxy, could show to the Church that we have done an injustice to the Greek Fathers by reading them, as well as the Bible, through "Augustinian glasses."[1]

Augustine[2] lived at the time when the decay of the Roman Empire began to be politically obvious.[3] He was born a hundred years after the death of Origen, and he died one year before the Council of Ephesus and twenty-one years before Chalcedon. Thus his life span falls into the period of the later parts of the Arian controversy and the beginning of the great christological tension between Alexandria and Antioch. Yet his works give little indication that these theological controversies deeply affected him. But was he not in the same Church with the Eastern Fathers? Did he not live in the same North

---

[1] It is very moving to read the words of the aging Harnack in the introduction to his collection of thoughts of Augustine, *Augustin* (Tübingen: J. C. B. Mohr, 1922), p. xxiii, where he says that the brutalities of the world war ought not trouble us, for civilization and a "new Augustinianism" would help create a "Christian-Augustinian" covenant of justice and peace. This or nothing, in Harnack's judgment, would lead us to real freedom!

[2] A most helpful introduction to Augustine is now available in English translation: Hans von Campenhausen, *Men Who Shaped the Western Church* (New York and Evanston: Harper & Row, 1964), pp. 183–276. Cf. also the Catholic introduction by Eugène Portalié, S.J., *A Guide to the Thought of St. Augustine* (Chicago: Henry Regnery Company, 1960), which contains a good bibliography.

[3] Cf. H. v. Campenhausen, "Augustin und der Fall von Rom" in *Tradition und Leben* (Collected Essays; Tübingen, J. C. B. Mohr, 1960), pp. 253 ff.

Africa with the Alexandrians? Yet his Church presented another climate, suggested different questions and received from him a theology which was not understood in the East, because Eastern piety and theology no longer fed the West. Augustine stood at the beginning of the Western ecclesiastical and theological isolation which has today become a political and cultural reality in the division between East and West.

Augustine's theology shows in every step of its development[4] the influences under which this great spirit became a Christian and a theologian, influences which he tried to overcome or at least thought he had overcome by making them a part of his life and theology. Scholarship[5] has long agreed on the following three important intellectual and spiritual influences on Augustine's thinking. The degree of importance of each of them is controversial, but most interpreters concede that all three belong to the complete picture of Augustine's thought world.

1) The world view and ontological thought structure of *Aristotle*[6] was mediated to Augustine chiefly through Cicero's *Hortensius*, although already within the climate of Neo-Platonism. It was this Neo-Platonized Aristotelian framework which Augustine later filled with his theological thoughts. The universe is seen as a pyramid with matterless form at the top and formless matter at the bottom. Moreover, Aristotle's concept of *gravitas*, presented in his physics, is translated by Augustine into anthropological categories: every being has the tendency to follow the downward pull into the lower spheres of lesser being. Evil has no being and can be spoken of only in relation to the good, i.e. to being and ever-higher being. But it is downward toward evil, non-being, that all beings tend to fall. Augustine the Christian teaches later that mankind *has* already fallen, that what is ontologically "impossible" has become a reality: mankind

---

[4] Cf. the critical and still unsurpassed study of Karl Holl, "Augustines innere Entwicklung," in *Gesammelte Aufsätze zur Kirchengeschichte* (Tübingen: J. C. B. Mohr, 1928), pp. 54–116.

[5] Cf. Carl Andresen (ed.), *Zum Augustin-Gespräch der Gegenwart* (Darmstadt: Wissenschaftliche Buchgesellschaft, 1962), with eleven contributions, mostly by French scholars, and a bibliography of 120 pages (cited hereafter as "Augustin-Gespräch").

[6] Cf. Rudolf Schneider, *Seele und Sein, Ontologie bei Augustin und Aristoteles* (Stuttgart: W. Kohlhammer, 1957), which demonstrates Augustine's dependence on Aristotle's concepts of analogy, potency and act, categories and the four causes.

has become a *massa perditionis*, a mass of sinners doomed to perdition. The originally free spirits abused their freedom by affirming
themselves rather than God. The result is not deficiency but degradation to another order. Self-restoration is now impossible, since the
gravitas downward has had its effect. Only a *gravitas* upward could
restore mankind; this is provided only by God himself, who by grace
gives *caritas* to the hearts of men. *Caritas, amor dei*, is the love
toward God which at the same time denies the world with its inner
laws of *gravitas*. Augustine's systematization of the state of mankind
(or the pre-existent spirits or non-fallen angels) before the Fall is
well known: they were free both not to sin and to sin, *posse non
peccare* and *posse peccare*, but they chose the latter. After the Fall,
they were unable not to sin, *non posse non peccare*; sin has become
not only a "bad habit" but an ontic status. After the acceptance of
grace, the believer is again free not to sin, *posse non peccare*, and
this means mainly that he is able to fight the *concupiscentia carnis*,
the lusts of the flesh. And finally, in the eschatological status, the
redeemed can no longer sin, *non posse peccare*. It is obvious that this
theological scheme combines Aristotelian ontology with Origenistic
ideas, for it was Origen who developed the notion of a movement
from the pre-existent state of men to the fallen state and from there
to the redeemed state. But Augustine went beyond the mere concept
of restoration by affirming that the redeemed enjoy a higher and
firmer form of freedom than did the pre-existent spirits.

But more important than this systematization is the more "existential" interest in the question of how man can attain the *caritas* which
draws him to God. Augustine had received the philosophical version
of this question directly from Cicero's *Hortensius*; and to this question Neo-Platonism, later in the form of Christian Neo-Platonism,
provided the answer. Man is by nature filled with the hope of being
elevated to something higher than himself[7]; but how can this striving toward elevation (*celsitudo*) be directed toward good and not
toward evil? How can man attain happiness? He cannot of his own
ability, for he belongs to the human race, which participates in
Adam's sin.[8] It is at this point that Augustine's doctrine of grace
comes in. But we must keep in mind that the basis for the doctrine of

---

[7] *De civitate Dei*, XIV, 11 and 13, *passim*, and *Enchiridion* 25, *passim*.
[8] *De civ. Dei*, XXI, 12, and already *De moribus ecclesiae catholicae* of the year
388, chaps. 1, 19, 35, 40, *passim*; cf. *Enchiridion* 26, 27, 33, 108, *passim*.

grace is to be sought in the *recognition of man's predicament* and in man's striving toward liberation, elevation or eternal happiness. Karl Holl emphasizes this by saying that "the influence of Paul has not reached into the ultimate depth" of Augustine's thinking but that the basic "eudemonistic tendency" has remained "untouched" in its "orientation of all striving toward (man's) own self."[9] To put it positively, we can say that this adopted basis of Augustine's theology is the beginning of the Western discovery of individual personality, and Augustine has understandably been praised for this. But to put it negatively—and this is a theological judgment—we must say that this discovery marks the beginning of the Western isolation from Greek patristic thought and of the founding of a Christian anthropology which can only very artificially be brought into harmony with the Old and New Testaments. After Augustine, Western theology never gave up the individualistic question: How can I obtain grace? Although it may sound premature and careless, we should not shy away from the statement that Luther's search for a gracious God, from which stems the emphasis on justification, is well in line with this Augustinian concern. And we may add that this search also describes well the various theologies of "personal encounter," among them Bultmann's views on man's liberation from his predicament through the kerygma.

2) Not unlike Aristotle's ontology, *Manicheism* too reached Augustine in the dress of Neo-Platonic thoughts. The Manicheism that influenced Augustine was no longer the original Persian religion but a later type of outspokenly "Christian Manicheism." Augustine, as an auditor, belonged to the Manichean sect for a period of almost nine years. Here he found what popular philosophy was unable to present: an honest confrontation with the question of the reality of evil in the world and in the course of history.[10] The Manichean concepts are still recognizable in Augustine's later ethical thoughts, and their influence on his doctrine of predestination is undisputed. But he attempted in a congenial way to combine the dualistic views of the Manicheans with the apparently contradicting monistic trends in popular Aristotelian philosophy, a combination seemingly fully justified by the Bible. Thus the later Augustine must not be one-

[9] Karl Holl, *op. cit.*, p. 111; cf. *Enchiridion* 26 ff., 64 ff.
[10] Cf. Alfred Adam, "Der manichäische Ursprung der Lehre von den zwei Reichen bei Augustin," *ThLZ*, No. 77 (1952), pp. 38 ff., and "Das Fortwirken des Manichäismus bei Augustin," *ZKG*, No. 69 (1958), pp. 1 ff.

sidedly labeled as a dualist, as though his doctrine of predestination were the key to his theology, nor yet as a monist, as though he had been unaware of the Church's task to face seriously the problem of world order and of evil in the world. Of all the philosophical influences upon Augustine, the Manichean underwent the strongest transformation, although there is no denying that Manichean dualism maintained its place even in the latest writings of Augustine. We cannot discuss here, however, the delicate problem of the relation between Augustine's concept of predestination and the rest of his theology. It has been said that there is no harmony between the two, and the history of Augustinianism seems to confirm this observation, for medieval theology was no longer able to hold together what Augustine had embraced in his thought. The problem itself, however, continued to occupy the minds of Western theologians, first in the form of a sharp distinction between the *Corpus Christianum* and the non-Christian world (reflected in the appropriation of Augustine's *civitas* concept in the distinction between the worldly and the spiritual powers) and secondly in the form of Luther's differentiation between "world-person" and "Christ-person." The West has inherited from Augustine the difficulty of assigning a proper place to traditional "dualism" within the whole of theology, a difficulty which Augustine himself was unable to eliminate from his thinking because it was his only bridge to the reality of the world. If it had not been for the Manichean influence on him Augustine's theology would have taken an even more directly Neo-Platonic course. If this is a correct description of the inner connection between Augustine and our contemporary problems, it follows that we today, approaching reality and history in a manner entirely different from that of Augustine, can dispense with the problem of dualism and with the difficulty of incorporating it into theology. But this negative conclusion of course does not suggest a positive answer to the problem of evil, an answer which depends on the proper theological understanding of reality and history. At this point we merely notice that existentialist theology today operates with a negative approach to history, as if the Manichean corrective, which Augustine apparently needed, were still the only possibility.[11] The same applies to popular piety, especially in Amer-

---

[11] Cf. as an illustration of this approach in contemporary theology, G. Ebeling's statement: "The sober way to express our real situation is to see our failure and fall, that is, to see guilt and death, which go together. . . . This is the

ica, which is unduly concerned with the question "Who will be saved and who will not?"

3) The *Neo-Platonic* influence upon Augustine's theology presents much more complex problems than do the other influences which have been mentioned so far. It is not even correct to say that Augustine was "influenced" by Neo-Platonism: *he was a Neo-Platonist*. No learned interpretation[12] has attempted to belittle this fact. Only the evaluation and chronological fixing of the various steps of Augustine's development are controversial. We are not concerned here with the details of this problem but note only that Roman Catholic interpreters as a rule are not afraid to call Augustine a Neo-Platonist, since for their theological tradition the statement that Neo-Platonism is "in harmony with Christianity" is less problematical than for Protestants. Concerning the development of Augustine's thoughts, we admit, of course, that it is important to pay attention to the difference between Augustine's early philosophical and introspective period at Cassiciacum and the highly ecclesiastical tenor of the thoughts of the aging bishop of Hippo, who shows indications of disappointment and resignation and who seems partly to regret his

---

reality of our existence, that in the end we have no future. And if we now think about God concretely, in relation to this reality, then we have to hold firm to this contradiction, that on the one hand we hear in our existence the brutal and unambiguous words, 'You have no future,' and that on the other hand to say that God *is* can only mean that we do have a future." *The Nature of Faith*, p. 75. It is interesting to notice that many adherents of the post-Bultmannian tradition show relatively little interest in the social and political tasks of the Church today. Some aspects of this question will be discussed further in Chap. VI.

12 From a great number of publications I mention only Pierre Courcelle, "Die Entdeckung des christlichen Neuplatonismus," in *Augustin-Gespräch*, pp. 125–181. (The thesis is that Ambrose mediated to Augustine both Neo-Platonism and the Christian faith.); Erich Frank, "Augustin und das griechische Denken," *ibid.*, pp. 182–197; and the utterly naive Christianization and justification of Neo-Platonism in the defensive article by Paul Henry, S.J., "Die Vision zu Ostia," *ibid.*, pp. 201–270. Preceding these studies, Harnack and P. Alfaric had drawn attention to Augustine's Platonism, but Ch. Boyer (1920) had refuted this; W. Theiler (1933) had maintained that Augustine knew only Porphyry and not Plotinus, but Paul Henry proved the acquaintance with Plotinus (1934; cf. also *JThS*, No. 36 [1937], pp. 1–23). Still others have spoken of two "conversions," the first to Neo-Platonism and the second (around 400) to the Christian faith. (Walther von Loewenich, *Von Augustin zu Luther* [Witten: Luther-Verlag, 1959], speaks of a third step, Augustine's turn to eschatology at the end of his life, p. 19.)

dependence upon the Platonists.[13] To neglect the theological difference between the *Soliloquia* and other earlier writings, on the one
hand, and *De doctrina christiana* and *De civitate Dei*, on the other,
would of course mean to revert to the period before the nineteenth
century, i.e. before historical scholarship began to see the importance
of a thinker's development; (but medieval and Reformation theology
did read Augustine without this critical understanding). Nevertheless, the Neo-Platonic (and Aristotelian) question determined the
theological answers of even the old Augustine, who "never ceased
even then to be a Platonist and a philosopher."[14] If the comparison
is permitted, it would perhaps be meaningful to point out our present
difficulties with Augustine by saying that during his life Augustine
traversed the way from egotistical-introspective philosophical questions to an intolerant ecclesiastical position which found its climax in
a doctrine of predestination (without Christ and with cruel descriptions of the fate of the damned) which deprives the believer of his
joy and certainty, whereas many postwar theologians today find
themselves on the move from a doctrinally well-defined Protestant or
Catholic concept of Church and theology into the open fields of
"mere humanity," politics and social concern, taking their freedom
seriously and searching for meaningful tasks. It is only natural that
such moves do not imply the denial of the points of departure; Augustine remained faithful to his initial questions, and we must hope
that theology in the immediate future will maintain contact with its
Protestant Reformation or Roman Catholic heritage.

The manifestations of Augustine's Neo-Platonism in his writings
are manifold. Most important is his view of the *meaning of life*.
Not only the *Confessiones* but also the exegetical writings (and his
choice of Biblical texts) and the later dogmatical works show clearly
that the ideal of the *vita beata* stood at the center of his theological
concern. R. Lorenz indeed calls the *vita beata* the *Zentralproblem* of
Augustine's theology.[15] God, the highest being and the *summum
bonum*, is the true goal, *telos*, of man's striving, according both to
popular Neo-Platonic and to Augustine's thinking. But Augustine was
enough of an intellectual to maintain that the *visio beatifica*, the
blessed vision of God, does not exclude rational thinking but rather
stimulates and initiates thinking. But it is a *new thinking*, an activity

[13] *Retractationes*, I, 1, 4.
[14] H. v. Campenhausen, *Men Who Shaped the Western Church*, p. 207.
[15] R. Lorenz, *RGG*, 3rd ed., Vol. I, p. 743.

of the new man, as the Pauline epistles had also taught and as Anselm later unfolded the concept. It is *thinking* in the form of love and based on faith, not a mystical giving-away of one's own self.[16] Ordinary human thought, related to the reality of this world and of history, is a constant "war"[17]; but the vision of God leads to peace, to the *pax* of the *contemplatio rationalis* which is the down payment for the eschatological state of eternal bliss.[18] The problems of death and of this-worldly time disappear when the *visio Dei* occupies the heart and mind of the believer. Then God can be "enjoyed," the intellect no longer resists God, and the body no longer resists the human mind. The *fruitio Dei*,[19] the enjoyment of God, is sharply distinguished from man's intellectual and spiritual attitude to the things of this world, which can only be *used*. Thus the psychological categories of "enjoying" as over against "using" must serve the theological purpose of defining the difference between man's approach to the world and his position before God. The consequences of this concept have been disastrous. Augustine not only prepared the way for Bernard's excessive and ethico-politically very questionable mysticism, but he himself laid the foundation for a definition of church-state relations and for a self-evaluation of the Church which not even the Reformers were able to extirpate. The invitation to the *fruitio Dei* found entry into Reformation theology as well, e.g. into the Westminster Shorter Catechism with its formulation that a "man's chief end is to glorify God, and to enjoy him forever." This statement is in itself perhaps justifiable, although its meaning is not clear apart from the Augustinian roots; but it is certainly not protected against the misinterpretation that *therefore* the world and its sensuality cannot be enjoyed and must be left behind by the believers. And it is just this devaluation of creation which is so centrally important in Augustine's theology precisely *because* it is juxtaposed with the attitude toward God. Augustine did, however, try to do justice to the double command of love by stating in many different words and at different times in his life that love toward God should be *accompanied* by *caritas* toward men. But it is quite obvious that

---

[16] Cf. Ephraem Hendrikx, O.E.S.A., "Augustins Verhältnis zur Mystik," in *Augustin-Gespräch*, pp. 271–346.

[17] *De civ. Dei*, XIX, 28.

[18] *Ibid.*, 18th book.

[19] Cf. R. Lorenz, "*Fruitio Dei* bei Augustin," ZKG, No. 63 (1950), pp. 75 ff., and "Die Herkunft des augustinischen *Frui Deo*," ZKG, No. 64 (1952/3), pp. 34 ff.

he assigned greater value to the first half of the command than to the second. And is it not true that any competition between the two betrays a faulty concept of "love toward God" in the first place? Indeed, Augustine taught (and practiced) that God is to be loved through men, and that therefore our neighbor is to be loved only because God is ultimately the recipient of this love. We will later discuss[20] the inner contradictions of such a doctrine. In fact, after his conversion Augustine attempted to win some of his early friends to the Christian faith, but realizing that he was having no success he dropped them! This is a concrete example of the catastrophic ethical consequences of the theological double notion "using/enjoying" (*uti/ frui*). The shelteredness of the Church during the Constantinian period apparently made superfluous a critical examination of this aspect of Christianized Neo-Platonism; and Abelard as well as the philosophers of the Renaissance, the only critics of this aspect, were unable to replace Augustine's ethics with something equally strong and influential.

Following these observations on Augustine's teaching on the "meaning of life," a further examination of the impact of Neo-Platonism on Augustine and on later theology would have to center on the concepts of God, grace and the Church. Before entering into this discussion, we should mention in passing that Augustine's hermeneutics are a good case in point of this Neo-Platonic influence. Despite his repeated affirmation that the literal sense of Scripture is to be taken seriously (an affirmation in accordance with his training as a professional rhetorician), he accepted, initially from Ambrose but later on the basis of his own reflection, the allegorical method of interpretation. The same Neo-Platonic doubleness which we have observed in Augustine's attitude toward man (through whom God is loved) appears here in relation to the written words. It was in accordance with his ontology that he developed his philosophy of language[21] with the double notion of "sign" and "reality," *signum* and *res*: language is of significatory character, so that the *signa* become transparent for the metaphysical reality which is not bound to space and time. Contemporary theological attempts to utilize various types of language philosophy for biblical exegesis and for theological interpretation in general are indebted to Augustine's congenial combination of the rhetorical tradition (stressing the literal sense) and the

[20] See Chap. V.
[21] *De doctrina christiana*, esp. book III.

Origenistic allegorical method, strange as this may appear. But the basic concept which permitted Augustine this combination and which underlies much of contemporary hermeneutics as well is the assumption that *that* part of the content of the text *which matters* is timeless, i.e. applicable to different contexts at different times.

This survey of the impact of three philosophical influences upon Augustine was a necessary prelude to the remaining parts of this chapter. But the description of these influences, indispensable as it is for an interpretation of Augustine, does not exhaust the task. Augustine was more than a compiler and systematizer of three important religio-philosophical streams in late antiquity. "Augustinus Magister,"[22] the teacher and theologian of the Western Church, reinterpreted the Catholic tradition and selected from it what was to become the material for further theological work in the West. This accomplishment is a genuine theological one, and our respect and admiration for it should never be diminished by the criticisms that spring from our present understanding of the Church's task today. But what, we must ask in pursuit of our inquiry, is the genuinely theological rootage of Augustine's thinking? Despite the undisputed fact that no other theologian of the Western Church has presented to posterity such an overwhelming amount of new material, it may be justifiable to follow Harnack's judgment[23] when he observes that Augustine's *piety* was the power that absorbed, selected and transformed the traditional dogmatical and ecclesiastical content without deliberately adding new content to it. Harnack draws attention to Augustine's early exposition of the Early Church's creed, the *De fide et symbolo* of the year 393, and compares it with the latest, the *Enchiridion* of 421, observing that Augustine always remained a traditional theologian to whom it never occurred to alter the content of the early creedal conceptions. Harnack maintains that Augustine's views are rooted so strongly in his own piety that many of them "are nothing but theoretically interpreted emotions."[24] Harnack did not mean this in a derogatory sense, as he can harmonize this statement

---

[22] This was adopted as the title of the International Augustine Congress in Paris in 1954.

[23] See the third chapter of his *History of Dogma*, Vol. III.

[24] *Lehrbuch der Dogmengeschichte*, Vol. III (1909; now Darmstadt: Wissenschaftliche Buchgesellschaft, 1964), p. 92. Harnack was not the only scholar who passed this judgment. Karl Holl, who in many points disagreed with Harnack, emphasized a similar view by saying that Augustine's understanding of grace after his conversion was but a change of "taste" from Platonic *eros* to Christian *caritas* (*op. cit.*, p. 94).

with the observation that Augustine remained essentially a traditional theologian of the Early Church. It is indeed amazing that the *dogmatical* content of theology was not enlarged, while it is obvious and generally known that Augustine discovered and utilized entirely new *categories* with which the believer could *appropriate the traditional content*. Thus Augustine's theology was "hermeneutics," to use the term in the modern sense. But is it not true that the formulation and employment of these new categories stemmed from Augustine's Neo-Platonism? This may be too simple a conclusion, and one may prefer Harnack's reference to Augustine's "piety." But we must not give up asking: Was this piety really different from Plotinus' *opsis makaria*, the blessed vision of the trans-empirical and supernatural "highest good"? Admittedly Augustine's life and theology were embedded in prayer—and this he had in common with the Eastern Church—but was it really the prayer of the *Church*, so characteristic of Eastern piety, and not rather the prayer of the pious individual Augustine, who was *therefore* unable to think of the Church other than as an institution which guarantees the correct transmission of tradition and the reception of divine grace which leads to salvation? Despite his enormous respect for the Bible, Augustine lifted his hermeneutical categories not from Biblical texts but from his Neo-Platonic individualistic piety, which he superimposed on Scripture and Catholic tradition.

Augustine's familiarity with Greek patristic thought is a problem in itself.[25] It is undisputed that he knew of the major issues of the Eastern theological debates. But we have little reason to judge that he accepted the strongest parts from the Eastern tradition. Had he really read and understood what we have called the "best part" of early Greek tradition, he would have had every possibility and freedom to present it to his Western audience. But this was not the case. Rather he accepted, partly through Ambrose, the world-denying tendencies of Greek theology, and had a rather low opinion of the value of Eastern Christology for personal (Western) piety. Although he agreed with the "orthodox" conclusions and wrote polemically against the Arians and the Apollinarians, he did not feel enriched by

[25] Berthold Altaner has the merit of having examined in greatest detail Augustine's relation to the Greek theologians. Fourteen of his learned publications are listed in *Augustin-Gespräche*, p. 532, and Altaner has provided a summary in "Augustin und die griechische Patristik," in *RevBen*, No. 62 (1952), pp. 201 ff.

the theological and liturgical work of the Eastern part of the Church. Medieval theology followed him in this attitude, as can be seen for instance in Peter Lombard's *Sentences,* which pay almost no attention to the Greek Fathers. And the picture does not really change in Reformation theology; Luther's[26] and Calvin's knowledge of the Greek Fathers came mainly from *catenae* and other medieval collections of certain passages. We must conclude that Augustine stands at the beginning of the Western tradition which received from the Eastern Church only fractions of theological insights and that he preferred to choose the rather unfortunate Greek theological climate of Neo-Platonism. Thus we regard as confirmed our initial hypothesis that Augustine's theology does not embrace Western and Eastern *theological* tradition but rather combines Western ecclesiology with Greek philosophy.

The Western neglect of the Eastern doxological approach to Christology resulted in the medieval type of theology which was concerned primarily with God rather than with God in Jesus Christ. In the following pages we will attempt to substantiate the thesis that this development was a legitimate outcome of Augustine's theology. Jesus Christ's was a temporary function, since the Church could usurp his priestly office, even more so after the isolated Christian medieval world was established. God was at the center of attention, and it is not at all surprising that Aristotle's philosophy experienced a medieval renaissance, serving as it did to solve the problems concerning God.

b) *The Eternal Church and the Transitory Christ*

Augustine's interpreters seem to agree that his understanding of *grace,* a concept which became characteristic of his theology and controversial in medieval discussions, was first formulated in *Ad Simplicianum* in the years 396–97. The early Augustine conceived of grace as a work of man, though prompted by the gifts of God, while the mature Augustine is said to have abandoned this concept in favor of an understanding which assigns the origin, power and effect of grace solely to God.[27] Whether this latter understanding necessarily

---

[26] Cf. Ernst Wolf, "Asterisci und Obelisci zum Thema: Athanasius und Luther" in *EvTh* (1958), pp. 481 ff.

[27] Cf. the discussions by Étienne Gilson, "Die christliche Freiheit," in *Augustin-Gespräch,* pp. 399 ff., and John Burnaby, *Amor Dei, A Study of St. Augustine*

implied the doctrine of the irresistibility of grace is controversial, for Augustine always maintained the idea of man's free will. Man's real freedom, however, was to be found only in his obedience to God. Thus the understanding of grace is necessarily connected with the concept of election, since the obedience to God is the outcome of man's having been elected out of the "mass of perdition" to the vision of God which unites the believer eternally with the life-giving power of God. Those who are not elect continue to abuse their free will, while the elect begin to use it in the proper way, i.e. in accordance with their destiny as elect. *Grace affects and directs the will of man*, a notion which was taken up and unfolded further by William of Occam, who in turn influenced Luther.

But why, according to Augustine, does God elect some to obedience and consequently to grace, which is the partaking of God's own life-giving power? The traditional answer is that Augustine referred to God's freedom not to have elected any man at all, since he did not owe man anything. The argument runs like this: God in his justice is not obliged to save any man, but the fact that he decided to save some merely indicates his great mercy. Gilson, however, has demonstrated[28] an earlier (Protestant) suspicion that the answer is not so simple. He shows that in Augustine's theology justification must logically precede election, for God cannot base his election upon a righteousness which does not yet exist; consequently he must create it before electing righteous men. But why does he elect them? It cannot be because of faith, Gilson concludes on the basis of *Ad Simplicianum*, but must be because of God's pre-knowledge of each man's circumstantial situation: God foresees a man's situation, i.e. the factors which influence and determine his *will* and his *works*, and foresees his own joy over these works, and *therefore* elects the man to the reception of grace (i.e. eternal salvation) *without* jeopardizing his free will. Thus "divine predestination" is, as Gilson summarizes Augustine, "nothing other than the infallible foreknowledge of the future works."[29] Gilson further stresses the fact that

(London: Hodder and Stoughton Ltd., 1947), pp. 226–241 (see *Augustin-Gespräch*, pp. 540 ff., for forty-seven more titles on Augustine's doctrine of grace).

[28] Gilson, *op. cit.*, pp. 420 ff. Cf. Augustine's own difficulties with this all too simple answer in his discussion of Rom. 9:16, *Enchiridion* 99, and of I Tim. 2:4, *ibid.*, 103.

[29] *Ibid.*, p. 423 (FNS 29–30; my translations).

Augustine had developed this understanding on the basis of the Pauline epistles before his acquaintance with Pelagius. Augustine's problem was not that of "free will" over against divine election; but he attempted to unfold the inner relations between grace and freedom, and freedom is "the proper use of the free will."[30] And it is God who foresees this proper use.

Assuming that Gilson's detailed examination truly reflects Augustine's doctrine of grace and freedom, we cannot help raising the question whether Augustine really deserves the praise of having "rediscovered" the Apostle Paul's teaching on grace and justification. Gilson himself opens his study with the words: "The true significance of grace can be grasped only on the basis of the evils for which grace is the medicine."[31] It is in accordance with this statement when Lorenz summarizes[32] that "the doctrine of the universal causality of grace was prepared by Augustine's Neo-Platonism," for grace leads to the love of the eternal, prompted by illumination from that which is loved, the eternal or God, who is "the life of the soul."

Admittedly, Augustine tried hard to show that grace is not dependent on merits, but his complicated logical and speculative detours do not ultimately remove the idea that God justifies only the just, not the sinner. It is not surprising that later medieval theology shortened Augustine's detours and plainly fell back into a concept of grace based on a definition of merits. It was already with Gregory the Great that grace was understood as something which the Church administers and dispenses. But it is also true that a thin stream within later tradition tried to preserve Augustine's insights into a grace which at least *precedes* human merits. The reason for the difficulties which medieval theology had with Augustine's doctrine of grace lies in Augustine himself. He was more interested in the effect of grace than in a careful definition of its *origin* in God and its having become an *event* in Jesus Christ. The emphasis on the effect permitted later scholastic theology to unfold the concept of a process of the salvation of man, caused by the *infusio* of a new *habitus*. Although

---

[30] *Ibid.*, p. 436.
[31] *Ibid.*, p. 399; cf. Augustine's complex treatment of this axiom in *Enchiridion* 9 and 22.
[32] *RGG*, 3rd ed., Vol. I, p. 745. Bonaventura has fully understood Augustine's trend of thoughts and expanded them into his theology of illumination; cf. my evaluation of Gilson's and Bougerol's books on Bonaventura, in *ThZ*, May–June 1966, pp. 225 ff.

Augustine would not have been happy with this, his own thoughts permitted such simplification and alteration to Aristotelian thought forms. For grace, according to Augustine, is essentially a mediation and transmission of divine power into the human soul, a power that enables man to take delight in God and to deny the lusts of the world.

The artful connection between the concept of grace and the doctrine of predestination has not removed the anthropological basis of these theological thoughts. On the contrary, it has explained and confirmed this basis. Thus, as seen from the "side of man," grace can be understood only in relation to the concept of the evil from which man must escape. The following chain of thought appears to summarize Augustine's thinking: Grace comes from God as an unaltering life-giving power, and the understanding of it depends on the recognition of evil (of the whole realm of matter); this depends on the theological notion of the *massa perditionis* which in turn depends on the (later: anti-Pelagian) concept of the Fall, and the significance of the Fall can be seen only in the light of the doctrine of predestination; but predestination is preceded by justification, the understanding of which depends on recognizing God as the supreme good and as perfect righteousness, who out of his freedom justifies man by giving man grace. Justification itself can be described by another chain of thought: God knows in his foreknowledge the situation of each man, i.e. the factors which will determine his free will and works; man will perform these works because his favorable situation is preserved by God and because his will is aided by the illumination of grace; God will then take delight in man's works and recognize in him the true love and humility of Christ, and he will forgive him the "lesser sins" and protect him against "mortal sins," thus preserving and protecting him in the number of the elect which is the Church.

We merely note at this point the enormous importance of *individual* justification and salvation in Augustine's theology. We observe that the formulation of this justification and final salvation is *in answer to man's question* and search for overcoming his natural self and the evil of the world. Augustine's mode of presenting these theological thoughts is non-historical, although he operates loosely within a framework of redemptive history. But his real interest is in the "historicity" (*Geschichtlichkeit*) of the believer's encounter with God. The parallels to trends in contemporary theology are obvious. We leave aside at this point the often lamented uncertainty of salvation in Augustine which keeps the believer in constant fear, for according to Augustine there is little or nothing to assure the believer of his acceptance. He must live in constant *repetition* of his "overcoming himself" without being liberated to a new state of life. His "heart will be restless" as long as he lives. An obvious parallel may be drawn between this theology and some of the more disconsolate aspects of existentialist theology.

Before investigating further such possible parallels, we must return to our theme and relate it to ecclesiology. How did Augustine connect his interest in the individual's vision of God and in salvation with his doctrine of the Church, which obviously takes an important place in his thinking? Well known are his *notae ecclesiae:* The Church is "one," kept together by the same love that is between the persons of the Trinity; the Church is "holy" as the true body, the *corpus verum*, although here on earth it is still a *corpus permixtum* since the unholy, the non-elect, can also belong to its outward structure; the Church is "catholic," i.e. world-embracing; and finally, it is "apostolic" so far as the origin of the content of its teaching is concerned. But how is the believing individual related to the so-defined Church? Two oft-cited sentences may help answer this question. The first is taken from Cyprian[33]: *salus extra ecclesiam non est*,[34] there is no salvation outside the Church. This sentence is quite understandable and meaningful if *salus* means participation in the priestly work of Jesus Christ. This is what the "best part" of the Eastern tradition had *de facto* thought: the people of God are those who vicariously listen and speak, pray and act on behalf of the rest of mankind. If *salus*, however, means that an individual reaches his final destiny of being accepted rather than rejected by God, the sentence becomes a juridical one, and there can be no doubt that Augustine, like Cyprian, interpreted *salus* in this second sense. The anti-Donatist writings make this more than clear: the Church is that divine institution which gives a home to the elect even in this world and time, although the non-elect also dwell in this home and partake of the *communio sacramentorum* as though they truly belonged to the *communio sanctorum*. The Church, therefore, is the realm within which the *ecclesia praedestinata*, the predestined, perfected and

[33] Cyprian, Ep. 73 (21).
[34] Augustine, *De baptismo contra Donatistas*, IV, 17, 24. Cf. *Enchiridion* 56–63.

heavenly Church is now being prepared. The task and work of the present Church is the *preparation* of her individual members for her future.[35] Thus the definition of the individual determines the definition of the Church and of the future.

The second sentence, "I would not have believed the Gospel if the authority of the Catholic Church had not moved me [to it],"[36] seems at first sight to contradict our finding that Augustine's ecclesiology is based upon his concept of the pious individual and his destiny. The sentence is again open to two interpretations. One would be represented in Luther's fine statement: "He who wants to find Christ must first find the Church. How else should one know where Christ is and his faith, if one would not know where his faithful people are? And he who wants to know something of Christ must not trust in himself nor build a bridge into heaven by his own reason, but go to Church, visit her and ask her."[37] But the alternative interpretation is Augustine's and is again a juridical one; Augustine has a basically epistemological interest when he deals with the relation between human thoughts and divine reality, and the acceptance of thoughts other than man's own (evil) thoughts is a matter of authority. The Church is instituted to provide the safeguard for the correct transmission of supernatural thoughts. Again: the Church serves the interests of the believing individuals. The first of our two sentences warned the believer not to seek the *vita beata* outside the Church and the second confesses in positive form that Augustine has really found the Church to be what it promised.

Inasmuch as Augustine's concept of grace depends on his understanding of the fallenness of man, his ecclesiology depends on his view of man's need to be redeemed from his imprisonment in selfishness and worldliness. *It is sin which glues mankind together, and it is the awareness that sinful worldliness must be overcome which ties the believers together in the Church.* The piety of those who have found their home in the Church is patterned upon the *humilitas*

---

[35] We cannot here enter into the debate which Wilhelm Kamlah has aroused by maintaining that Augustine's ecclesiology is exclusively eschatological (*Christentum und Geschichtlichkeit*, 2nd ed., 1951), an opinion refuted by J. Ratzinger and others. Our interest is taken care of by the above summary statements.

[36] *Ego vero evangelio non crederem, nisi ecclesiae catholicae me ammoveret auctoritas* (*Contra Epist. Manichaei*, 5, 6).

[37] Luther, WA 10, I, 1, 140, 8f. (my translation).

Christi, so that they now abstain from all boasting and all lusts of the flesh.[38] But this is almost the only occurrence or necessary function of Jesus Christ in Augustine's doctrines of grace and the Church; it would be possible to reproduce large parts of Augustine's theology without mentioning Christ at all. Grace and salvation occur between the two poles of God and man, and Christ only appears in a general and timeless manner when Augustine makes reference to the trans-intelligible world in which Christ is the representative of God's form-giving ideas. Even in the emphasis on Christ's humility, Christ is no necessary part of Augustine's concept of grace and of the Church. The tragic result was that his theology, although it took its point of departure with the individual who is in need of redemption, failed to give final assurance and certainty to the individual.[39] This outcome is well described by two quotations from different theological quarters. H. v. Campenhausen writes: "Only with Augustine did the idea of predestination attain the gloomy inevitability which made it 'the horror of Christian thought in all ages' (Heinrich Barth). How does this come about? The answer leads us to the ultimate weakness of Augustine's theology, a weakness which merely culminates in the doctrine of grace."[40] And B. Altaner says: "From the beginning Augustine's doctrine of grace which is based on a frightening conception of God has roused opposition within the Church, and subsequently has caused grave errors."[41]

In his *De civitate Dei*, Augustine goes beyond the mere application of individualistic Neo-Platonic categories, and seems rather to return to biblical-historical patterns of thought. His elaborate explication of

[38] We meet again the strong emphasis on "boasting" (*kauchāsthai*) as the opposite of Christian existence in Bultmann, e.g., *Theology of the New Testament*, Vol. I (New York: Charles Scribner's Sons, 1954), pp. 190–269, the part entitled "Man Prior to the Revelation of Faith." H. v. Campenhausen summarizes Augustine by saying: "The sole object of Augustine's teaching on grace is to rebuke the pride of man who is imprisoned by himself and who deceives himself" (*op. cit.*, p. 265), a statement which could equally well serve as a summary of Bultmann's theology.

[39] It appears that other great systems of thought, such as the social teachings of Thomas Hobbes, or Hegelianism and Marxism, suffer from the same inherent problem. In a more complicated way this is also true of existentialism; any system that begins with the individual in one way or another will ultimately fail to answer the individual's needs and questions. Recent critical publications by Marxist philosophers demonstrate well this difficulty within Marxism.

[40] *Op. cit.*, p. 264.

[41] Altaner, *Patrology* (New York: Herder and Herder, 1961), p. 526.

the dialectical relation between the two *civitates,* the *civitas* of God
and of the world, affects the conception of the Church. We will not
enter here into the controversy as to the possible identification of the
two *civitates* with the empirical Church and the Roman State; while
one group of interpreters (represented, e.g. by H. Scholz) saw in the
civitates merely allegorical exemplifications, the other group (e.g.
Karl Holl) unhesitatingly identified the *civitas Dei* with the Church
and the *civitas terrena* with the Roman State. It appears that both
interpretations are right in their emphasis on Augustine's desire to
distinguish sharply between "Church and World," as we would put it
today, but that both are wrong in overlooking the fact that a (Neo-)
Platonist cannot be forced to separate a transcendental idea from a
historical manifestation. "Allegory" and "identification" are categories which do not lend themselves to the interpretation of Augustine in this matter. But one result is certain and is well established by
Augustine's later anti-Donatist writings: he conceived of the Church
as something which will not fade away at the end of time. Whatever
stand we take in the interpretation of *De civitate Dei,* and irrespective of W. Kamlah's thesis of the utterly eschatological character of
the Church, we cannot help stating that Augustine taught the existence of an *eternal Church* whose earthly manifestation is, as it were,
the prolongation of the *eschaton* backward into history. Thus Augustine adds a third system of history and eschatology[42] to the two
existing ones. The earliest Church apparently thought of a *millennium* which would begin after the return of Christ; the expectation
was that then the Christians would *rule* with Christ, while at present
they had to suffer. But already at the time of Justin Martyr[43] this
expectation seems to have been disappearing. Hippolytus of Rome in
his *Chronicle* introduced openly the thought that the expectation of
the *millennium* was futile. And it is not by accident that Hippolytus
contributed much to the strengthening of the position of the Church
in the sense of an authoritative institution for the future salvation of
its present members.[44] But Hippolytus clearly dropped the idea of
the *millennium.* Augustine, then, *combined the first with the second
notion and the result was his concept of the eschatologically authoritative Church.* The Church experiences the millennium now! She has

---

[42] Especially *De civ. Dei* XX, 5–9, and *Enchiridion* 54–56, 84ff., *passim.*
[43] *Dialogue with Trypho,* 80; here Justin admits that not all Christians believed
    in a *millennium* to come.
[44] Cf. the list of passages and the discussion in my study on Hippolytus (see
    Introduction, FN 3).

eschatological authority now, and her statements and judgments have eschatological finality. She rules now with Christ. But *over whom* does the Church rule today?

The answer, though shocking, is clear and cannot be discussed away: The invisible, true *ecclesia praedestinata*, dwelling within the visible Church, rules over the world. Or, to state it from the point of view of the tasks of the *civitas terrena: the world must serve the Church*.[45] The world exists because of the Church, and in order to aid, support and protect the Church. And the possibility of dispensing with Jesus Christ as the permanent priest of the Church, i.e. the usurpation of Christ's priesthood by the post-Augustinian medieval Church, invites the sentence: *The Church is the priest whom the world must serve.*

Both Protestant and Catholic authors have repeatedly drawn attention to the fact that "Augustine paved the way for St. Thomas Aquinas, who attempted to provide the medieval Inquisition with a theological foundation," as Altaner puts it.[46] But the Inquisition is merely a symptom. While the later Eastern Fathers (e.g. Eusebius) naively hailed Constantine and Theodosius, and indeed accepted theologically unjustifiable privileges and practices, it is Augustine who must rightly be called the theological architect of the "Constantinian" Church, as we use the term today. Augustine agreed with the idea of using the power of the state against heretics, and judging from his concept of grace and justification we must admit that his position was consistent with his basic presuppositions. If it is true that the sole purpose of the Church is the protection and preparation of the believers in order to save them from this world and to lead them to the eternal vision of God, it is also true that God in his omnipotent rulership over the whole creation, who knows no other goal than the salvation of the elect, will use all human beings, believers and unbelievers alike, to serve and aid his Church. One cannot deny that there is a beauty and an ultimate consistency in this un-Biblical thought.

We will have to discuss later[47] the extent to which the Reformers, who also concentrated on individual justification, were able to over-

---

[45] Cf. the competent but rather tolerant study of the political implications of Augustine's ecclesiology by Herbert A. Deane, *The Political and Social Ideas of St. Augustine* (New York: Columbia University Press, 1963).

[46] *Patrology*, p. 532.

[47] *Vide* part d of this chapter, as well as chaps. IV and VI.

come the idea that the world is to serve the Church. We merely note at this point that Calvin apparently accepted Augustine's combination of the two types of eschatology, *viz.* that he too thought of the present state of the Church in terms of a present *millennium*.[48] In any case, Western theology carries the burden of the Augustinian heritage, for the strong emphasis on the individual's *vita beata*, justification and salvation leads either to an institutionalized Church or to a spiritualistic anti-Church mentality so typical of much of contemporary Protestantism.[49]

c) *The Enjoyment of God and the Separation of Nature and Grace*

One could obtain the impression that Augustine's theology is nothing but a magnificent praise of the *Christus praesens*. But this would be a deception. The early Augustine tried to discipline himself in the art of viewing before his spiritual eyes the incorporeal realities. He valued the liberal arts because of their pedagogical function toward this end.[50] He even doubted whether a person not trained in these disciplines and not gifted with the ability to conceive of the trans-intelligible could ever have a vision of God.[51] And after his conversion he still taught the seven steps in which the vision is reached.[52] And the later Augustine continued to praise the vision and enjoyment of God as the highest good and chief end of man. He even defined the Church as the best structured society for the purpose of the enjoyment of God.[53] But he had great difficulties in connecting his concept of the enjoyment of God with Christology. In his unfolding of the doctrine of the Trinity he begins with God in his

---

[48] Cf. Elwyn A. Smith, "The Impact of St. Augustine's Millennialism on the Function of the Church Tradition," *JES*, Vol. 3, No. 7 (Winter 1966), pp. 130 ff., esp. pp. 142 ff.

[49] A third alternative is flight into the social tasks of Christians—at least a useful occupation. It is certainly true that the lamentation of the younger theologians over the institutionalization of our present denominations cannot easily be met by "moral" arguments, nor is it simple to rebuke the desires of many of our theological graduates to do anything rather than serve in a local parish. The sickness of our Western theological situation is very deeply rooted.

[50] *De ordine*, I, 24.

[51] *Ibid.*, II, 26.

[52] *De animae quantitate*, 70 f.

[53] *De civ. Dei*, XIX, 13.

oneness and unity and proceeds from there, applying Plotinus' categories of intelligibility.[54] Within the process of the vision of God, Jesus Christ holds only an auxiliary function. Christ's own obedience unto death is a lasting pattern and model for our attitude toward God, as well as a sign of God's mercy toward us. But Christ is neither the subject nor the object of the *visio* and *fruitio Dei*. Thus his *presence* in the congregation is not conceived as theologically important. God is present, or omnipresent, but not God in Christ.[55] And the omnipresent God is in Augustine's view an unchangeable, timeless and trans-historical Spirit. There is *no time* for God, time[56] belongs entirely to the realm of creation. But God's timelessness is conceived as a blessing, in fact it is with this timelessness that for Augustine theology stands or falls. If it were not for God's trans-historical existence the human soul would gain nothing in the *visio beatifica*. But now everything is gained: conversion from the desires of this present world, and contemporaneity with the saints of the past and future, most of all with Jesus himself. "Were you there when they crucified my Lord?" is also answered by Augustine in the affirmative.[57] Moreover, it is only on the basis of this concept of the timeless God that Augustine was able to unfold his doctrine of predestination, which, as we have seen, is directly tied to the understanding of grace and justification. From the point of view of God, there is *only one time: the present*. The sharing in this present time equals the confrontation with God's presence. And this experience is the meaning of life. We are reminded of the already cited sentences of Bultmann in which he says that the advent of Christ is "an eternal event which occurs again and again in the soul of any Christian in whose soul Christ is born, suffers, dies and is raised up to eternal life . . ." the Christian becomes a "contemporary of Christ" and "time and the world's history are overcome." "In every moment slumbers the possibility of being the eschatological mo-

---

[54] Cf. Thomas Wassmer, S.J., "The Trinitarian Theology of Augustine and his Debt to Plotinus," *HThR*, Vol. LIII, No. 4 (Oct. 1960), pp. 261 ff., an examination of Augustine's high praise of Plotinus, a praise which "knows no limits" (p. 268) and declares Plotinus "consonans evangelio" of John.

[55] Cf. Stanislaus J. Grabowski, *The All-Present God* (St. Louis: Herder, 1954).

[56] Cf. *Confessiones*, XI, 14 ff. This and other relevant passages are discussed by W. B. Green, "Saint Augustine on Time," *SJT*, Vol. 18, No. 2 (June 1965), pp. 148 ff., in relation to Plotinus' *Enneads*.

[57] The answer in the affirmative occurs frequently in his writings: *ibi eramus*, there we were.

ment. You must awaken it."[58] This is not the praise of the *Christus praesens* but rather a *representation* or *reenactment* of the historically known Christ by virtue of a strictly timeless concept of God. At the risk of overstating the case, we may call this concept of God *deistic*. For the decisive acts of God lie in the past, at least to the extent to which a "past" exists. There is a "past," of course, to the human mind, and the assertion that what appears as the "past" to the human mind is to God the present is a theological construction which is nevertheless based upon the "past." If this is true, it would follow that Augustine's statements about the *eschaton* are likewise constructed on the basis of the human understanding of the past, a past, however, which does not exist for God but only for man's limited mind. And this is indeed the case.

The enjoyment of God in the present is not christologically tied to the newness of the risen man, Jesus Christ. Rather its understanding is derived exclusively from a concept of God which must by necessity define God as timeless, although in the eyes of man he appears as the one whose actions of the "past" can be reenacted in the present. The reenactment, however, is for the sake of final salvation, and consequently Augustine teaches that history is running toward its fulfillment. He denies the cyclical idea of history,[59] as he knew it through the Pythagoreans. Nevertheless, his idea of fulfillment is shaped by his concept of the fate of the believing individual after his death. Augustine's interest in purgatorial fire[60] and other elements of popular piety indicates well his individualistic approach to the promise of eschatological fulfillment. It is only consistent with this interest that Augustine focuses on the description of the true Christian, rather than of Jesus Christ. The true Christian is the believer who is perfected in wisdom, *sapientia*,[61] which is the climax of his having climbed the seven steps of the recognition of God and of himself. The process described by the seven steps is not a mystical one: the sixth, which opens the beginning of the vision of God, is the *intellectus*. It is here that the enjoyment of God begins and it is from here that the believer can finally climb higher to the *sapientia*, which is by

[58] See Chap. I, FN 44–47.
[59] E.g. *De civ. Dei*, XII, 14.
[60] E.g. *Enchiridion*, 68, 69, *passim*.
[61] *Enchiridion*, 1, 2; in addition to the early form of this doctrine in *De animae quantitate*, cf. *De sermone Domini in monte*, I, 2, 9 ff. and *De doctrina christiana*, II, 7, 9 ff.

all means an activity of the human intellect, inspired and aided by the Holy Spirit. Medieval mysticism adopted from Augustine merely the concept of the elevation from the worldly to the beatific status, but often with the exclusion of the intellect, whereas scholasticism stressed the function of the intellect by deemphasizing Augustine's pious interest in the vision of God. Augustine is the father of both medieval mysticism and scholasticism. Different as were their interpretations of the Augustinian heritage, they had in common a negative attitude toward the world and a non-historical approach to the history of Israel and to the coming of Jesus of Nazareth. And in this they interpreted Augustine correctly.

Western theology has taken from Augustine the theological license to separate divine grace from the world and from history, and that means from *nature*. Within this license is contained an outspoken intellectualism and its counterpart, apparently its opposite, the mystical approach to God. But the former was more powerful than the latter, as is demonstrated by the interesting fact that Western theology always suspected that mysticism could lead to heresy, whereas theological intellectualism seldom met this suspicion.

The separation of nature from grace is the inevitable result of a theology in which Christ holds merely an auxiliary function. Nature *must* be evil, otherwise the whole system would collapse. For a non-christological understanding of grace presents the following impasse: As soon as grace is separated from Christ, who was *man* in Jesus, it cannot *affect* nature; it can either be nature, as in natural theology, or else it must bypass nature, as in Augustine's thinking. Consequently medieval theology, having its roots in a theology which presented this alternative, had always two possible avenues: natural theology or spiritual theology. But in both cases grace is separated from Christ, who is thus no longer an essential part of theology in the sense that theological reflection begins and ends with him who is confessed to be both God and man. The great intellectual accomplishment of medieval theology is the artful combination of the two avenues. Going beyond Augustine, Thomas Aquinas "divinized" nature and "naturalized" grace, while the other medieval tradition, Scotism, followed more strictly Augustine's high evaluation of the human will, though attempting nevertheless to combine the two avenues. Thus the question of the relation between nature and grace remained an important theme in Western theology. The disadvantage of this polarization was visible not only in the obvious degradation of nature as over against grace, but also in the unfortunate juxtaposition of reason and faith, of works and faith (in Reformation theology) or of law and Gospel (in Lutheran theology).[62] Necessary as these distinctions may be, they all imply that God has reserved for himself a special realm. If this is so, it follows logically (a) that certain (or most) parts of human life and activity are outside of this realm, which means that God's rule is limited; and (b) that those who desire to be with God must try to leave the world and history behind. The traditional form of the separation of nature and grace implies a limitation of God's rule and a negation of at least certain parts of his creation. The ecclesiastical and ethical consequences of such a doctrine are well known. Medieval monasticism is a relatively harmless example compared with the horrible extermination of Jews and of other non-Christians in the late Middle Ages, not to mention the Crusades with all their cruelties and bloodshed in the name of the Church. All these manifestations are indicative of the idea that parts of creation are autonomous, i.e. outside the realm of grace and the will of God, and must therefore either be destroyed or else be brought by force under subjection to God (or the Church).[63] While certain factors in Reformation theology and, more effectively, the impact of the Enlightenment have persuaded the Church to dissociate herself from such cruel imperialism, the basic thoughts of the Augustinian and medieval tradition regarding nature and grace have not yet been overcome. "Religion and politics" are still separated by the majority of the Christians, and learned theological publications still justify and expound the difference between the "spiritual" and the "worldly" realms either by utilizing the Lutheran distinction between law and Gospel, or by referring to a more shallow theological rationale, or even by directly advocating the difference between the sacramental realm of the Church and the sinful realm of the world and of history.

Augustine's and his mother's vision at Ostia[64] can fairly be called

---

[62] Cf. B. A. Gerrish *Grace and Reason, A Study in the Theology of Luther* (Oxford: The Clarendon Press, 1962).

[63] Bernard of Clairvaux, whose thinking is perhaps furthest away from what modern Christians can understand, sanctioned a Crusade against the Wendish people in 1147 with the motto: "Conversion or destruction!"

[64] *Confessiones*, IX, 10. Cf. the study by P. Henry, S.J. (FN 12); A. Butler (*Western Mysticism*, 1920) and especially F. Cayré (*La contemplation*

the beginning of this theological position, although earlier reports of visions, such as that in the *Passion of Perpetua and Felicitas*, had of course strongly influenced popular piety. But none of them was theologically as powerful as Augustine's. He not only assigned a legitimate place to the experience of a "vision" but declared it as well to be the center of the Christian's life and of theological reflection. His description of the blessed hour was read, memorized and imitated by generations of believers all through the centuries, and their impression was certainly correct that here they were grasping the heart of Augustine's theology. Indeed, the fading away of the world consciousness and the disappearance of time in periods of sole and most intense concentration of the *"esse"*[65] of wisdom are described as the wonderful fruits of the vision. This grace is to be had only if at the same time all desires are directed away from the world and concentrated on God.

It is high time that this Augustinian creed, despite all its beauty, be replaced today by the humble though nevertheless daring confession that we Christians today have never had such visions of God and we do not desire to have them; we desire to have a *vision of man because of God and not a vision of God in spite of man*. But such a creed is possible only on the basis of a christological understanding of the knowledge of God, for Christ "is the icon of the invisible God" (Col. 1:15).

Augustine's theology cannot be a praise of the *Christus praesens*, since Christ is to him neither the object nor the subject of the vision of God which occupies such a central position in his theology. The timeless God is omnipresent, according to Augustine's thinking and experience, but this presence implies and necessitates the destruction of time and the negation of history. Presence which is identical with timelessness ceases to be presence. This fact is illustrated by Augus-

---

augustinienne, 1927, and many other publications) had labeled Augustine as a mystic, while E. Hendrikx (FN 16) showed the intellectual character of Augustine's *visio beatifica*; the essays of twenty-three authors on this question are listed in the bibliography in *Augustin-Gespräch*, pp. 503–505.

[65] *Confessiones*, IX, 10, 24. The tenth chapter, reporting the vision, should be read in the context of the following chapters. In chap. 12, after the death of his mother, Augustine said: "But she neither died unhappy nor did she altogether die." The possible connection with Horace's *Odes*, III, 30, is not of great interest, but the *de facto* denial of the reality of death should alarm us; it is in harmony with the denial of the world and of time as described in the vision in chap. 10.

tine's separation of nature and grace, which resulted by necessity from his theology in which Christ takes an inferior position. The Church, however, receives a position superior to the rest of mankind, from which she is separated. Western theology after Augustine was thus required to face unfortunate alternatives: natural or spiritual theology, sacramentalization or spiritualization of grace; and the various attempts to harmonize or combine the two possibilities wasted valuable intellectual and spiritual power for many centuries.

In the last part of this chapter we will now examine the impact of Augustine's individualistic interest in the encounter with God on the later concentration of justification as presented primarily by Reformation theology.

d) Personalism: Static Eschatology Projected into Ecclesiology

Augustine's combination of early Christian millenarianist eschatology with Hippolytus' non-millennarian ecclesiology resulted in a static understanding of the Church and the *eschaton*. The biblical aspect of fulfillment in the *eschaton* was projected by Augustine into the experience of the *visio Dei* in the *present*. The beatific vision anticipates the final fulfillment to such an extent that the expectation of the fulfillment becomes unimportant and superfluous. God is not expected to perform decisively new acts in the future; the hope of the Christian is almost entirely directed toward the reception of grace which leads already in the present to the full vision and enjoyment of God. Augustine of course admitted that the moments of such vision are brief, and in his later life he conceded that many would not reach the blessed experience during their lifetime, but only after death. Bernard in like manner complained that his own visionary experiences always passed away so quickly. But these concessions do not change the fact that with Augustine the Western Church learned to project future eschatological expectation into the realm of the believer's existence in the Church. Thus eschatology not only becomes "realized eschatology," to use C. H. Dodd's term, but it also receives its definition in relation to the individual. The hope of the Church is replaced by the individual hope of the single believer. Later Catholic theology provides the proof of this statement; Roman Catholic dogmatics has never shown much concern for biblical eschatology, rather the fate of the individual after his death moved into the center of attention. And the situation in Protestant theology is not much better; Protestant popular piety is also interested primarily in the future life of the individual believer after his death, and academic theology has only rarely provided correctives to this individualistic view. Among these exceptions we think of Luther's attempt to overcome medieval individualistic eschatology (though crippled by his difficulties with the apocalypticism of the *Schwärmer*), of some Confession Books of the suffering Reformed churches in post-Reformation time, of certain trends in pietism, of father and son Blumhardt in the nineteenth century and finally of sermons and scholarly publications of the persecuted churches in the twentieth century. But on the whole one can say that Western theology has not been able to overcome the individualistic conception of eschatology. Moreover, any attempts to rehabilitate certain aspects of apocalypticism have almost always been refuted as fantastic and sectarian. Existentialist theology has not changed this situation, but on the contrary has confirmed and strengthened the Augustinian approach to "realized eschatology." It is here that the projection of the eschaton backward into the Christ-event and the "event of my faith" has been more fully developed than ever before in the history of theology; the hope of the Christian is entirely directed toward the *present encounter* with God. In other words, God is no longer seen as the God of the Exodus, who moves with his people through history which is hastening toward its fulfillment, but rather God is understood statically. *And this static God is expected to reveal his mystery by repeated epiphanies in the encounter with the individual believer.* This is the Christian hope. It is all that remains after God has been declared to be timeless and static, and after his dealing with mankind has been reduced to the description of the personal encounter between him and the believer. Augustine's conception of eschatology, projected into ecclesiology, has prepared the way for modern Western personalism.

It is an extreme judgment of W. von Loewenich, using modern terminology for ancient thoughts, when he says that Augustine discovered the "existential character of knowledge" and was "the founder of the existential concept of faith," the *Confessiones* being "the beginning of the philosophy of existence."[66] But there is some

---

[66] Walther v. Loewenich, *op. cit.* (cf. FN 12), pp. 40 and 42. Cf. also Erich Frank, *Augustine-Gespräch*, pp. 182 ff. and 381 ff. and Carl Andresen's introduction, *ibid.*, pp. 35 ff., on the controversy as to whether Augustine can really be called the father of the philosophy of existence.

truth in this statement. Augustine was certainly the first influential
theologian who focused his interest on self-reflection and "self-
understanding." Whether his self-accusations regarding his boyish
"sins" in his youth are "pathologically exaggerated," as the historian
Jacob Burckhardt said, or whether they should be interpreted as
strictly theological evaluations, it is true that Augustine not only
based his concept of grace and justification on his understanding of
(his) sin but that *he also defined the status of being justified as the
reception of a new self-understanding.* Luther's self-accusations are
in proximity to Augustine's, although Luther's doctrine of justification is unquestionably christological, while, as we have seen, this
cannot be said of Augustine's thinking. Luther, according to Hamel's
study,[67] did not accept from Augustine (a) the idea of the *merita*
which are necessary for justification, (b) the concept of the *gratia
cooperans* and (c) the doctrine that because of God's righteousness
God can justify only the righteous man, the *iustus*. But Luther certainly did not challenge Augustine's individualistic approach to justification on the whole, as is visible in Luther's strong emphasis on the
"pro me," i.e. the understanding of the work of Christ *for me.* Later
Lutheran theology has, of course, gone further in this direction than
did Luther,[68] but Luther is nevertheless responsible for the general
approach. His rather problematical concept of "saving faith," the
fides salvifica, which can be distinguished (scholastically and abstractly) from the *fides historica,* clearly shows the inherent danger.
Moreover, Luther, not unlike Augustine, operates with a concept of
the timeless God, not only with reference to the hidden God, the *deus
absconditus,* but even when speaking of the justifying God, the *deus
revelatus,* for the antinomy of man's simultaneous righteousness and
sinfulness is resolved only by the insight that *for God the future is
already present,* i.e. the final salvation of the individual already now
determines God's attitude to the yet sinful man.

---

[67] Adolf Hamel, *Der junge Luther und Augustin,* 2 vols. (Gütersloh: Bertels-
mann Verlag, 1934–35). Hamel limits his study to the doctrine of justification.
Luther became acquainted with Augustine in 1509–10 when commenting
on Peter Lombard, but used him more freely in 1513–15 when working on
the Psalms. The dependence on Augustine's *De spiritu et littera* is especially
strong. The commentaries on Romans, Galatians and Hebrews show Luther's
admiration for Augustine, but Luther did not, according to Hamel, accept
Augustine's idea that *concupiscentia* is primarily sexual; rather, it is man's
desire to love his own ego, which is also Bultmann's view.
[68] Cf. Hans-Joachim Iwand, "Wider den Misbrauch des *pro me*" in *EvTh,*
1954, pp. 120 ff.

If it is questionable whether Luther (and Calvin) took the sinfulness of man as the starting point of their concept of justification, there can be no doubt that existentialist theology (as well as popular piety) proceeds in this way. Moltmann observes that it is consistent with the Augustinian tradition that in existentialist theology the kerygma presupposes a misery (*Not*) which it turns to the good; in other words, that the question presupposes an answer which it indeed gives.[69] He calls this a "strange reciprocity" between God's coming to man and man's coming to himself, and he concludes that this theology presupposes a theological anthropology which "Jesus verifies," a *"theologia naturalis* of modern existence." Moltmann, however, wants to protect Augustine by saying that modern existentialist theology, though having accepted the Augustinian tradition, has not done justice to Augustine himself, to whom the distress (*die Not*) of man comes from God himself. This statement can be challenged, but Moltmann is certainly right in seeing the connection between Augustine and Ebeling, whose thinking he criticizes. That the distress and human predicament comes from God, thus indicating that the anthropological basis of the doctrine of justification is nevertheless actually a theological one, holds true only in Luther's theology. To him the human predicament and the insight into man's lostness comes from the *law* which accuses man of his sins (law understood exclusively as *lex accusans*), and the law is seen as over against the Gospel. And it is evident that Bultmann and Ebling, with little concern for the Old Testament, have replaced the traditional Lutheran concept of accusation by the *law* with the idea that today it is the *world* which convinces man of his limitations, lostness and destiny for death.[70] This shift is indeed important and makes manifest that the accepted anthropological basis precedes the christological understanding of the kerygma. But we would maintain that this approach represents a shift away from Luther and back to Augustine, whose theology is apparently "spiritual" and philosophical enough to have pleased not only medieval mystics and nineteenth-century liberal Protestants but also late twentieth-century theologians of "encounter" and of existence.

Without attempting to belittle the differences between Augustine,

[69] Jürgen Moltmann, "Anfrage und Kritik zu G. Ebelings 'Theologie und Verkündigung,' " in *EvTh*, Jan. 1964, pp. 25 ff.; this observation on p. 31.
[70] Cf. G. Ebeling, "Erwägungen zur Lehre vom Gesetz," *ZThK*, 1958, pp. 270 ff.

medieval mysticism, post-Schleiermacher liberalism and contemporary existentialist theology (including its Catholic counterparts), we cannot help observing that the *individual believer* occupies a central place in these theologies. The Lutheran tradition especially, culminating in Bultmann and Ebeling and also in Tillich, has stressed the importance of Pauline justification on this very basis. But while Pauline justification operates little with the idea of the "terrified conscience," the theologies just mentioned are deeply rooted in this notion. The conscience becomes the testing ground, the *forum spirituale* of the soteriologically understood biblical message. When the conscience is freed toward the future, then man has reached the goal of what has been promised him. When the conscience is troubled, however, man needs the message that corresponds to his "terrified conscience." The Study Report of the Lutheran World Federation in preparation for the meeting in Helsinki in 1963 showed full awareness of this typically Lutheran heritage: "With Luther, the judicial process takes place in the conscience itself. Hence his tendency to introspection. Here he is an heir of Augustine, who was the first to know a conscience in our sense, and of the medieval practice of confession and penance."[71] The report continues by drawing attention to Athanasius, and it shows the necessity of limiting the empha-

---

[71] *Justification Today*, Studies and Reports, Supplement to *Lutheran World*, No. 1, 1965, p. 32. The contribution of an unnamed discussion partner is given on the same page: "We are not agreed that there is in the Church a false spiritualizing of the concept of sin. Bonhoeffer, of course, in one of his Letters from Prison reacts strongly against what he calls spiritual methodism in which one always portrays man at his worst and no longer gives any place to the good in him. The incorrect line stretches far back. It is already to be observed in Augustine who understands the fifth petition of the Lord's Prayer in such a way as to infer that sin must be present. And then he tries to magnify this sin as much as possible. But it is precisely this magnification of sin which Paul in Romans 6 rejects. But that is what happens, when the sin of the heart is separated from the act. That, however, is not only a Lutheran tradition, but really a Western tradition. It is important to me that there should be undertaken from this standpoint a different valuation of the history of dogma, and particularly of the relation between East and West, for one can usually see in Protestant histories of dogma an underestimation of the East, originating with Augustine, because the fathers of the East speak as easily as Paul about free will and about the Christian's possibility of not sinning, and because they speak so little of the Christian's being a sinner. In this respect, many of these Eastern fathers could be more biblical than the fathers of the West. We must see once more that for the Christian sin has been extinguished, destroyed, forgiven." Dangerous as this statement is, it contains much truth.

sis on the *"pro me"* and the *"pro nobis"* in the understanding of the work of Jesus Christ, lest the "personal and existential reference" to the doctrine of justification should be allowed to have "absolute importance."[72]

Historically speaking, Luther's emphasis on the personal-address character of justification came from the voluntarism of Duns Scotus and William of Occam, on the one hand, and from mysticism with its stress on the superhuman, i.e. merely divine righteousness, given by God into man's soul, on the other hand. Luther's combination and clarification of these insights is his great merit, but it is regrettable that his exposition of the imputation of "alien righteousness," the *aliena justitia Christi,* preserved and confirmed the subjective-individualistic thought forms of Augustine and his medieval followers. Exaggerating only slightly, we may conclude that Luther merely gave a new answer to Augustine's soteriological questions. This is also Reginald Prenter's opinion when he complains that Reformation theology continued the medieval interest in the "mediation of grace" to the individual. "It may be said that the Reformation gave a new answer to the medieval question of salvation. The means of the mediation of salvation is now the word . . . the pattern of thought is still that of mediation, not the New Testament pattern of incorporation. Herein lies the individualism of the Reformation."[73] Prenter also observes what we have made a central point of this present book,[74] *viz.* that the Constantinian existence form of the Church caused a certain understanding of justification which today, after the Constantinian period, requires revision. "When the church was no longer a church encountering a non-Christian world but lived in a *corpus Christianum,* then the conception of incorporation had lost its power and vividness and perhaps even its truth."[75]

But modern existentialist theology still continues with the ques-

---

[72] *Ibid.*, p. 35.

For Luther's concept of conscience, see Ernst Wolf, *Peregrinatio* (Munich: Chr. Kaiser Verlag, I, 1954, II, 1965), "Vom Problem des Gewissens in reformatorischer Sicht" (I, pp. 81 ff.), and also "Gewissen zwischen Gesetz und Evangelium" (II, pp. 104 ff). For a new, constructive approach to the "social character" of justification, based on the interpretation of Galatians, see Markus Barth, "Gottes und des Nächsten Recht," in *Parrhesia* (Zurich: EVZ-Verlag, 1966), pp. 447 ff.

[73] *Ibid.*, p. 41.

[74] See Introduction and FN 4.

[75] *Op. cit.*, p. 41.

tion, typical of the Constantinian period of the Church, as to how
man's terrified conscience can receive liberation, absolution and the
permission to look hopefully into the future. The claim that this
theology is more relevant to the needs of modern man than other
theologies is questionable, to say the least. It is based upon an abstraction of what "modern man" is and this abstraction determines at
least partly the content of what is being declared important. While
the Church in the nineteenth century, still feeling secure in the Constantinian mentality, felt it important to ask "How can we convert
others to the Christian faith?" many quarters in so-called modern
theology, denying the Constantinian privileges, have merely modified
the question by asking "How can we tell others the (eternal parts of
the) Good News?" Both approaches are based uncritically and unhesitatingly on the idea that the decisive events, or facts, or truths lie
in the *past* and must be transmitted to modern man. We have already
observed that hope is thereby individualized, and that in function and
importance the Church is thus reduced to an assembly in which this
transmission occurs in the most practical and efficient manner. The
necessity of the Church, however, is readily sacrificed as soon as it
seems feasible to use other channels to transmit the word of liberation to troubled consciences. Such is the outcome of the Western
concentration on justification. Not only is the Christian hope distorted into an egoistical expectation concerning one's own self, but
what is worse and more difficult to repair: there is no place for
adoration, no necessity for worship, no joy in prayer. The one half of
the Church's priestly task, the vicarious prayer on behalf of others, is
abolished. And the other half, the preaching and working "on behalf" of God for the benefit of others, is carried out in individualistic
form and within the framework of a hidden Constantinianism. The
Christus praesens with the dimensions of memory and hope no
longer stands at the center. *His* past and *his* future have been replaced by *my* hermeneutical method to apply the historical/risen
Christ to the present, and by *my* expectation to be liberated to *my*
future. "God's coming to man" has indeed become, to use Moltmann's expression, "man's coming to himself." The history of the
God of the Exodus with Israel and with the Church has become the
history of repeated epiphanies, making manifest time and again the
same eternal truth, thus leaving the Christian ultimately without
hope, and leaving the Church without concrete tasks. The believer is

totally dependent on his *faith* and theology is therefore faith-centered. The examination of the articulation of faith is, consequently, an analysis of speech events, and theology is *"Sprachschule des Glaubens,"* the language school of faith. Ebeling's recent book on Luther[76] interprets Luther from the standpoint of this approach; and it is noteworthy that the book contains not a chapter on Luther's concept of the Church, although Iwand's Luther studies had shown the understanding of the Church as the key to Luther's theology. Could it be perhaps that Ebeling is right in interpreting Luther's theology as not necessarily implying the Church when unfolding the *sola fide*, by faith alone, on the part of the believer as primarily for the sake of liberating his "terrified conscience"? We have made this observation in the case of Augustine; the interest in the individual's liberation from the lusts of the flesh to the *vita beata* is so dominant that it provides the basis for an ecclesiology. And we have already concluded that this ecclesiology opened the door to the two apparently contradicting views, the institutionalization and the spiritualization of the Church.

These critical remarks about existentialist theology and the neighboring non-academic theological positions should not belittle the undisputed advantage of these approaches over the ice-cold and impersonal atmosphere of classical Protestant Orthodoxy, or for that matter of neo-Thomistic Roman Catholic theology. Modern "personalism" would indeed be preferable if we had only the choice between the objectifying language of scholastic orthodoxy and existentialist theology. But the aim of this chapter is to show that the alternative is not a genuine one. What today claims to be "modern" in the form of taking seriously man's self-understanding appears in historical analysis as but a modification of the Augustinian and medieval heritage of the *mediation of grace to the individual*. This today becomes the application of the *kerygma* to the "solitary exister" for the good of his conscience in order to "free him for the future." *We need a far more radical alternative to traditional Western theology.*

The exclusive concentration on justification must give way to a broader understanding of Church and theology, an understanding which is more strictly christological and therefore adaptable to the

[76] Ebeling, *Luther, Einführung in sein Denken* (Tübingen: J. C. B. Mohr, 1964).

great variety of situations which exist in the ecumenical Church in different countries and cultures. A point of departure could be Karl Barth's relocation of the *locus* of justification[77] away from the center of theology to a subcategory of the doctrine of reconciliation. Although his unfolding of the christological conception of justification as one of the three parts of reconciliation is still in the traditional, i.e. "old-fashioned," language, his concentration on the self-humiliation and exaltation of Christ is indeed "modern" and more radical than other theological approaches of our time. It is perhaps because of his language and conservative (in the true sense) frame of reference that many contemporary theologians have not become aware of the challenge and stimulus of this part of his work. It is not by accident that the modern reader has often preferred the aphoristic and non-systematic suggestions of the later Bonhoeffer to Karl Barth's voluminous and highly systematic *Church Dogmatics*. But there is little doubt that Bonhoeffer[78] would today take sides with Barth rather than with existentialist theology. The christological dimensions of Barth's understanding of justification prepare the way for the concept of the priestly task of the Church.[79] There is no avoiding dealing with a reformulation of classical Christology if the separation of soteriology from the rest of theology, or the exclusive interest in soteriology, is to be made impossible. But the Augustinian-Lutheran heritage has presented many difficulties with regard to this reformulation of classical Christology. The existential, soteriological interest has become so strong a part of Western theological tradition that the methodological and epistemological problems concerning "objective" statements about God and Christ seem almost insurmountable. Bultmann's demythologization program, followed by the discussion about non-objectifying language, and taken up in different form, e.g. by Paul van Buren's interest in linguistic analysis, are impressive indications of Western theology's difficulties with classical Christology. They all relate themselves to the Augustinian heritage, partly by adopting Augustine's central interest and questions, partly by reacting against his answers or the modification of his answers as presented by Reformation theology.

[77] Barth, *CD*, IV, 1.
[78] Eberhard Bethge's definitive Bonhoeffer biography, to appear shortly (Munich: Chr. Kaiser Verlag, 1967), stresses this point against the attempts to make Bonhoeffer the father of "speech event" theology and of today's anti-Church theological intellectualism.
[79] See our discussion in Chap. VI.

By way of summarizing this chapter's historical findings which are of systematic interest we can formulate the following theses:

1) Augustine did not accept the strongest parts of Eastern theological tradition but rather combined Western ecclesiology with Greek philosophy.

2) Augustine's adoption of Aristotle's concept of the structure of the universe created the ideology of sin, the recognition of which precedes all other theological insights. The "eudemonistic tendency" in Augustine's theology cannot be denied.

3) His Manicheism introduced dualistic thoughts to his own thinking and to later theology. Later forms of the doctrine of predestination as well as of ecclesiology and the negative evaluation of world reality and history are shaped by this influence.

4) His Neo-Platonism is apparent in the central position of the ideal of the *vita beata,* the vision and enjoyment of God. This exclusively soteriological interest only seemingly praises the *Christus praesens;* in reality it operates with a strong concept of the timelessness of God. This view has affected Augustine's ethics; our neighbor is not to be loved for his being a fellowman but because we love God through him.

5) Augustine's doctrine of grace was simplified in later medieval theology so that the latent anthropological basis of justification became openly accepted. The mediation of grace remained the theme of theology and reappears today in the post-Lutheran dress of existentialist theology.

6) Augustine's concept of the Church is molded by his projection of eschatological fulfillment into the present. It is the Church which has final authority; whereas Jesus Christ is assigned a merely auxiliary function, the world is to serve the Church. This concept paved the way for the Inquisition, the Crusades and other manifestations of the Constantinian concept of the Church, not overcome by the Reformers and either accepted or totally reversed into a spiritualized understanding of the Church by contemporary Western theology.

7) Augustine's timeless God invites the thought of reenacting God's actions of the past, thus conceiving of God in terms of a God of epiphany rather than of history. Nature and grace must be separated, since the non-christological conception of God does not tolerate a non-spiritual idea of grace. Later medieval theology was faced with the choice of "naturalizing" grace or spiritualizing nature. This

unfortunate alternative has occupied the minds of theologians for centuries.

8) Augustine's individualistic interest in the encounter with God was not altered by the Reformers, although theirs is the merit of having recognized the weaknesses in Augustine's concepts of grace and justification. An expression of this individualism is Augustine's and Luther's overly strong emphasis on personal sin, almost entirely excluding the corporate and political aspects of sin and guilt. Consequently, redemption was also seen by Augustine as restricted to the subjective and private realm of human life.

9) While Luther taught that it is God in the law who accuses man, existentialist theology today substitutes the world for the law, thus falling back into Augustine's negative valuation of history and the world. The accusation, i.e. the recognition of man's predicament, is realized in man's conscience, and consequently it is the conscience which becomes the recipient of the Good News. The questions of the "terrified conscience" demand an answer which the kerygma provides.

10) The Augustinian and later Western concentration of justification blocks the way to joyful adoration in the awareness of the *Christus praesens*. The Church merely serves as an instrument to transmit the kerygma, an instrument which is readily replaced by another as soon as it should become apparent that another is more useful.

These pages, filled with harsh and critical statements about Augustine's theology and its impact on Western theology, should not be taken by us as permission to dissociate ourselves lightly from the most respected and beloved Father of the Western Church, whose confession we today must make our own:

> "We bear on our foreheads the sign of Christ, and we do not feel ashamed of this sign as long as we bear it in our hearts. His sign is his humiliation. The Magi from the East recognized him by a star; and this sign, given by the Lord was heavenly and bright, but he has not willed that a star should be his sign on the foreheads of his believers, but his cross."[80]

[80] *Tractatus in Ioannis evangelium* III, 2.

Part Two

SYSTEMATIC IMPLICATIONS

Concerning the Presence of Christ

IV

"Atheistic Christology" as Radical Augustinianism

ONE OF THE RESULTS of our study so far has been the insight that Augustine and subsequent Augustinianism created and preserved within Western theology a one-sided interest in individualistically understood justification, i.e. in the "personal encounter" with God, at the expense of the corporate understanding of the Church. We have also seen that classical Christology did not fit the framework of Western piety. It was not refuted, however, but was treated as an isolated theological topic which was related to the rest of theology by using "justification" as a bridge. The *Christus praesens* was understood as a self-manifestation or epiphany of a timeless God, either in the form of an actualization of the ancient message in the proclaimed Word or in the form of a sacramental reenactment of the event of the incarnation. Theological reflection, consequently, was "past-centered" and the Church's hope was reduced to the expectation of rewards and eternal life after the individual's death or it was banished to the realm of suspect speculation of a sectarian type.

In order to prepare the theses of our final chapter, we will now discuss the systematic theological difficulties which have arisen in recent years with regard to "speaking of God." For centuries Western theology "knew too much about God," as Professor Outler once put it, so that the Enlightenment, Kant and more radically existentialism presented a shock which determines many aspects of contemporary theology. The growing awareness of the end of the Constantinian era has apparently been translated by many theologians into epistemological problems. But we will maintain that the decision to concentrate on philosophical questions, to let theology even *begin* with philosophical-anthropological questions, is not the proper and most helpful reaction to the awareness of the new situation of the Church. On the contrary, this approach equals a falling back into the thought forms of the Augustinianism which was typical of the Constantinian era. If it were correct, which it is not, to make the "desires of the modern world" the starting point of theology, we would nevertheless maintain that the "world" (and who is that?) desires more to hear the theologians speak theologically than to hear us unfold our internal philosophical preconsiderations. It is the theological value of the complexity of these preconsiderations which will occupy our attention in this chapter.

a) What Sense Does It Make to Speak of God?

At the latest, it was with Thomas Aquinas that theology began to operate within the framework of *ratio* and *fides*,[1] reason and faith. Augustine's highly evaluated *sapientia*, wisdom, was redefined and thereby changed into *scientia*, science. Theology became a *scientia conclusionum*, a scientific art of making conclusions. Augustine's emphasis on illumination was weakened and replaced by the idea that the content of revelation is not *contra rationem*, against reason, but *supra rationem*. The contents of faith can be neither proved nor disproved by philosophical operations, but philosophy is considered helpful for the clarification of the *praeambula fidei*, the "preambles" of faith. In fact, however, theological speech became indistinguishable from philosophy. Despite Luther's attempt to free theology from its philosophical bondage, Melanchthon reintroduced into Protestant thinking the more or less Thomistic concept of the relation between theology and philosophy. He too taught that revelation is not *contra* but *supra rationem*.[2] Following this approach, Johann Gerhard spoke of a "threefold use" of reason.[3]

[1] Thomas Aquinas, *Summa Contra Gentiles*, I, 1–9.
[2] Cf. Wilhelm Neuser, *Der Ansatz der Theologie Philipp Melanchthons* (Neukirchen: Buchhandlung des Erziehungsvereins, 1957), pp. 18–40.
[3] Johann Gerhard, *Loci theologici* (1610–22).

It is understandable that the eighteenth century with its radical departure from the undisturbed use of the philosophical apparatus caused an enormous shock. The theologians after Kant showed great caution in the application of traditional, orthodox categories with regard to God. Schleiermacher's congenial attempt to base theology upon faith and yet maintain the Christocentric emphasis of the Reformers[4] seemed to have saved the situation. But the post-Hegelian theology showed discontent with Schleiermacher's concentration on faith, although Schleiermacher's influence remained strong, even in Roman Catholic theology. Bultmann's and Ebeling's theological programs, with their reemphasis of the basic importance of faith, indicate the latest forms of this influence. The influence, however, was indirect, for Schleiermacher's thoughts had been modified by Albrecht Ritschl's passionate attempt to eliminate metaphysics from theology.[5] Ritschl's system was especially influential in Anglo-Saxon theology, yet without accomplishing the abolition of metaphysics from British and American theology. Finally, we must mention Karl Barth—unknowingly partly paralleled and preceded by P. T. Forsyth—who made the first attempt at reworking and overcoming the whole complex of problems in this matter. Barth's strictly trinitarian approach to the problem is conservative in intent and language, yet radically revolutionary in comparison to the nineteenth-century attempts at solving the theological and philosophical questions concerning "speaking of God."

This all too brief historical introduction is intended to show but one point: the most recent European and American discussions about the possibility of "speaking of God" are not at all as modern as the participants would have us believe. Theirs is an *apologetic interest*, although they are sufficiently influenced by Barth not to admit this. They are discontent with Bultmann's unreflective and naively presupposed "theism," but they take their departure from the point at which Bultmann has arrived, *viz.* the importance of the new understanding of my existence in the light of the future.

One of the first exponents of this new theology in Europe was Herbert Braun (in cooperation with his colleague in Mainz,

[4] Cf. the famous Christocentric paragraph No. 11 in *The Christian Faith*.
[5] Cf. "Geschichtliche Studien zur christlichen Lehre von Gott," in *Gesammelte Aufsätze*, ed. O. Ritschl (Freiburg/Leipzig: J. C. B. Mohr, 1896), Vol. II, pp. 25–176.

Manfred Mezger); and his antagonist is Helmut Gollwitzer.[6] A famous public debate between Braun and Gollwitzer took place at the
University of Mainz on February 13, 1964.[7] Another public discussion which has been widely noted and commented upon took place
between Walter Künneth and Ernst Fuchs in the village church at
Sittensen on October 12, 1964. Braun's position is summarized for
the purpose of the discussion in Mainz in three theses. Following an
introductory thesis, the second thesis maintains that the proper understanding of the New Testament does not presuppose the existence
of a "supra-worldly God who speaks in the New Testament and who,
in his acting, interferes in the world." The third thesis states that the
authority of the New Testament is derived not from the concept of a
God who exists before he is heard but from the *event* of the listening
which "draws me" into the matter itself; God dwells in this event. In
the course of the discussion Braun expounded the main points of his
previous publications by defending the idea that God is the "Whence
of my being-moved-about" (*Woher meines Umgetriebenseins*) which
comes to me *only* through my neighbor, who is par excellence Jesus.
Despite various streams within the New Testament, the stream of
tradition which depicts Jesus as the one who demands obedience is to
be considered the dominant one. Jesus meets us as the one who
"fraternizes" with the discriminated, and it is in him that the "Thou
shalt" is always accompanied by the "You are permitted." This is the
specialty of the Christian faith over all other religions, and it is this
very fact which also excludes the possibility of ontology in theology
or of "objectification." The one-sided "Thou shalt," so typical of the
homo religiosus, the religious man, is destroyed by Jesus. The climax
of the old law, the love toward the neighbor, is exemplified in its
"encounter-character" by Jesus. Christology has no other task than
to indicate God's "yes" to man.

Gollwitzer's answers, systematically presented in his book of
1963, and formulated with passion and temperament in the discussion in 1964, show his willingness to understand Braun's main intent.

[6] Helmut Gollwitzer, *Die Existenz Gottes im Bekenntnis des christlichen* Glaubens (Munich: Chr. Kaiser Verlag, 1963). Engl. transl. by James W. Leitch,
The Existence of God as Confessed by Faith (Philadelphia: Westminster Press,
1965), admittedly a hurriedly published contribution to the current discussion
though hardly justifying Thomas J. J. Altizer's harsh and schoolmasterly review in the *Christian Advocate*, Oct. 7, 1965, pp. 9–10.
[7] The discussion is now published, including subsequent comments, in two small
volumes, *Post Bultmann Locutum*, Vols. I & II (Hamburg-Bergstedt: Evangelischer Verlag GmbH, 1965), ed. Horst Symanowski and Hans-Werner Bartsch.

Gollwitzer rightly points out that all theology since Schleiermacher has agreed in a negative evaluation of the opinion that God must "first" be accepted abstractly before his concrete word can be heard and accepted. He draws attention to the dangers in Thomas' and Melanchthon's theology, which indeed seemed to have fallen into undue objectifications. But Gollwitzer strongly disagrees with Braun's logical abstraction that "the subject is known only by its predicates": e.g. with reference to I John, "God is Love" is a sentence which cannot be reversed to "Love is God." It is the *subject* (God) that receives a predicate in the form of a fulfillment of the Old Testament expectation, a conclusion which is yet not identical with the philosophical idea that man must "first" accept the abstract idea of a trans-worldly God before hearing or saying anything further.

Braun's position is that of an exegete who has been shocked by the dogmatical implications of his exegesis. His views, consequently, cannot be of lasting interest to the historian and systematician. Gollwitzer, on the other hand, cannot abstain from giving theological answers to philosophical questions, for Braun's questions appear in the dress of philosophical formulations; Gollwitzer's position is, therefore, not ultimately satisfying. This is the price for his fairness in taking so seriously the position of his opponent. (Quite similar are other authors' reactions against Bishop Robinson's philosophically even more dilettantish propositions.) The problems which Braun (and Robinson for that matter) has raised are not new in the history of theology. But the favorable reception which Braun (and Robinson) has experienced among intellectuals inside and outside the established denominations indicates well how little academic theology has been willing and able to acquaint the general public with the essential parts of its work. Thus Braun (and Robinson) has the merit of having stimulated anew a discussion which unfortunately had hitherto not reached out into the non-theological circles in the Church. The reception of his publications uncovers the guilt of the preachers of the last forty or even one hundred years.

The problem itself, however, is more complicated than has been shown in the discussion in Mainz and in the controversy about Bishop Robinson's *Honest to God*. In the same year in which Gollwitzer's book against Braun was published, Paul van Buren presented to the English-speaking theological scene his propositions, which deserve to be taken more seriously than those of Braun and Robinson.[8] Gollwitzer's and van Buren's books are equal partners, the authors are both systematicians, and van Buren has studied under the same Karl Barth whose theology has so decisively molded Gollwitzer's thinking. Yet their positions are extremely opposed. A confrontation of their views will be helpful in order to crystallize the dogmatical problem of the complicated contemporary theological situation.

Whereas Gollwitzer's book is, despite its rich historical references, "intra-German," i.e. lacking references to publications in the English language and to linguistic analysis in particular, van Buren's book aspires to be an example of Anglo-Saxon theology which takes "a frankly empirical method which reflects the thinking of an industrialized, scientific age."[9] But it is strange that almost all the theologians whose works are mentioned in this book are Continental Europeans. Moreover, van Buren does not deal with those Europeans who are concerned precisely with his problems, e.g. H. Braun and in a broader sense Fuchs, Ebeling, Käsemann, Pannenberg and Løgstrup. Instead van Buren relies heavily upon the British linguistic analysts who know little about theology, as he himself admits.[10] His book has a strongly autobiographical flavor; the author wants *not* to "make the Gospel relevant to the secular man of today"[11] but to understand what *he* believes. The first part of the book introduces an

[8] Paul M. van Buren, *The Secular Meaning of the Gospel* (cf. above, FN 3 of the Introduction). It is with hesitation that I here present critical thoughts against the book of my friend to whom I owe so much. The fact that this present book is dedicated to him should indicate that I do not at all consider the continuation of the discussion between his and my positions as fruitless. Since the writing of this chapter, two review articles have come to my attention with which, however, I can only partly agree: Langdon B. Gilkey, "A New Linguistic Madness," reprinted from *JR* in *New Theology*, No. 2, pp. 39 ff., and Harmon R. Holcomb, "Christology Without God," separate reprint by Colgate Rochester Divinity School from *Foundations*, Jan. 1965.

Another book deserves to be taken seriously: *The Death of God* by Gabriel Vahanian (New York: George Braziller, 1957 and reprints); but Vahanian states his case more in terms of cultural analysis than in the form of systematic theological discussion and we may be justified in omitting it in the present discussion. Cf. now his recent collection of essays, *No Other God* (*ibid.* 1966), which, in addition to personal conversations, seems to me to indicate that Vahanian does not intend to forsake solid theological work.

[9] *Ibid.*, p. 120.

[10] *Ibid.*, p. 104; cf. p. 101. How can van Buren take seriously such trivialities as are summarized on pp. 94 ff.? Indeed, he later dismisses his star witnesses.

[11] *Ibid.*, p. 11.

interpretation of Chalcedon which tries to do as much justice to the Greek Fathers as possible. Remarks on Bultmann are followed by a discussion of linguistic analyses (Hare, Ramsey, Miles, Braithwaite, having begun with Flew). Van Buren then claims to be equipped to move into the subject itself: Jesus of Nazareth, the meaning of the Gospel and the problem of theological statements. His main intent is "clarification," a word that occurs as often in his book as does the word "encounter" (*Begegnung*) in Gollwitzer's. The "reconstruction of the kerygma and Christology" should be performed with the help of linguistic analysis; but van Buren has admitted in conversation that perhaps Kant, or any "writer of common sense," could have done the same service of clarifying. What is it then that is to be clarified? It is the "meaning of history,"[12] which does not lie in history itself but which arises out of reflection upon history. This clarification is utilized for the understanding of what is called "Easter," and is connected with the fact of Jesus' being "free." Van Buren maintains that the notion of freedom "does not lead us so easily onto the slippery ground of the nonempirical."[13] Having nothing against the "freedom of Jesus,"we should yet ask: Why is this notion more acceptable (to the secular man within me) than any other formulation provided by the New Testament texts? Van Buren avoids speaking of God because of the "metaphysical" character of such speech; but is the speech about the "freedom of Jesus" less metaphysical? If on Easter Jesus' freedom became "contagious,"[14] and if this means that here Jesus "had become the point from which they (the disciples) saw the world and lived in it," then this is truly, as van Buren calls it, a "historical perspective."[15] But this is what theology has commonly called "faith," and it is certainly of another quality than the empirical-pragmatical assertions which alone are, according to van Buren, understandable to modern man. Is it possible, even from a "merely" philosophical point of view, to make "empirical" observations, and consequently *statements*, which do *not* contain a "metaphysical" element of cognition? It would appear that the history of philosophy has shown with sufficient clarity that absolute empiricism is absurd. Van Buren's employment of linguistic

---

[12] *Ibid.*, p. 114.
[13] *Ibid.*, p. 123.
[14] *Ibid.*, p. 133.
[15] *Ibid.*

analysis is not convincing as a means of demonstrating that modern man (or any man) is now in the position to have access to the Easter event in a merely empirical-pragmatical way. Does van Buren really provide answers to the questions which he at first takes so seriously when discussing classical Christology? As does Gollwitzer, it would seem that van Buren too gives *assertions* where the reader rightly expects explications and verifications. For van Buren's final claim is that "The issue of faith can be at least made comprehensible by logical analysis."[16] If "logical analysis" means the contribution of the British linguistic analysts, van Buren has not shown their unique contribution to the problem; if it means "clear logical thinking," certainly nothing can be said against the attempt to employ it. If "comprehensible" means "expressed in consistent terms, understandable on the basis of its presupposition, Easter," one would certainly have to agree; if it means more than this—but van Buren does not say it does—we would have to judge that the Gospel is "descandalized." Van Buren calls his approach "tentative," and we will have to respect this reservation. Nonetheless, his position could have been considerably strengthened, even in its tentative form, if only instead of the "freedom of Jesus" he had said something like "submission in obedience to his mission as depicted in the Old Testament." This approach would have done more justice to the Biblical texts; and, dogmatically speaking, the "historical perspective" of which he speaks would have been preserved up to the point where it would again make sense to speak of the "Father" or of "God." We will not argue with van Buren that *today* in American theology *it may be necessary not to speak of God* but only of Jesus Christ in the light of Easter. But to conclude that *we cannot speak of God* is to make an assertion which does not follow from van Buren's own presuppositions and which denies the "multistoried" character of theology. This denial could well mean a return to the mentality of philosophically cemented theological "orthodoxy."

Gollwitzer's book faces the same questions. He too takes seriously the problem as to whether the recipient of the "revelation" in Jesus Christ must necessarily reach conclusions and make statements about the one whom Jesus reveals. But while van Buren faces a neglected *epistemological* question which causes him to rethink critically his own theological background (Karl Barth) and its dogmatical an-

16 *Ibid.*, p. 192.

swers, Gollwitzer takes up a neglected dogmatical question and confronts it with H. Braun's epistemological assertions and restrictions. Van Buren, therefore, is inclined to give philosophical answers to theological problems, whereas Gollwitzer does the opposite. Gollwitzer takes as his point of departure the problems of existentialist interpretation. His references to Kant are most helpful and his remarks about Ernst Bloch's atheistic interpretation of the biblical news are stimulating. But does he put anything concrete against or in the place of Bloch? His employment of the category of analogy is intended to provide the key to the problems of biblical anthropomorphisms. When it comes to the central question of "speaking of God," Gollwitzer extends a call for help to "personalism," with a good number of references to Martin Buber and Eugen Rosenstock-Huessy. The emphasis on "personal encounter" indicates that Gollwitzer stays in the same Augustinian tradition which is represented in an extreme form by Bultmann, whom he criticizes, however. Does not the reference to the "God who comes" or "who reveals himself" or "whom I encounter" give a dogmatical answer to an epistemological question? Gollwitzer puts a postulate, or a "creed" we might say, against Bloch,[17] and against Ebeling's "language-event" he argues: "But the neutral term *event* cannot possibly replace the notion of person, the confrontation of I and Thou."[18] Why not, we should ask? Is a notion identical with that to which it points? Can it really be Gollwitzer's opinion that the correct usage of terms saves one from error, and *vice versa*? His stress on the personal character of the encounter with God, expressed linguistically in the form of

---

[17] Gollwitzer, *op. cit.*, pp. 80 ff. (German text); pp. 97 ff. (English tr.). Bloch's three volumes *Das Prinzip Hoffnung* (1954–59) are not translated into English. They represent a most interesting combination of Marxist eschatology, Jewish religious tradition, and partly understood Christian elements. Bloch's concept of hope, it seems to me, is ultimately reducible to a network of *wishes*. This is also the fate of any Christian theology which operates on the basis of the analysis of the present without any reference to promises and fulfillments. A most competent analysis and careful evaluation of Bloch's philosophy of hope has recently been presented by Heinz Kimmerle, *Die Zukunftsbedeutung der Hoffnung, Auseinandersetzung mit dem Hauptwerk Ernst Blochs* (Bonn: H. Bouvier Co., 1966). The results of Kimmerle's investigation challenge, it seems to me, Moltmann's theological appropriation of Bloch's thought and also supersede Sauter's interpretation (*vide* above, Chap. 1, FN 67), Cf. also the little volume by Wolf-Dieter Marsch, *Hoffen worauf? Auseinandersetzung mit Ernst Bloch*, (Hamburg: Furche Verlag, 1963).

[18] *Ibid.*, p. 143 (my emphasis).

analogical speech, does not convincingly show a middle way between the two errors, an *analogia entis* on the one hand and a positivistic theology of the "benefits" which come from God through Christ on the other. Gollwitzer may be right in seeing that the cognitive questions concerning "speaking of God" cannot be answered at all, but he does not really say this. It would have greatly simplified the whole discussion had he admitted this to begin with. For his final conclusions are all of the quality of creeds or confessions: we cannot formulate any "is-sentence" about God,[19] but we depend utterly on himself, "receiving ourself from him as it-self comes to light in the encounter with him." And finally and most clearly: "To affirm God's existence means: to will that God is, and no other and nothing else."[20] Thus the restricted and qualified "theism" of which Gollwitzer speaks to the surprise of many seems to be the philosophical form of his theological assertion: that when speaking of Jesus as the revealer one will also have to speak of the one whom he reveals. One cannot speak of the arrow without speaking of the archer. Or, as Gollwitzer said, in the public debate with Braun, we not only know the "predicate," we also know the subject of the predicate.

What can we conclude from these two theological approaches? First, we should draw attention to the fact that both authors seem to have omitted the trinitarian approach to the problem.[21] Both concentrate on the christological approach. One will readily agree with Gollwitzer that mere "is-sentences" about God are useless because of the implied identity between the being of God and the being of the creation. God "is" not in the sense in which I am. But Gollwitzer's claim to be able nevertheless to speak of the existence of God is based upon the revelation in Jesus Christ in history, i.e. within the realm of being about which "is-sentences" *can* be made. Yet does not this information create the following impasses: God's being not only rests within God but is revealed in the man Jesus *within* creation and history; but does this not imply that God's *revealed being* no longer *is* but *was*? The awareness of this impasse could then vindicate van Buren. A second observation that parallels the first is that neither van Buren nor Gollwitzer speak of prayer, that is to say, of

[19] *Ibid.*, p. 165.
[20] *Ibid.*, p. 172; the emphasis on the "will" again resembles Augustine's thought.
[21] This is also E. Jüngel's judgment; cf. *Gottes Sein ist im Werden* (*vide* above, Chap. I, FN 78).

the *Christus praesens;* the creedal character of Gollwitzer's arguments against Braun seems to serve as a substitute for the *Christus praesens.* It is at this point that we must continue our theological reflection.

The question at issue is, "What sense does it make to speak of God?[22] But should we join in and make this question our own? Is it not a modified version of the medieval interest in the proofs for the existence of God? Should we not rather ask: To what extent is it necessary to speak *of* God after having accepted the fact that we speak *from* him and *to* him? In other words, the latter question asks why we ask the question at all. *The fact, received by tradition, that we do speak of him* invites the question not whether this is possible (because it *is* done) but to what extent this is necessary. What "degree of urgency"[23] is there to do so? We speak of God not because we have encountered him but because we remember him in ongoing expectation. God has no philosophical qualification which is "meaningful" or "meaningless," although he has unfortunately received such qualifications; but the "God of Abraham, Isaac and Jacob," the "God of the Fathers," the "God of the Exodus" is *remembered* in the tradition of Israel and of the Church. *The remembrance becomes expectation because of his presence in the congregation.*

This statement is to be expounded further. We have said earlier (in Chapter I, a) that the Church is the matrix within which the presence of Jesus Christ is recognized. The recognition of his presence is at the same time the acceptance of the importance of earlier witnesses of the presence of Christ in times past and also the anticipation of the future occurrences bearing witness to his presence. Or, in other words, the Church is the locus of the intentionality (an ancient scholastic term, utilized by the philosopher Brentano and passed on to his pupil Edmund Husserl) of the corporate personality of the believers of perceiving in the appropriate way the message of

---

[22] This is Bultmann's basic question; cf. his article with this title in *ThBl,* IV (1925), pp. 129–35 ff.; transl. "What Sense Is There to Speak of God?" in *The Christian Scholar,* Fall 1960, pp. 213 ff., and "The Idea of God and Modern Man," in *Translating Theology into the Modern Age* (No. 2 of *Journal for Theology and the Church;* New York: Harper & Row, 1965), pp. 83 ff. (trans. from *ZThK,* 60, 1963, pp. 335 ff.). For basic information, cf. David E. Jenkins, *Guide to the Debate about God* (Philadelphia: The Westminster Press, 1966).

[23] *Vide* above, Introduction, FN 6 and Chap. V, d.

the Bible and of later tradition. Tradition is the articulation of this intentionality, i.e. the fence, horizon and stimulus for interpreting the Old and New Testaments and later tradition in a manner corresponding to the subject matter of these earliest witnesses. We also have concluded that the Church's corporate consciousness is shaped by what she has perceived, and that ultimately (as a statement of confession of faith) this shaping is the work of the *Christus praesens*.

What do these observations mean in the context of our present discussion? First, they suggest that van Buren's and Gollwitzer's negations or assertions concerning the possibility of uttering "is-sentences" about God appear to be rather abstract and artificial. A married man is not to ask whether he can utter "is-sentences" about his marriage partner or the covenant in which he finds himself. Rather, he is asked whether he knows that he is married and whether he is aware of the necessities and limitations of speaking about this very fact whenever he himself fells compelled, or when others urge him, to give account of his situation. The Christian finds himself within the stream of tradition which asserts in terms which are appropriate and comprehensible, or only too often inappropriate and incomprehensible, that the election of Israel in times past *matters*, and, since most likely his ancestors are to be sought among the Gentiles and not the Jews, that he is now involved in the continuation of the same history of which Israel's history is the beginning. Now what sense does it make to speak of this?

Secondly, our initial observations suggest that the category of "encounter" as a means of solving the theological questions concerning the "knowledge of God" is of very limited value. Thinking simultaneously of various biblical accounts of what one may call "encounters," such as Jacob's wrestling with a demon or angel when crossing the Jabbok (Gen. 32), or Moses' experience of the burning bush (Ex. 3), or Samuel's hearing the voice of God at night (I Sam. 3), or the annunciation to Mary (Lk. 1), or the two disciples' confrontation with the risen Christ on the road to Emmaus (Lk. 24), or of Paul's experience on the road to Damascus (Acts 9)—we can safely formulate the following theses concerning "encounters" with God:

> 1) An encounter with God, i.e. the understanding (by the recipient and by later hearers of the account) of an "epiphany," presupposes a prior knowledge of God.

2) We are justified in substituting the term "expectation" for the term "knowledge of God." For an "encounter with God" presupposes an expectation of God in one form or another, which is not to deny that the *time* and *form* of the encounter, even the content of it, may well have been surprising to the recipient. But the *novum* which surprises him is only "new" as over against the "old" which he remembered.

3) Time, place and mode of the "encounter" can be recalled in the recipient's memory at any time; it can also be remembered by others through the medium of oral or written reports. But the *content* of it, i.e. God himself, who is said to have constituted in the encounter a partnership between himself and the initial recipient—this content can only be received, be understood, proclaimed or explained by those who not only remember the encounter itself (or the reports of it), but also the expectation which preceded it. This is to say that only those who trust in the preceding promises and who hope in future actions of God can make any sense out of reports of "encounters" with God which happened during the time between the promises and their hopes.

4) "Encounters," therefore, are not the primary mode of the cognition of God. They are no more than invitations to the believers to participate with others in the stream that goes from promise to fulfillment. They are "on-the-way" fulfillments of certain aspects of ancient promises, strengthening, though often irritating, the hearers' confidence in the credibility of the reports of God's promises of old.

5) "Visions" or direct encounters, or accounts of experienced "encounters," are in themselves obscure, although they are openly available to examination, recital and memorization. The obscurity of Jacob's crossing the river Jabbok and of his wrestling with somebody who blessed him and gave him a new name is in itself no greater than the obscurity of the crucifixion of Jesus or of his resurrection. All three were only understood "in retrospect," that is to say, after those who perceived these events or who

heard of them, connected these events with preceding
promises and with their own hopes toward further imple-
mentations of what the promises had said. This insight
into the ongoing work of Jahweh was the sole reason for
the transmission of tradition (for what other reason
should anyone be interested in Jacob's journeys?). And it
was only because of this insight that the men on their way
to Emmaus understood in retrospect what had happened
to them. "Did not our hearts burn within us while he
talked to us on the road, while he opened to us the Scriptures?" And likewise, the occurrence of the resurrection
"itself," the result of which allegedly was witnessed by
women visiting the tomb, caused horror and fear. It was
not until the appearance of the risen one himself that the
Easter horror was turned into joy, and immediately these
events were interpreted as events "in accordance with the
Scriptures" (I Cor. 15:3, 4), i.e. in accordance with the
memory of earlier expectations.

These textual and dogmatical observations are to be held in contrast to the abstract insistence on the importance of "encounters" as
the sole access to meaningful "speech about God," or to the denial of
it. This is not to say, however, that "encounters" have no place at all
in the discussion about Israel's and our "knowledge of God." But their
function is subordinate to the general scheme of promise and fulfillment. It could be argued, of course, that "the stream of tradition" of
promises and fulfillments by infinite regress is reducible to a "first
encounter." This is not so, however. If one wanted to speculate
about the origin of Israel's awareness of Jahweh, one would have to
say, exegetically, that the earliest records were written by those who
had already accepted a certain interpretation of the political event of
the Exodus, and, dogmatically, that a nexus of various interpretations of diverse political and social (and why not religious?) events
and occurrences crystallized into certain anticipations, the fulfillment
of which retroactively validated certain aspects of such interpretations. One does not, however, gain much insight from such analyses,
beyond the almost trivial statement that a minimum of *two* validating
fulfillments were, logically speaking, necessary to enable Israel to say
that there is indeed consistency and reliability in Jahweh's promises.
But the thought is at least valuable to the extent to which it shows

that anticipations connected with interpretations *precede* the understanding of "encounters" with, or epiphanies of, Jahweh. In expanded form, the observation about the minimum of two consistent occurrences is perhaps not as useless as may first appear: the first gives rise to an expectation and the second confirms the first. The second is understood on the basis of the first, but it is not only the first which interprets the second: the second also reinterprets the first. This is undoubtedly what happened textually regarding such occurrences as the burning bush and the plagues, the plagues and the Exodus, the Exodus and Sinai, and the Exodus and the coming of the Messiah. This logic is different from typology because it does not interpret texts, rather it interprets Jahweh's faithfulness on the basis of texts.

We stated that "encounters" function in a manner which is subordinate to the general scheme of promise and fulfillment. And we called the "encounters" "on-the-way" fulfillments of earlier promises. With this we mean to indicate that private visions or encounters belong to the realm of the exceptional, but that the account of them, as perceived and "celebrated" by others, is certainly not without significance. But if it is true—as we hope to show in Chapter VI— that the *Christus praesens* is shaping the Church's memory and hope, it follows that the awareness of the *Christus praesens* is the very liberation from the egotistical hope of receiving a private vision of or encounter with God. One must consider the implications of the exegetical observations that Jahweh was "present" in Israel primarily in the modes of memory and hope and secondarily in the modes of appearing in "encounters" as well as in the work of charismatic leaders. But these secondary modes of his presence were certainly embedded in the stream of recalling the ancient promises and of Israel's reaching out in hope toward the final implementation of what Jahweh had begun to do. There are no compelling reasons for saying that this mode of cognition has changed with the advent of Jesus and the records of this in the New Testament; on the contrary, it is the New Testament's main emphasis that that which was reported to have happened opens believers' eyes to the reception of Israel's election and turns their hearts in expectation to the advent of the Kingdom. Augustine's *visio* and *fruitio Dei* concept is really quite remote from the Bible's central thrust, and so are modern theology's concerns to affirm or deny the significance of encounters or epiphanies.

Braun's emphasis on the encounter "in my neighbor," and van Buren's thought that Jesus' freedom is "contagious," as well as Gollwitzer's stress on the "encounter," are as such not valueless categories. But none of them can serve as a basis upon which "speaking of God" really makes sense, theologically or philosophically. If the "presence of God" is prematurely translated into personal categories, statements about God will have to become descriptions of a personal experience which in all probability is meaningless to another person.

"Speaking of God" is a risk taken by those who receive the memory of the Church and who are led by this memory into expectation. What they say about "God as he is remembered" and "God as he is expected" is indeed historical, political, person-bound and in any case "earth-bound." But what they say about "God as he is now with us" is prayer or doxology. It is only at this point that the concrete decision becomes possible as to whether doxological speaking to God must necessitate theological speaking of God. This decision cannot be made abstractly. It is certainly possible that in certain places and at certain times such speech should not occur, for our initial question: What sense does it make to speak of God? is in itself and abstractly to be answered: It makes no sense to speak of God. The sense is the Christus praesens, who makes the Church participate in his priestly function for the world and on behalf of the world, opening the eyes of the believers to the past and to the future and inviting them to address God in doxological language.[24] But when doxological speech, which formally articulates what I would like to call a "synthetical judgment," is retranslated into historical speech, which formally consists of "analytical judgments," the result is indeed what Ebeling and others call "objectifying language," which means the separation of prayer and theology, piety and scholarship. Heinrich Ott observes astutely in his book on Heidegger: "Must not all theological speech in its cause and execution, if not externally and directly visibly yet internally and in truth be prayer?"[25]

---

[24] Van Buren's idea of "historical perspective," Braun's concept of the "event of listening" and Gollwitzer's insistence on the "subject" of the revelation of Jesus are not now as far removed from one another as it first appeared.

[25] Heinrich Ott, Denken und Sein, p. 192; vide above, Chap. II, FN 23, and our discussion on the "best part" of Greek patristic theology in Chap. II). Heinrich Ott reports that Buber, whom he visited shortly before his death, said: "A God about whom one can talk is not a God to whom one can pray."

b) The Controversy over Non-objectifying Language

Our statements about the memory and hope of the Church, the dimensions of the presence of Christ, demand some further qualification. Memory is transmitted and expressed in the form of language, and language is shared by many. The narratives of the Old and New Testaments in their transmission in the tradition not only *use* language but make and *create* language. Some contemporary authors have called this a "language gain," which occurs when the "revelation conquers language." It is at this point that E. Fuchs and K. Barth are close together, for both have stated in their own terms what the Reformers had already taught and what medieval theology was unable to deny: that language "as such" is incapable of "speaking of God" or of transmitting "revelation." Revelation conquers language. Interpretation, therefore, is the discovery of this conquest. But the memory of the Church is time and again reestablised by interpretation. The hope of the Church, on the other hand, is dependent upon the language of the past, for there is no other language than language of the past. It is in and because of language that man is a historical being, since it is by using language as well as by "being used by language," i.e. by listening, that man takes part in the past that lies behind him. His using language and his being used by language can again cause a "language gain," as everyone knows who retells a story. Proclamation, therefore, is (formally speaking) the risk of hoping that the transmitted language of tradition will experience a "language gain" between the proclaimer and the hearers. The mere repetition of ancient formulae is no proclamation; a "stolen" confession can be a denial of that which is being confessed.

If this is true, we cannot say with Thomas Aquinas that theology is a *scientia conclusionum*. If this were so, the hope of the Church would no longer be directed toward God in Christ himself, but rather toward the possibility of formulating once and for all what is "true" at all times. The danger could then not be avoided that "language conquers revelation," which formulation is perhaps the shortest and most concise definition of scholasticism. The language used for this purpose is "objectifying language." If Käsemann[26] and other adherents of existentialist interpretation have in mind *this* meaning of

---

[26] Ernst Käsemann, e.g. *Exegetische Versuche und Besinnungen*, Vol. I. (*Vide* chap. I, FN 9), pp. 224 ff. (German text); pp. 48 ff. (Engl. transl.).

the term "objectifying language," nothing at all should be said against it. But some of them go further than this. Their true opinions come to light when they speak positively of "non-objectifying language." The Cross of Christ then becomes a "speech event," i.e. my own being crucified, and the resurrection becomes my own reception of faith and consequently of a new self-understanding. It can be asked whether this fall-back into Augustinian-individualistic categories does not invite a new beginning of objectifying language. For this replacement of objectifying language with the language of existentialist categories is in fact a *subjectification of historical events*. It is for this reason that we have tried to stress the importance of the memory and hope of the *Church*, rather than of the individual. Language is used by many, and by using language (and by being used by language) the individual steps into a stream of tradition. Therefore the question: What sense does it make to speak of God? is too abstract a question. The Church before us has already spoken of him, and we are left with the question whether the "conquest of language by the revelation" demands still today that we speak of God. In other words: *The question of the necessity has priority over the question of the possibility*; and this statement is meaningful as an empirical-historical, not merely as an axiomatic-dogmatic assertion. It appears that existentialist interpretation advocates the opposite. But the opposite is the admission that man's speaking is prior to his forefathers' and to God's speaking, at least logically; and is this not a meaningless assertion? Is the central question of the Christian faith really this: What *can* I say? Is it not rather: What *must* we say as members of the Church which has spoken in the past and will speak in the future?

Moreover, is it not true that seemingly "non-objectifying" statements will through long use automatically become objectifying statements? Let the following statements serve as examples. It has become fashionable today to say "God *is* not, but he *happens*." And regarding justification it has become acceptable, as we have seen, to formulate: "I become free for my own future." There is little reason to say that these sentences are incorrect as such, leaving aside here the disadvantage of their narrowness. And it is also clear that they are intended to be "non-objectifying." They are expressions of the insistence that God cannot be captured as though his being and his doing were exhaustively describable in ways which are analogous to objective definitions of facts. Rather, these sentences are "dynamic," not "static." All this is understandable and praiseworthy. But what force prevents them from falling into a dogmaticism of "dynamics," i.e. into a new form of objectification? The longer they are used, the more they will tend toward a new objectification. Theologians who deny this either lack self-criticism or knowledge of the history of theology. When the Greek Fathers employed the Platonic and later the Aristotelian terms for the (approximate) description of that which in truth cannot be grasped in language, they knew of the limitation and incompleteness of their undertaking. But later centuries, as is well known, used the same terms within a cemented framework of scholasticism. The historical character of language makes it impossible to abstain totally from objectifications.[27] But the coercive attempt to avoid them at any price may easily lead into a new form of docetism, a denial of the Word having become flesh. The philosophical form of this approach is manifest today in the various attempts to "overcome the subject-object split." Is this aim really justified in the light of the tension between the present and the eschatological future? It appears that the desire to overcome this split is parallel to the Augustinian projection of eschatological fulfillment into the present. The subject-object split is a true description of world reality and history. And it is only in eschatological expectation that the meaning of history and the "overcoming" of the subject-object split can be anticipated.

These thoughts lead us back to the categories of memory and hope. The biblical "picture" (for the biblical writers are fond of anthropomorphisms) of the eternal God who is not timeless invites and necessitates the thought that God in Jesus Christ has a history himself and that the *Church is taken into his history.* The Church's language expresses this history in the modes of promise and fulfillment. The forms of reception of these modes of language are memory and hope. They do not exclude the importance of the present; on the contrary, they constitute the present as that which *was* expected and which *will be* remembered. This is visible in quite practical and concrete events. The Christian deals with others not "out of the

[27] Eduard Schweizer has remarked concerning this problem that "We should joyfully dare to make objective statements," *EvTh,* July 1964, p. 41 (*vide* above, Chap. I, FN 8). Cf. now his recent public address as rector of the University of Zurich, *Was heisst "Gott"?* (Zurich: Orell Füssli, A.G., 1965).

moment" and on the basis of an expected epiphany or momentary illumination but because he remembers the promise that his doings will not be in vain; and in his present occupation he lives from hope to hope. If he were to neglect the memory of the promises, he would deny forgiveness; if he did not live from hope to hope, he would deny the fulfillment of the eschatological promise. By pressing both into the "moment," i.e. by reenacting the past existentially to himself, and by projecting the fulfillment into the present, he would forfeit both and deny that God in Christ has a history. But his memory of the promises of the past, received and verbalized by others, invite him to *learn* God in Christ; and his hope in God's final fulfillment (the articulation of which is possible in only very *general* terms) pushes him to meet his situation with time-bound "little hopes" (the articulation of which is possible in quite concrete terms) in the light of the ultimate hope. His reliance on the ultimate hope enables him to have again such hopes. If it were not for the ultimate hope, the Christian could have only wishes, not hopes. For *wishes* grow out of the moment; but *hopes* are dependent on the hope for final fulfillment. *Wishes* are based on the analysis of the moment's incompleteness and lack; they absolutize the moment and its immediate history and project that which is lacking into the future. Once wishes are fulfilled, they cease to exist; and if they are disappointed, they must either be forgotten or repeated. But endless repetition of disappointed wishes is absurd and shows the imprisonment of wishes within the structure of the moment and its immediate history. Wishes grow out of the "now" and the "behind," but *hopes* come from the "ahead." With regard to a particular situation or person, particular hopes are concretizations of a larger network of hopes. Their fulfillment does not mean the end of their existence but the invitation to further hopes, both regarding the particular object and also regarding the next larger context or situation. And conversely, their disappointment does not mean that they are to be forgotten or meaninglessly repeated, rather that they be risked anew in relation to the next larger context. (This is, structurally speaking, the Christian's attitude toward the death of a particular person; the failure of a particular effort to reach reconciliation or peace; or the experience of "unanswered" prayers.) Whereas wishes are engulfed and imprisoned by history, the *ultimate hope*, which permits particular hopes on the levels of ever more limited application, is "history-embracing" (cf.

Chapter I, a and b). The content of the ultimate hope is not an-chored in the language of Israel's or the Christian's memory of ancient promises, but it transcends the possibilities of such language. The closer language moves to the content of the ultimate hope, the less concrete it becomes. But this is not justifying the statement that hope itself (either in its ultimate content or in its application on specific levels of human existence) is a "language event." Rather, the "lan-guage event" is prompted by the content of the ultimate hope. This prompting, it appears, is the truly eschatological nature of the struc-ture of the Christian faith. Thus *eschatology*, in this not too fashion-able understanding (when compared with its usage in much of con-temporary theology), *enables the Christian to have access to the present*. The stronger the hope, the more direct and passionate is his involvement in the present problems and tasks of the Church and the human situation in general.

So far we have only advance propositions, which in part will have to be examined more fully in the last chapter. At this point they are primarily relevant to the problem of language. We have seen that the memory as well as the hope of the Church can only be expressed in language forms of the past, for there are no other forms. This is especially interesting with regard to statements about hope. It is logically obvious that a "language of the future" does not exist. The-ology has always been tempted to circumvent this fact by trying to employ abstract-philosophical language for the description of the eschaton. But the biblical writers as a rule chose the opposite ex-treme: the eschatological and apocalyptic passages of the Old and New Testaments make deliberate use of "old," concrete and anthro-pomorphic language games. This demonstrates the insights (a) that a language of the future is dismissed as a speculative imagination which would destroy in advance the concreteness of that which is being hoped for, and (b) that the future is tied to the same God who is already known in the language of the past. The employment of artificially "modern" language is therefore not as necessary and helpful as may at first sight appear.

Anyone who enters into a discussion about the theological implica-tions of language and its use must face criticisms and challenges from three different quarters within contemporary theology. The advocates of a new form of proclamation, evangelization and mission insist that modern secular man no longer understands the traditional language of the Church. While this may very well be true, the mere employment of modern terms neither produces a new content, appropriate to the situation of our time, nor does it guarantee greater understandability. The second challenge, theologically far more interesting, comes from the originally Continental European theological trend which insists that "objectifying language" must at any price be avoided in theology. We have already discussed some merits and disadvantages of this. But one critical observation remains yet to be made: Is the distinction between "objectifying" and "non-objectifying" language really more than a programmatic *theological* statement? Is it a categorization which is tenable and meaningful when tested against the structure of language itself? There are good reasons for denying this. The simple distinction between these two types of language appears as rather naïve in the light of recent linguistic analysis and language philosophy in general. Existential theology on the Continent has displayed little, if any, familiarity with technical-philosophical linguistic analysis, although on the whole it has taken more seriously than English-speaking theology the directly theological implications of the quest for the nature and use of language. This is not to suggest that without familiarity in this discipline theological work could not be pursued, but it does mean that theologians must at least try to grasp the mapping of the landscape of the problems at stake when they enter into a quest which has been central to the inquiry of other scholars. Instead, most of the treatments of the problems of language by existentialist theologians are characterized by a certain vagueness, a poetic or even a "mystical" approach to the phenomenon of language. This observation is not to judge the theological intent or content of these authors, but it draws attention to the irony that much of their theological writing is lacking the very precision and lucidity which are at the heart of their theological program and their criticisms of traditional theology.

The third challenge comes from linguistic analysis as a philosophical discipline. It has become fashionable among some of the younger theologians to judge any theological utterance or publication by applying the "razor" of the analysts, often to the extreme of ridiculing the publications of those theologians who obviously have not *read* in the field of linguistic analysis. Not to have read in this field, i.e. not to be able to use the proper jargon, is of course no proof that a certain writer's utterances are "senseless." It is to be expected that this exaggerated criticism will, before long, diminish and will be recognized as having been typical of a period of transition in theology. Such shifts of emphasis have already occurred within linguistic analysis itself. Whereas Bertrand Russell attempted to anchor language in empirical cognition, an approach which was radicalized in logical positivism, centering on the "verification principle," more recent concepts of linguistic analysis have stressed the importance of the *use* of words in language.[28] The investigation of the use of language in different language games is considered superior to the abstract interest in (empirical) verification. It would be an exaggeration to say that modern linguistic analysis has shown full awareness of and sufficient interest in the historical character of language. But the tendency is in this direction.

The question is difficult to answer as to whether the employment of linguistic analysis in theology is really promising. So far no truly revolutionary contribution has been made on this basis, for van Buren's approach has not convincingly shown that the clarifying function of linguistic analysis could not be performed by another philosophical method. Nevertheless, the stress on the *use* of language, or words within language games, is sufficiently interesting and helpful to be brought into theological discussion. But it is not the purpose of our study to pursue this theme further. We raise only one dogmatical quesion: How can the dangers of classical nominalism be checked which would force theology to test all statements over against empirical cognition, or, in accordance with more recent trends, over against compatible statements? So long as this would be advocated merely for the purpose of clarification, one should not hesitate to agree. But as soon as it would imply that words are *the matter itself*, we would once more face the medieval problem of nominalism. The use of language would then destroy the "language gain," because language would "conquer revelation." Theological reflection would become "world-verification theology"[29] whose ke-

---

[28] Cf. the critical evaluation of the presuppositions of the steps of this development in J. O. Urmson, *op. cit.* (*vide* above, Introduction, FN 1), pp. 188 ff. Robert W. Funk's recent book, *Language, Heremeneutics and the Word of God* (cf. Chap. I, FN 70), is an attempt to pull together the Continental theological emphases on language and the British-American findings in linguistic analysis. To illustrate the above remarks about those theologians who are obsessed with linguistic analysis: just prior to the official publication date of Funk's book, I was told that the author "knows nothing about the analysts!"

[29] Cf. Chap. I, c.

rygma would be that minimum which appears as applicable in all times and situations. There would be "nothing new under the sun" and the language of prayer would be absurd, since it is not basically interested in verification, understandability and applicability.

c) *The Difference Between Doxology and Metaphysics*

We must briefly return to the question whether it is possible or necessary to abolish metaphysics within theology. We have mentioned that the Continental European trend of abolishing metaphysics goes back to Albrecht Ritschl's theological intentions, and we have drawn attention to Paul van Buren's new approach to this problem, which he examines on the basis of a deliberately Anglo-Saxon empirical philosophical method. These two theological intentions are by no means identical. It is even questionable whether it would in principle be possible to bring Continental and Anglo-Saxon theologians together in conversation on the question of metaphysics. The former have, consciously or unknowingly, gone through the school of Kant; the latter have not.

It is not impossible, however, to advance a definition of metaphysics which would be acceptable to both parties. Using Aristotle's basic distinction between matter and form, we can say that the Western mind has conceived of metaphysics as that *kind of consistent thinking which is concerned with the trans-empirical*. This broad definition can be split into two subdefinitions: metaphysics can either be *speculative*, i.e. interpret the whole of reality by starting with a highest general principle, or it can be *inductive*, i.e. strive toward a general world view by starting with a synoptic view of the interpretation of individual things or events. Which of these two types of metaphysics is helpful or destructive in theological use? It appears that the first type, although it has been utilized by theology for a long time, distorts theology and damages its integrity. A. Ritschl's criticism is chiefly concerned with this type. But the second type seems to be van Buren's target, presupposing that the first is meaningless anyway.[30]

---

[30] It goes without saying that the distinction between speculative and inductive does not do justice to the problem of metaphysics on the whole. How untrue this would be is shown by Stephen C. Pepper, *World Hypotheses, A Study in Evidence* (Berkeley: University of California Press, 4th ed., 1961; 1st ed., 1942).

The question now is not only whether van Buren is *philosophically* right in asserting that cognition is possible without metaphysics of the second type; but the question which concerns us more directly is whether the *categories of the reflection about this problem are relevant at all to theology*. Of course we cannot exempt theology from unavoidable philosophical problems. But neither can we say that the task of theology is sufficiently described by the problems of the mode of cognition. Man's possibilities of cognition do not determine the content of what theology talks about, nor do they *limit in advance* what can be talked about. For theology is concerned with the one who makes necessary and possible the recognition of himself. It is clear, however, that the language in which this recognition is verbalized is not derived from the trans-empirical; on the contrary, the Bible and the tradition of the Church affirm that no other than this-worldly language exists. And it is within this language and within history that the content of that (of Him) which embraces history and which causes a "language gain" is verbalized. The *recognition* of this content, or better, the *discernment* of *this* rather than another content, is confessed to be the very work of God. Many cities have been destroyed, but the destruction of Samaria was confessed to be a judgment; many peoples have been led into exile, but Israel's exile and subsequent liberation was confessed to be God's work; many men have been put to death on a cross, but Jesus' Cross is confessed to be God's judgment. Why is this so? The answer is *not* that any kind of interpretation of historical events necessarily implies a non-empirical factor which enables the interpreter to have a synoptic view of the past. Although this is true too, it would not take care of the uniqueness of the Church's speaking about events. The Church's *acceptance* of the biblical (and later, even contemporary) interpretations of events is an acceptance in *faith*, and that means an acceptance in the awareness of the *Christus praesens*. If the Church were not the Church *today* she could not understand and accept what the Church has said in the *past*, e.g. about Samaria, the exile and the crucifixion; nor could she say anythng about the Crusades, Auschwitz, Dresden, Hiroshima or, for that matter, a joyful event or the fate of an individual man. But this continuity between the Church in the past and the Church today does not necessitate that today's statements be identical with the statements of the past. Critical reception is necessary and possible, for the Church today is neither forced nor able to use the language and adopt the world view of the Church in centuries past. Her language form and her world view are not the factors which constitute the Church or which provide patterns for the interpretation of contemporary events. That which constitutes her ever anew is God's faithfulness, the manifestation of which is the *Christus praesens*. It is in the awareness of the *Christus praesens* that the memory of the Church becomes transparent to the one who is hoped for in the future. Or to put it differently: the shaping of the Church's awareness of God's ongoing faithfulness—that *is* the *Christus praesens*.

How does the Church receive and express her awareness of the *Christus praesens*, or, more precisely, her awareness that the *Christus praesens* shapes, and ultimately *is*, her awareness of God's faithfulness? Is this a "metaphysical" speculation? Is it necessary or even helpful if the Christian asserts "the existence of an invisible world" or the like? No, God's will and work with the world cannot be had *without or outside the world*. God's having come into history in Jesus, God's having used the only language that exists, human language, cannot be spoken of in terms of trans-historical history or unworldly language.[31] But the difference between the Church's speaking of "something" or "somebody" in the past and future, and her speaking of *God* in the past and future (as he has come and will come in Jesus Christ) *lies in her speaking to him in the present*. Any great historical figure or historical force can be spoken *of* in terms that express their importance or goodness or evil or lasting influence; but God in Christ is also spoken *to*, he is addressed. Although the Church speaks of God's doings in the past in the *same* language in which one speaks of Napoleon, Lincoln, Gandhi, Hitler or Stalin, neither the Church nor any man would seriously advocate that we can *speak* to these "history-causing" men. The category of *doxology* is unparalleled and in every way unique. Doxological speaking is not merely based on what the believers consider *possible*, but it is initiated, invited and necessitated by the one to whom this kind of speaking is addressed. Doxological speaking is in strange reciprocity with theological speaking. While the repeated experience and discipline of prayer allows, stimulates and enriches theological speech, it

---

[31] I have attempted to explain this point more fully in the chapter "The Worldliness of the Word" in *A Theology of Proclamation* (Richmond: John Knox Press, 1960 and 1963), pp. 47 ff.

is nevertheless true that the relation between these two kinds of speech is irreversible. Doxological speech must not be made the *beginning* of theological analyses; the language of prayer is of a different category from that of a narrative which demands analysis and interpretation. Prayers must not be analyzed; they must be prayed. They are directed not toward man but toward God.

These statements must be expanded further. We will first reflect upon the formal criteria which permit or necessitate the distinction between narrative and doxological language, and we will conclude with a discussion of the relation between metaphorical and doxological language.

By "doxological language" we mean the whole complex of utterances (in the Bible and later Church tradition) which are *directly* prayer, i.e. petitions, thanksgivings, praises, etc., or *indirectly* related to prayer, such as liturgies, including narrative parts, and names, titles, ascriptions, designations, attributes and even "definitions" used with regard to Yahweh or Jesus, but not necessarily addressed to God. The indirect relation to prayer may be vague and obscure, even based upon a misunderstanding of earlier utterances or texts (as textual and historical criticism may demonstrate). This broad definition of doxological language is assigning an important place and function to *prayer* within the whole structure of theology. And to say this is indeed our intent. We have concluded earlier that theology does justice to its subject matter by taking seriously the fact that he who thinks theologically finds himself in the "stream of tradition" which leads from promise to fulfillment. Theology's point of beginning is not man's existential need, predicament or doubt, but his present involvement in the "stream of language," we might say, which causes his thoughts, doubts or agreements. With regard to doxological language, we can say that prayer is the *prayer of those before us.* It is not the invention of something new, but a new concretization of old language, not unlike the address language which little children learn from older ones to address their parents, or the language which young lovers "borrow" from others to express themselves. This mode of language is not necessarily less direct or concrete than reporting language, even if the latter appears in the dress of scientific reports. With respect to the Old Testament, we have little reason to deny that both doxological and narrative language occurred side by side and that neither of the two is preferred

at the expense of the other. Our modern inclination to prefer in
theology historically verifiable sentences to those of doxological
character—and in general our Western separation between scholarship and prayer—has only occurred on account of the supposition
that reporting language is of a higher "density" or concreteness than
is address language. Prayer is suspect of being "metaphysical" in the
speculative sense. For the following reflection on the formal differences between narrative and doxological language we omit references to the many historical reasons which have prompted the suspicion of prayer's being necessarily a speculative-metaphysical
matter.

   Exegetical as well as theological reasons invite the statement that
a speculative-metaphysical categorization of prayer is detrimental to
the genuineness of prayer. The Church prays "out of the depths" as
Psalm 130:1 says, not "out of the heights" of trans-empirical
knowledge and wisdom. Prayer is carried by the power of the
Church's memory and risked in the hope of its fulfillment. It is
permitted and possible only because of the presence of God in
Christ, or in biblical terms: "in the Holy Spirit." Formally speaking, the difference between doxological speaking and explanatory
theological speaking is the following. It is proper to distinguish with
Kant between analytical and synthetical judgments. "Analytical" is
a judgment whose subject contains a predicate: e.g. "All bodies are
extended." "Synthetical," however, is a judgment whose predicate is
not contained in the subject, e.g. "All bodies are heavy." Moreover,
if a synthetical judgment is based upon or related to experience (or
historical recognition), it is a judgment *a posteriori*. If, however, it
grows out of reason, it is a judgment *a priori*.

   What is the use of these distinctions for our theological reflection?
"Merely" historical assertions operate on the basis of transmitted
historical evidence in the form of reliable information. The sentence
"Samaria was destroyed" does not contain "God" as its subject or
as its predicate. It is as such not a unique statement and it can of
course be made by any historian. Because of our interest in understanding the Church's unique statement that some sentences of this
type should be understood as having "God" as their subject or predicate, we utilize in modified form Kant's distinction between analytical and synthetical judgments. We call the understanding of the
reception of historical information "analytical," but we use the term

"synthetical" to designate the type of statement which calls God the subject or predicate of the analytically received and understood historical information,[32] e.g. "The destruction of Samaria was the judgment of God." This synthetical judgment about Samaria's destruction, is therefore a "synthetical judgment *a posteriori*." Judgments *a priori* would lead to a theology which is structurally identical with "speculative metaphysics," as we have called it. But the statement that such synthetical judgments (*a posteriori*) are "based upon" and "inseparable from" analytical judgments does not mean that the former are *caused* by the latter. This would equal the assertion that theology is caused by history, or, more precisely, by historiography. This, in turn, would mean that any responsible historian who is cognizant of such information as "Samaria was destroyed" or "Israel was delivered out of Egypt" would *ipso facto* become a believer. Rather, the *cause* for making the "synthetical judgment" that it was *God* whose judgment caused the destruction of Samaria or the deliverance from Egypt lies in *addressing* God in prayer *as the one to whom* this statement is made. The *basic* form of this synthetical judgment is the prayer or doxology: "You are the one who destroyed" or "who delivered." It is for this reason that God in the Bible is spoken of in historical terms which become his "names," e.g. "the God of Abraham, Isaac and Jacob," or "God who delivered us from Egypt." It is in prayer that the interpretation of history becomes most concrete, and it is because of the prayer of the Church in the past and in the present that the Church today has an *interest* in the knowledge of the destruction of Samaria, in the deliverance from Egypt, in Abraham and Isaac, in short, in the Bible and in later tradition. If it were not for this, the interest in such information could easily be exchanged for an interest in other texts which provide historical information.

Admittedly, this formalistic categorization of analytical and synthetical judgments is only of limited use. The point is merely this: Synthetical judgments (e.g. "Samaria's destruction was God's judgment") do not *result* from analytical exploration of historical facts, nor would the Church have any particular interest in these facts if it were not for the believers' forefathers' synthetical judgments and for

---

[32] This is not to disregard the fact that, in the process of the historian's work, the information, of which we say it is "analytically received," was elucidated on the basis of "synthetical judgments."

their present involvement in addressing God as the one who bears these "historical names." But neither would the Church be able to make these synthetical judgments if it were not recorded that certain events took place which are open to analysis but which time and again were interpreted "synthetically" as being related to God, in whose awareness these synthetical statements were made. It is important to note, however, that synthetical judgments ("You are the one who delivered"), which are necessarily connected with analytical judgments, must not be taken as material for new analytical judgments. The decision to do this is the beginning of scholasticism. In theological terms: The relation between prayer and theology is not that the content of prayer is to be considered material for theological interpretation. Interpretation deals with *history*, and the reason or stimulation or encouragement *to perform this interpretation lies in prayer*. Thus we have again reached our thesis that only the living Church can understand the witness of the Church in times past. For the Church is not only "living" because she remembers, but more basically, she remembers because she is living. Her memory would be merely *fides historica*, faithful acceptance of historical facts, if she were not kept alive by the same Lord whose actions of the past she remembers and interprets. John's Gospel expresses this in various forms by saying that not only the Son reveals the Father but the Father reveals the Son. The recognition of this doubleness presents to the Church the constant task of doing both: thinking and praying, theological speech and doxological speech, historical interpretation and offering sacrifices of praise, thanksgiving and adoration. The confusion of these two activities would mean the end of one of them, either of thinking when mysticism succeeds or of prayer when historicism succeeds. And the confusion or false relation between doxology and metaphysics would invite the idea that doxological speech is made possible or even necessary by omitting and denying empirical reality. But God's actions in Christ can neither be interpreted in history nor can God in Christ be addressed doxologically when the Church desires to leave behind world reality and history. There is no other realm than this one for the understanding *and* adoration of what God is confessed to have done in the past and expected to do in the future.

In conclusion we must discuss briefly some theological aspects of the relation between doxological and metaphorical language. The problem of the logic of metaphors[33] is very complex and we touch upon it merely in the interest of further clarification of doxological speech. We must omit a discussion on the problem of analogy in its various forms. It suffices to mention that certain aspects of each, doxological, metaphorical and analogical language, may be characteristic of any of these three forms. But an identification of all three for the use of theology is more than confusing. It is surprising that Gollwitzer unhesitatingly speaks of analogical language when he means metaphorical address language, and that he speaks of metaphors when in fact he sets out to analyze doxologies, which may or may not contain metaphorical elements. If a relation between metaphors and forms of analogy is sought (despite the different realms of problems to which these terms refer), one could perhaps see a connection between metaphors and the form of analogy which the old logicians called analogy of proportion (each analogate contains something in which it is similar to the other). Metaphors such as "movie star," or "breathtaking view" are structurally related to analogies, but they are not uttered with the intention to be such. Likewise, such statements as "the hand of the Lord God fell there upon me" (Ez. 8:1) or "The Lord roars from Zion" (Amos 1:2) or statements that Yahweh "does not like to smell," that he "walks in the garden," is "jealous," etc., are of course not meant to be analogies.

With regard to Biblical texts and also Church tradition, one can say that metaphors are statements about God or his doings which are chosen by the writer because he considered them to be preferable to non-metaphorical, direct expressions. There may be two reasons for this preference. A metaphor lends itself in a pointed way to reminding the hearers of something they already know, but now hear in a new context and in a new application (e.g. "Yet it was I who taught Ephraim to walk, I took them up in my arms, but they did not know that I healed them." [Hos. 11:3]). In this case a metaphor is the best and briefest way of expressing a state of affairs,

---

[33] Cf. the suggestive, though not ultimately satisfying examination of metaphors and models in the sciences and in theology by Ian T. Ramsay, *Models and Mystery* (London: Oxford University Press, 1964). I am also indebted to a mimeographed article by E. W. Van Steenburgh of the University of Michigan, "Perspective, Root and Prescinding Metaphors." Cf. also Max Black, *Models and Metaphors: Studies in Language and Philosophy* (Ithaca, N.Y.: Cornell University Press, 1962), esp. pp. 25 ff.

given the limited time the speaker has the attention of the hearers, and presupposing prior knowledge on their part. Another reason for the employment of a metaphor is to express that which is ineffable, but of which the hearers may think that it *can* be expressed in descriptive language. Thus Yahweh's direct contact with man is expressed "And they heard the sound of the Lord God walking in the garden in the cool of the day" (Gen. 3:8), or the eschaton is depicted as a geological transformation (Is. 40), as peace between wild beasts and sheep, or as the coming "down" of the new Jerusalem (Apoc. 21), etc. All of these metaphors have in common that they are theoretically capable of *reinterpretation.* The narratives and the memories of the fathers' doxological affirmations that these promises are really trustworthy—these are *open* to reinterpretation by the hearers. In other words: the narrative which stands behind the metaphorical acclamations of Yahweh as the rescuer are known to the hearers, and the person who uses these metaphors knows it. This is also the case with the metaphors used for the second reason: Israel is supposed to know that the eschaton *cannot* be defined in descriptive language, that Yahweh's face, dwelling place, voice, etc., *cannot* be likened to empirical reality, and the metaphor serves to remind the believers of these barriers.

If a metaphor is used without the hearers' assumed knowledge of the content of the "story behind it," or even without the speaker's knowledge of this, then it is an open invitation to believe the absurd. There is no doubt that, because of Israel's and the Church's being bound to tradition, legitimate metaphors have time and again been used in this irresponsible way. Metaphors have then ceased to be the "shorthand" for longer sermons or explanations, and instead they have been abused and turned into "objects of faith."

Doxological language shares with biblical metaphors the following elements: (a) it is based upon narratives about events, or upon the memory of earlier doxological affirmations (e.g. Jacob's prayer prior to his crossing the Jabbok: "O Lord who didst say to me, 'Return to your country and to your kindred, and I will do you good' . . . Deliver me, I pray thee, from the hand of my brother . . . for I fear him . . . But thou didst say, 'I will do you good, and make your descendants as the sand of the sea . . ." Gen. 32:9–12); (b) it is a condensed form, a "shorthand," of longer statements known to the speaker and his hearers; (c) it is used for the same two reasons metaphors are used, *viz.* to express in a short form better what can be expressed in detail in the form of less pointed speech, and to prevent blasphemous descriptions of that which cannot be described; (d) it, too, is vulnerable to the same abuse, i.e. its original meaning can freeze into a misunderstood formula.

Doxological speech, of course, is not necessarily metaphorical. Any "language game" is capable of becoming part of doxological speech. The distinctive mark of doxological speech is its original rootage in prayer, and, in a derived manner, its proximity to creeds, confessions and creedal affirmations. *All* forms of doxological speech have in common that their content is synthetically *derived* from narratives, interpretations and—although this is a source of errors and distortions—from other doxological speech as it is transmitted by tradition. It is originally, but not necessarily, address language, and its transposition into propositional form is highly problematical because the hearers of propositional statements may not know of the original rootage. They may perceive a doxological statement as an invitation to form further judgments about the subject matter of the statement, judgments which are not contained in the statement. For example: Israel experienced the Exodus and praised Yahweh as the one who had elected Israel to be his people (original doxological speech); later, for the purpose of teaching later generations, Israel defined Yahweh as the one who had elected her (derived doxological speech). This development is understandable and legitimate. But when it was applied to the doctrine of predestination, as in Calvin for instance, the derived doxological statement that "God elects" only too easily slipped into the form of propositional statements from which further deductions were made. Statements related to such notions as "predestination," "election," "providence," "creation out of nothing," etc., are, however, *as doxological* in nature as is the statement "The risen Christ is present in a worship service," or "present in the world," or the like. All of them are open-ended thoughts, originally rooted in address language, even if after long use and much deliberation some of them now appear to be less doxological, i.e., more "descriptive," than the others.

We conclude, then, that doxological statements are a peculiar part of the language of the Church, though not without parallels in ordinary address language, and that they are necessarily related to what we have called "analytical judgments" concerning historical events and their interpretations. They may appear in the form of metaphors, but not necessarily so. They are open-ended, ever risked anew in faith. Although they seem to lend themselves to conversion into propositional statements, their very origin forbids it, because they are not descriptions of speculative-metaphysical realities.

All this is not to deny the validity of the philosophical problem of metaphysics, especially of the metaphysical elements within so-called empirical cognition; but our deliberations were intended to show that this philosophical problem is not directly relevant to theology,[34] contrary to the many assertions by contemporary theologians, especially in America, where a new obsession with philosophy, especially with epistemology, seems, after long neglect, to be considered the mark of a true theologian.

d) *The Historical Jesus and the Scandal of Confessing God*

Ernst Käsemann has said on several occasions that "faith cannot have the historical Jesus as its basis."[35] This is almost a commonplace which confirms once more the result of Albert Schweitzer's "life of Jesus" research. But why then are the exegetes who are close to Käsemann now advocating a "new quest" for the historical Jesus? They do this apparently for the same reasons for which Mark was written, to counteract a speculative tendency in the Church. The present advocates of the "new quest" are all members of a group which we have labeled "Augustinian" so far as their questions and thought forms are concerned. Their "new quest" could well be a corrective to their individualistic-kerygmatic approach, and as such it should be appreciated and not criticized too quickly. Nevertheless, we must ask whether their labors have shown results which go

[34] I am leaving aside W. Pannenberg's suggestion that historical research and cognition *do* lead to the understanding and acceptance of the kerygma. This idea presupposes a concept of history and of reason which truly brings in metaphysics, although in a qualified manner. Cf. H. G. Geyer, "Geschichte als theologisches Problem," in *EvTh*, 1962, pp. 92 ff. Cf. also the helpful exposition of the concept of the Holy Spirit's function as Advocate in Hendrik van Oyen, *Theologische Erkenntnislehre* (Zurich: Zwingli-Verlag, 1955), esp. pp. 210 ff.

[35] Ernst Käsemann, *Exegetische Versuche und Besinnungen*, (*vide* above, Chap. I, FN 9), Vol. I. pp. 187 ff. *passim*, (German text); pp. 15 ff. (Engl. tr.); Vol. II, pp. 31 ff. (German text only).

beyond what Reformation theology already knew. It is possible that the emphasis on the true manhood of Jesus is one of these results. Apart from this, not much else can be detected as yet. Heinrich Ott's revision of Bultmann's concept of *Bedeutsamkeit*, "meaning-fulness," does open up some possibilities, but it does not convincingly show what it basically intends to say, *viz.* that the acceptance of the historical Jesus is of another quality than the reenactment of a historical event for use in the present.[36] Faith, according to the New Testament, is neither an act of man nor a mode of cognition but is, as Eberhard Jüngel says,[37] something which "comes to man"—it is something that "happens with man," it "takes man into a new history." This sounds abstract, but it is the abstract expression of the concreteness of the presence of Christ in the congregation, through which presence the memory of the past becomes transparent to God in Christ who not only *was* but now *is* present.

Why should theology in its concentration and dependence on Jesus Christ be "atheistic"? Of course this term has generally been avoided (with the exception of journalistically minded theologians), but there is no denying that the tendency is in this direction. Braun and van Buren are the exponents of a movement the strength of which should not be underestimated.[38] The renunciation of confessing and *thinking* God can in fact only take the form of a renunciation of *speaking* of him. Moreover, the decision to forgo speaking of him can only be a decision *ad hoc*. If it were a decision *in*

[36] Heinrich Ott, *Die Frage nach dem historischen Jesus und die Ontologie der Geschichte* (*vide* above, Chap. I, FN 29).

[37] Eberhard Jüngel, *"Theologische Wissenschaft und Glaube,"* in *EvTh* (July 1964), pp. 419 ff., esp. p. 430. To be precise, however, we should say that, at least according to the Pauline writings, *pistis* has a threefold meaning: God's faithfulness to Israel and the Church, Jesus Christ's trust and obedience, and the believers' faithfulness which corresponds to God's faithfulness. This third meaning of *pistis* has, of course, cognitive dimensions, but they are subordinate to the first and second meanings and do not cause their recognition.

[38] The movement is strong amoung younger theologians on the American scene. Bishop Robinson, however, has disqualified himself as a member of this group because of his highly religious and metaphysical statements toward the end of his book *Honest to God*; cf. the passages on prayer, which Rudolf Otto could have written.

Cf. also the interesting collection of essays by Catholic and Protestant authors in *Is God Dead?* (*Concilium*, Vol. 16, ed. Johannes Metz; New York: Paulist Press, 1966), and H. Gollwitzer's forthcoming book *Von der Stellvertretung Gottes* (against Dorothee Sölle's *Theologie nach dem Tode Gottes*), which I have been privileged to read in proof.

principle it would imply that we "lose" Jesus Christ too. For the awareness of the *Christus praesens is identical with the awareness of God,* of God as he qualified himself in Jesus Christ. And without the *Christus praesens* we lose the historical Jesus. Only a separation between the "doctrine of God" and Christology, as Augustine tolerated it, could permit speaking of God without Christ as well as speaking of Christ without God.

The *"ad hoc* decision" not to speak of God for the time being, however, may have its merits. If this is what van Buren means, we can benefit from his suggestions; and it is possible that this is his opinion because of the "tentative" character of his theological reflection. But in the case of Herbert Braun it seems obvious that his "atheism" is of a more dogmatical and lasting kind. If the decision to be *silent* in the matter of possible speech about God is made for *ethical* reasons, it may be another form of adoration; if it is *dogmatical,* it leads the speech of Christ into absurdity. By this we mean to say: We Christians have not only spoken too much and done too little in centuries past, we have in particular *spoken too much about God,* as though we and everybody else knew him. Thus God has become a "supreme being" in legislative debates in America and a target of anti-religious propaganda in the Marxist world, as well as a symbol of colonialism in the memory of the younger nations. The result was, as H. Richard Niebuhr puts it,[39] with reference to a period of the past, that "a God without wrath brought men without sin into a kingdom without judgment through the ministrations of a Christ without a Cross." If we mean to be silent about God because we feel ashamed of the distortion of our speaking in generations past, we act responsibly. The decision to speak or not to speak of God is thereby an ethical decision. But while we have certainly spoken too much "to the world," i.e. to the non-Christians, we have not yet spoken enough to each other. Only the false idea that the members of the Church are to be addressed as if yesterday they were still non-Christians can suggest the thought that in the Church too we must be silent about God. Insofar, however, as the Church shares the world's distorted views of God, we may even be silent about God in the Church too, but only in preaching and teaching, not in doxology. A Church that feels ashamed of its ir-

---

[39] H. Richard Niebuhr, *The Kingdom of God in America* (New York: Harper & Bros., a Harper Torchbook, 1959), p. 193.

responsible speaking of God in the past to the extent that it gives up prayer ceases to be the Church. For the Church is different from other sociological groupings in her ability to see and accept her sins of the past and nevertheless to risk a new confession despite the burden of the past.

It must be repeated: God *is* not in the same sense in which I *am* or in which I can say a certain object *is*. A God *about* whom "one can speak" is not worth being prayed to. The confession of God's "is-ness" in this sense would be "metaphysics." But doxology, i.e. the verbalization of praise and thankgiving, offered in worldly language and anchored in the memory as well as directed toward the expecta-tion of the Church, is liberated from the necessity of asserting an "invisible world" in which things or persons *are*.

We are left now with the basically trinitarian question concerning the relation between "God," the *Christus praesens* and the Holy Spirit. By way of concluding this chapter we merely mention some thoughts which intend to point the way toward an alternative to the Augustinian categories that still dominate the contemporary discus-sion about "speaking of God." It appears, we would suggest, that the ancient concept of "economic trinity" or "historic trinity" is not as bad as some of the Fathers had thought. The *mode* of God's approach to man is determined by God and not by the cognitive possibilities of man. The word "God" is indeed to be considered an abstraction or "summary statement." It had a history before it was adopted by Israel and by the Church. But Israel and the Church have filled the abstract term with *that* content which Yahweh has made known to them. The fine old doxology *"Te Deum laudamus"* should therefore not be translated "We praise thee, O God," but rather "It is thee whom we praise as God." We will discuss the relation between Yahweh and Jesus in the last chapter, but at this point it suffices to suggest that the distinction between the Holy Spirit and the *Christus praesens* is meaningful only for "pedagogi-cal" and (historically) explanatory reasons. The presence of the Spirit is none other than the *Christus praesens,* but we call him *Christus* because we *remember* him as Jesus Christ in whom Yah-weh was present and we *expect* him at the end of time not as an *unknown* but as a *known* name of "God." Confessing and praising the *Christus praesens* is an expression of the awareness that "God" has a history which runs from promise to fulfillment. Metaphorically speaking, we could say that the *Christus praesens* is "the heart of God," or the "guts of God," he is "that" in the God of Israel, in Yahweh, which "reminds" Yahweh of his faithfulness to man and which "reminds" man of his memory and hope and invites him to doxological speech. Thus it is because of this *name* that "speaking of God" is not *based* on the trans-empirical and trans-historical. But for the same reason it is *dogmatically* senseless to confess "Christ" but not "God," although it may be necessary for *ethical* reasons to be silent about God. The decision on this matter is a question of the "degree of urgency." What is ethically urgent is not identical with what is dogmatically necessary and possible.

V

"New Morality" and
"Anonymous Christianity"?

OUR PREPARATION FOR the theses of the final chapter requires a brief discussion of the ethical problems which parallel the dogmatical ones of the previous chapter. The great carefulness with which theology today most frequently approaches the problem of "speaking of God" is strangely related to an openly confessed interest and optimistic confidence in the facility of "speaking of man." Since "God" and "man" are the traditional categories of the exposition of Christology, we will now focus our attention on the problem of "speaking of man." We will detect in this matter the same Augustinian influence which has determined many dogmatical questions and categories. Of course we can give only a brief outline of the problems at issue without claiming in any way to do justice to the complexity of the ethical questions which are being dealt with in contemporary theology.

a) Unworldly Thinking About "the World"

Ever since Tertullian and Augustine, the world has not been seen as God's good creation. Theologians who did point to the goodness of the creation were generally considered to be at variance with the

Catholic tradition and were suspected of Pelagianism. The main barrier between the Church and "the world" was created and defended by the Church herself. This remained true even and especially during the period of deliberate world domination by the Church. Leaving aside the influence of the Renaissance, an influence of a special character, it was at the time of the Enlightenment that the Church began to discover "the world." In recent times it has become fashionable—partly with the help of Bonhoeffer's thoughts, which are yet often misrepresented—to speak of "the Church" and "the world" in such terms that "the world" is valued most highly, the Church, however, often very negatively. The negative statements about the Church are understandable and in many ways justifiable if they are taken as an expression of the Church's insight into her own guilt. But the Church's praise of the world is often no more than the opposite and contrary of this admission of the Christians' own guilt. But if this is the motive, it hardly deserves to be taken as seriously as the insight into the goodness of God's creation. Moreover, it is often overlooked that the world does not need the Church's positive and pseudo-apologetic evaluation of herself. The world has never thought of the Church as anything other than a strange "part of the world," and therefore her praise of the world does not overly impress the world. Christians and hierarchs of the Church who think otherwise merely betray the fact that they secretly still adhere to the Constantinian ideal of the Church as the schoolmaster and moral superintendent of the world. It is questionable whether such churchmen really envision the *real world* today as it really is. Much of the Church's contemporary speaking of "the world" has an unworldly flavor. Sentences such as "the Church must open herself up to the world" (which is the tenor of *De ecclesia*,[1] the Constitution of the Church, Second Vatican Council, 1964) or "The Church must go out into the world" (the tenor of World Council of Churches publications) are certainly praiseworthy when compared with ecclesiastical pronouncements of the past. But do they not betray a hidden Constantinianism by silently denying that Christians are *ipso facto* human beings and therefore part of the world? If I already *am* somewhere, why then should I decide to *go* there?

---

[1] *De ecclesia*, Constitution on the Church, Second Vatican Council, Nov. 21, 1964; Engl. ed. prepared by George H. Tavard, National Catholic Welfare Conference, Washington, D.C.

A more complicated thought structure lies behind these problems. There is no agreement that "Christians" are "the Church" and that "human beings" are the world. At least the Catholic pronouncements have made it clear that the Church is considered to be "more" than the mere assembly of Christians. Thus Catholic and Eastern Orthodox theologians will readily speak of the sin of Christians but never of the *sin of the Church*. While Protestant theology as a rule does not elaborate this distinction, it does make a distinction between *men* and "the world." The recent expression of this distinction is reflected in the thoughts of Bultmann, Gogarten and Ebeling. We have already mentioned that Ebeling no longer considers (God's) *law* as the agency of accusation, tribulation and *"Anfechtung,"* but that the *world* has now taken over this function. Ebeling is in agreement with Gogarten that *today* the law is no longer "dangerous," but that *world reality* presents to the believer the troubled conscience and the difficulties of living his faith. Exaggerating the point, we could say that the demythologization of the Gospel has caused a remythologization of the world.

Admittedly "the world" is not simply identical with the sum of the people who live in it. We cannot enter here into the discussion about "principalities and powers" which has resulted in such differing theological positions as are represented by, e.g. Bo Reicke and Clinton D. Morrison. But without sacrificing the awareness that Christians are human beings to no greater or lesser degree than other people, we can safely say that the following three positions are incompatible with the priestly task of the Church: (a) the (Alexandrian) deification of the world, (b) the (Antiochian) separation between Church and world and (c) the idea that it is the task of the Church to transform the world so that it becomes the Church. In other words, the Church is neither identical with the world, nor is she separated from the world, nor is it her task to make the world the Church. The first and second opinions reflect a static, i.e., non-historical, way of thinking and the third relies on an invented promise that does not exist: there is no Biblical promise to the effect that the whole of America, Europe, the Soviet Union, etc., will ever "become the Church." The true solidarity of the Church with the world is destroyed both by the idea that the two are identical and by the idea that they are separated into two kinds of mankind. And the third notion, that of the conversion of the whole world, is a hidden form of Christian imperialism which does not trust God in Christ to deal with those who are not part of the Church. But it is this trust which enables the Church to live and work vicariously for those who are not the Church. This point will have to be discussed in the last chapter. We only note at this point that the solidarity between the Church and the so-called "world" is not established by the *sin* of mankind. Human beings are not linked together by the negative qualities of sin and guilt, as Augustine and also Kierkegaard taught, but rather by their being addressed as *men* in the man Jesus Christ. The Church knows that her members can freely enter into solidarity with non-Christians because as Christians they know of both forgiveness and their priestly task. They also know that their own lives may be more complicated and more burdened than the lives of non-Christians, for the vicarious work of Christians for others involves them in greater dangers and guilt than does the daily work of non-Christians.[2] "Everyone to whom much is given, of him will much be required" (Luke 12:48).

The present trend of assigning to the world the function of the *lex accusans*, the accusing law, is therefore in strange contrast to the fashionable slogans about "the Church and the world," or "the Church in the world." The latter are often no more than the expression of the guilty conscience of the Church regarding her past relations with non-Christians. But this expression should not invite one to think of an autonomous world which has its goodness or badness

---

[2] Discussing with Rolf Hochhuth, the author of *The Deputy*, the ethical implications of his forthcoming play on the British bombings of German cities, I tried to make the point that the British Christian who was *not* a pilot taking part in the operations was not "freer of guilt" than the pilots themselves. The following illustration served as an example: One of my former students told us in a class on ethics of his problem in the Korean War. From an aircraft carrier he took off every day with his comrades to strafe and drop small bombs into an area of North Korean barracks. Discovering in low flight that the people in the barracks were civilians, he notified the officer in command, who dismissed the information by remarking that the civilians were enemies too. The commander of the ship, however, who was subsequently approached, exempted our student from flying for a full week since he realized "that his conscience as a Christian" would have to be respected. The student remarked that "only then did my guilt become a reality"; he wished he could have done the killing instead of his less troubled comrades. Such is the vicarious existence of the Church for others, as it is partly expressed in Hochhuth's *Deputy* concerning the Christians in Germany and elsewhere regarding the murdering of millions of Jews, and as it was radically lived by the Catholic Christian Count Stauffenberg, who asked his priest for absolution before attempting to kill Hitler.

independent of the Church's knowledge of promise and fulfillment. For the Church is not the only recipient of God's promise and fulfillment. It is this fact which connects the Church with the world, and not the neo-Constantinian and secretly "imperialistic" idea that the reason for the Church's contact with the world is the hope for mass conversion. The "conversion" of individuals is merely the by-product of the Church's mission in the world. The Church's task with her fellowmen in the light of promise and fulfillment is the "humanization of history," as Paul Lehmann has frequently called it. But this humanization, we must add, demands a "demythologization" of Augustine's negative concept of world and history. Speaking of "the world" should be avoided as an abstraction; the interest of Christians is directed toward *specific* forms, places and problems of human life. There are good reasons for predicting that theological ethics, and theology in general, will focus attention on the questions concerning law, i.e. international, penal and other aspects of law. This emphasis would do justice to the necessity of concentration on specifics, rather than abstract generalities.

b) De-ideologizing Ethics and the "New Man" Ideology

The "new man" is certainly an important aspect in Pauline theology and in other parts of the Bible. But it should be said with all clarity that the "new man" is understandable, visible and recognizable only in Jesus Christ, the Second Adam. Ronald Gregor Smith[3] and others who have focused their attention on the "new man" have not directly denied this, but they have not taken the risk of facing this fact with all its consequences. Their concept of the "new man" is not sharply distinguished from the idea of the "modern man" who is said to be typical of the post-Renaissance and post-Enlightenment periods. Following these authors, less serious writers have begun their theological reflection with the abstraction "new man." Their intent is to transform "modern man" into the "new man," understood in a modern way. They make the *expected fruits* of the Holy Spirit the starting point of theological reflection. But this procedure has always in the history of theology proved to be dangerous. Although the intent to take man seriously is laudable, a theology which makes this its starting point will end up as an ideology. This

[3] Ronald Gregor Smith, *The New Man* (London: SCM Press, 1956).

is obvious, for instance, in Bishop Robinson's proposals concerning the meaning and task of the Church. His colleague Bishop Stockwood expresses the goal in the following vague and utterly empty sentence: "I decided that new methods would have to be used to break down the barrier of misunderstanding and apathy. *Somehow the Church had to convince the man in the street that Christianity was relevant.*"[4] The method of the "somehow" is apparently his chief concern, and the presupposition that the Church can and must "convince" betrays his hidden Constantinian imperialism, and finally the idea that "Christianity" is that which is to be seen as relevant makes it obvious that here the modern missionary is concerned more with a system or complex of thoughts, *viz.* an ideology, than with God in Jesus Christ. It is certainly possible and necessary to speak of "God in Jesus Christ" in entirely new terms, but it is uninteresting and intolerable to continue speaking of "Christianity" even in the attempt to modernize this old-fashioned complex of traditions. If our task were the search for an understandable and relevant ideology, it would not be advisable to examine hopefully the Christian tradition. Antiquity as well as modernity has produced better and more applicable ideologies than have the Christians who were too timid to rely on the *Christus praesens* and to let themselves be involved in his history.

It should of course be made clear that these theologically naive proposals are to be distinguished from the serious attempts, e.g. by Bonhoeffer, Ebeling, van Buren and other writers to grasp the problem of doing theology in a modern world. Nevertheless, their approaches breathe the same air as do the more journalistic versions; the latter represent the watered-down and often misunderstood (especially in the case of Bonhoeffer) version of their theology. The permissions for these evidently dangerous distortions are, however, indirectly given by recent serious theological authors. Ebeling, for instance, is not far from saying that the *true understanding* of world reality is *only* possible for those who have been renewed by justifying faith, i.e. by having received the new self-understanding which no longer tolerates the split between talk of God and talk of the world. But is this not an undue usurpation of basic human rights by the Christians and as such a result of the unhappy Western history

---

[4] Cited in Arnold Lunn and Garth Lean, *The New Morality* (London: Blandford Press, 1964), p. 89 (my emphasis).

of the relation between nature and grace? Indeed, the task of de-ideologizing ethics has not yet been accomplished. Thus "popular theology" in the local congregations still strives to find the characteristically *Christian* form of ethical actions without asking whether these forms really can and must exist (e.g. "Christian marriage"). Moreover, these ideologies seem to presuppose that we can know who "man" is, especially "modern man." But why is it that certain trends in contemporary theology show considerable timidity in using Augustine's directness in "speaking of God," while they unhesitatingly accept from him that we know what the "nature of man" is? Statements about "man" can be as "objectifying" as statements about God. For man *has* no "nature" about which we can speak with any hope of theological utilization.

Indeed, man *has* a history, a sex, a certain age, parents or children, friends and enemies, joys and sorrows, memories and hopes— but each in his own way and particular constellation. It seems that the only general statement which can be made about man is necessarily related to the man Jesus, and this relation shows the *tasks* which man has. This is true irrespective of the question whether or not the man is a Christian, because the Christian will not only speak of himself but work vicariously for others even if he never succeeds in "convincing" others of what he himself knows and hopes for. Irrespective of agreement or disagreement with non-Christians (or Christians) in matters of faith, the Christian will join hands with those who perform works which the Christian will also have to perform as fruits of his faith. And the opposite follows logically: The Christian will attempt to hinder such works and to change such situations as he cannot responsibly tolerate in the perspective of his faith, i.e. in his understanding of the history of the world in the dimensions of promise and fulfillment. He will do this hand in hand with non-Christians who have the same intent for different reasons.

Without going into detail at this point we can say that only the following de-ideologized and non-metaphysical (in the speculative sense) concept can help overcome the Augustinian heritage in contemporary speaking of man and his ethical task: *The actions of Christians are not by definition different from the actions of other men,* and that implies that by definition they are not "better" or more lasting than the actions of non-Christians. For what Christians do is not done *to* God as though he were the recipient of human actions. The Christians' actions are performed neither *to* God nor for the sake of their salvation (as Reformation theology also knew), but are done exclusively *for man because of God* in Christ. It would be absurd to suppose that God is the recipient of human actions, and therefore of human morality. The Augustinian competition between the two halves of the double command of love is irrelevant. Only man can receive what man does. But the Christian is that kind of man who does what he does *because* of what he knows of God in Christ, and this may imply that he will have to work *for man* in spite of man. This is the conflict of obedience which does not enter directly into the discussion here. The only act that man performs *to* God is prayer, and prayer is performed on behalf of others, including those who cannot pray. We can summarize this concept in the following way: Christians do not work *for* the Church and *for* God, but *because* of God (and *as* the Church) *for* man; but they offer thanks and praise and intercession *to* God for and *on behalf* of man. This is the priestly task of the Church.[5] The point of orientation is neither the "new man" as he indeed is described in the Bible, nor "modern man" as he is said to be found in today's world. The first orientation would be the error of beginning theology with the expected "fruits of the Spirit," and the second would be the attempt to establish an anthropological basis for theology. But both can be found only in the man Jesus: in him the newness which the Spirit creates has already become history (in the memory of the Church), and in him is that manhood which shows who man is meant to be and what his tasks are. Jesus "opens up" man both to himself (Jesus) and to man's fellowman.

Leaving aside the doxological aspect of the Church's task, is it true to say that non-Christians, e.g. humanists, can perform the *same* works which Christians are supposed to do? The answer is certainly affirmative. Would this mean that non-Christians can be "new men" in the same way as Christians are called to be "new men," *except* for the doxological function? Again, the answer is certainly affirmative. But this raises the question which today is being discussed in relation to the "New Morality." We will now turn to this problem.

---

[5] This will be discussed more fully in Chap. VI.

c) Christ Is Love—or—Love Is Christ?

The concept of "New Morality" is in part a British contribution to contemporary theology.[6] It would deserve to be analyzed sociologically and psychologically rather than theologically, but now it is already in the midst of theological discussion. In simple terms it is nothing else than the affirmation that the criterion for ethics lies in the inherent goodness of an action. H. A. Williams, one of the chief advocates of the seemingly new idea, comments on the Greek film *Never on Sunday*. A prostitute who helps a young sailor understand that he is not a failure but a real man with confidence and self-respect achieves the result that "he goes away a deeper and fuller person than he came in. What is seen is an act of charity which proclaims the glory of God. The man is now equipped as he was not before."[7] This is the illustration for H. A. Williams' doctrine: "Where there is healing, there is Christ."[8] We must hasten to admit that of course non-Christians can do as valuable and ethical works as can Christians. The reconciliation between a Communist husband and his wife, the forgiveness that a Moslem shows to his neighbor, or the love that an "agnostic" father gives his children are reconciliation, forgiveness and love which meet the recipients in no other way or lesser degree than if they had been given by Christians. Food parcels for hungry children need not have been mailed by Christians in order to accomplish their purpose. And forgiving love which restores joy and creates a new meaning in life or the "self-understanding" of a husband and a wife cannot possibly be looked down upon simply because the people who give and accept this love are not Christians. If there were goodness and human service only inside the Church, Paul could not have written Romans 13, and I Peter 2:13, which says: "Be subject for the Lord's sake to every human institu-

---

[6] The chapter entitled "The New Morality" in Robinson's *Honest to God* (London: SCM Press, 1963) is a summary presentation of this approach to ethics. Cf. also H. A. Williams' "Theology and Self-Awareness" in *Soundings* (Cambridge Univ. Press, 1962). Many other articles and press comments are cited in Arnold Lunn and Garth Lean, *The New Morality*. Cf. the critical essay by Hendrik van Oyen: " 'New Morality' en christelijke ethiek," in *Kerk en Theologie*, No. 16/3, pp. 237 ff. Edward LeRoy Long, Jr., has provided a history of this movement, "The History and Literature of 'The New Morality,' " in *Pittsburgh Perspective*, Vol. VII (Sept. 1966), pp. 4 ff.

[7] Cited in *The New Morality*, p. 60.

[8] *Ibid.*, p. 58.

tion, whether it be to the emperor as supreme, or to governors as sent by him *to punish those who do wrong and to praise those who do right,"* would be meaningless. The admonitions in the Epistles could not have used traditional ethical vocabulary if the authors had intended to express the opinion that there is no goodness outside the Church. In this sense we may as a borderline case agree with H. A. Williams that the prostitute in the Piraeus did something good for the young sailor. But is it not absolutely absurd to claim that this is the work of Christ and that it "proclaims the glory of God"? Is not the idea that reconciliation between a Communist husband and wife, forgiveness between Moslems or love between confessed non-Christians is secretly "Christian" an indication that *the "New Moralists" advocate a most subtle and tastelessly indirect form of Constantinian Christian imperialism?* Can they not leave alone the non-Christian fellowman who tries his best to give love and reconciliation—difficult enough without the memory and hope of Christ—and can they not abstain from conquering him with "Christian" categories? Apparently they cannot, for to be a Christian means to them to have a new self-understanding and to see a new "meaning in life." It is understandable that, if these are declared the chief factors of "Christianity" it follows logically that anyone who provides or receives such new self-understanding is labeled "Christian." Thus a theology which anchors itself in the praise of a new self-understanding dissolves itself. It cannot stand up to "modern man," who is no longer openly dominated and tyrannized by the intolerant usurpation of moral goodness by the Church, and who now develops his own independent self-understanding and ethical criteria. This "modern man" is frightening and must therefore be captured again with Christian labels. It appears that the Church's fear of man is the reason that she constantly speaks of man or of "modern man." The fear is that the characteristically "Christian element" of the Church is being taken care of by those who are not the Church. And we must conclude that, if the new self-understanding is this characteristic element, the fear is fully justified.

This recent development in certain quarters of contemporary theology would not have been necessary if the ancient criticism of Justin Martyr's doctrine of the "spermatic logos" had been taken more seriously and if Bonhoeffer's insights into the "world come of age" had been understood in their full depth. But as matters stand at present, Justin's doctrine still seems to be unchallenged, and Bonhoeffer's concept of the "world come of age" is bent to fit the Platonic and Stoic teachings of the Apologists. The departure from the *Christus praesens* to a theology of the *expected fruits* of Christ's work, individualistically understood, will indeed lead to the statement: Where there is healing there is Christ. Justin Martyr said for the same reason that Plato was secretly a Christian. And the "New Moralists" can say, leaving aside now as a borderline case the story of the prostitute, that Gandhi was a Christian, or that "where Gandhi worked there was Christ." Gandhi, however, knew what a Christian was and he consciously confessed to not being one.

The problem underneath the confusion is this: It is one thing to say that non-Christians can do as valuable and "good" works as can Christians, that they have in fact done these works and have put Christians to shame *and that therefore non-Christians de facto do what God in Christ wants man to do*. We may even add, if it is not already a commonplace, that "God uses these works for his own purposes," or the like. But it is another thing to say that *good actions tell who Christ is or that they are identical with his presence*. Certainly there are such things as "fruits of the Gospel" which are identical with human love, good will or sacrifice. This concept of the "fruits of the Gospel" is helpful and highly necessary for the Church's understanding of her involvement in the tasks which all men have in common. If this concept were not true the Church would have to dissociate herself totally from the non-Church; the isolated sect would remain for her the only form of existence. But the opposite is true. Granted now that actions in themselves are not by definition different when performed by Christians and by non-Christians, why and how should it follow that Jesus Christ is thereby *described* and made manifest in his *presence*? Neither is he described or proclaimed through human actions (of Christians or non-Christians), nor is the Church defined in her function by an analysis of her actions or by comparing her actions with those performed by non-Christians. In short, the idea of the "New Morality" which we have been discussing is based on a logical and theological confusion which is manifest in a confused terminology. Historically speaking, the "New Morality" is the end result of the so-called *beneficia* theology of which Melanchthon's sentence that to recognize Christ is to "recognize his *beneficia*" is a classical expression.

The advocates of the "New Morality" have the advantage of seeing: (a) that non-Christians can perform works which are of no less value than the works of Christians; (b) that the Church must not continue her ghetto existence; (c) that Christ's work and presence must not be confined to the walls of the Church. But they have certainly fallen victim to confused concepts regarding: (a) the difference between the presence of Christ and the recognizability of Christ; (b) the historical and corporate dimension of the Church and of her task, which is only in the end result and, so to speak, *ad hoc* paralleled by identical actions of non-Christians; (c) the priority of the understanding of the Church's function over the individualistically conceived idea of self-understanding. Moreover, we have seen that their concentration on self-understanding not only represents a continuation of Augustine's categories but also—which is much worse—betrays a hidden form of Constantinianism and "Christian imperialism," since it does not tolerate the fact that the consciously non-Christian man creates for himself and for those he loves a new self-understanding and "meaning of life." Thus we must conclude that what the "New Morality" says about the Church is by no means as dangerous (it is only insufficient) as what it says about "the world" which it intended to take so seriously.

The "New Morality" is strangely paralleled by a dogmatical thought which is indicated by the term "anonymous Christianity," which the Catholic dogmatician Karl Rahner has introduced into theological discussion.[9] Heinrich Ott has taken up this term and has shown[10] that Rahner's concept corresponds to Bultmann's interest in the liberation of man's existence to a new self-understanding. Both scholars seem to conceive of the newness in Christ in the existential categories of man's own self-reception and self-understanding. We may add that *De ecclesia* of Vatican II is not far removed from this approach, although the document stresses the importance of redemptive history and of the "plan of God." But the passage which speaks of the relation between the Church and non-Christians suggests concentric circles, the true Church being at the

---

[9] Karl Rahner, *Schriften zur Theologie* (Einsiedeln: Benzinger, 1962), vol. V, pp. 397 ff.

[10] Heinrich Ott, "Existentiale Interpretation und anonyme Christlichkeit," in *Zeit und Geschichte*, for Bultmann's eightieth birthday (Tübingen: J. C. B. Mohr, 1964), p. 367 ff. Ott's own conclusions are centering around Bultmann's concept of "meaningfulness" and are not very satisfying.

Center, other Christians surrounding it, and the non-Christians being located at the periphery, characteristic sentences being: "Nor is God far distant from those who in shadows and images seek the unknown God," and "Whatever good or truth is found amongst them is looked upon by the Church as a preparation for the Gospel."[11] These sentences are in line with the concluding remark that "the obligation of spreading the faith is imposed on every disciple of Christ."[12] This indicates that *De ecclesia* understands faith as a mode of cognition and it is for this reason that "faith" in "shadows and images" must be conceived as a preparation for "full faith." The tolerant tenor of the document is laudable and must be appreciated by everyone to whom the ecumenical contact with the Catholic Church is dear. But the non-christological understanding of the Church and of faith is nevertheless disturbing.

We are not concerned here with a lengthy discussion about "anonymous Christianity." But it is in line with the interest of our study to observe that theology in the post-Constantinian era is tempted to face the new situation by utilizing thoughts which once helped create the Constantinian era: Justin's and Tertullian's ideas that the universal Lordship of Christ can be expressed by referring to the "Christian nature" of the human soul, and by Augustine's concept of Christian world domination as well as by his interest in individualistic categories. What can be put in the place of these ideas? We have agreed with the "New Moralists" in some points, notably in regard to their openness in admitting that non-Christians can perform actions which Christians could or should also do. We have firmly disagreed, however, with their hidden "Christian imperialism" and with their exclusively individualistic categories. In fact, we have not been able to recognize any unique and helpful theological contribution of the idea of the "New Morality." The central ethical question is still left unanswered, for the assertion that e.g. the prostitute in the Piraeus has perhaps done something good is merely an *evaluation;* and the more sophisticated proposal that the goal of interhuman relationships is to gain a new self-understanding is likewise no more than an evaluation. Yet the central ethical question which has disturbed Israel and the Church as well as other people all through the ages is: *What* should we do, *when* should we

[11] *De ecclesia*, II, 16, *ed. cit.*, p. 18.
[12] *Ibid.*, p. 19.

do it, and *why* should we do it at all and not leave it undone? Neither Herbert Braun's emphasis on *Mitmenschlichkeit* (mutual neighborly love) nor Schubert Ogden's "authentic existence," nor, least of all, the suggestions of the "New Morality," go beyond the realm of formal assertions. The problem of the criterion is not faced.

d) *The Criterion for Ethics*

The question of the criterion for ethics is at the same time the question of the "degree of urgency." For example, it may be necessary and "good" to spend a lifetime fighting against the distribution of pornographic literature. But it may be more necessary and therefore "better" to spend one's life fighting anti-Semitism. And it may be still more necessary and most urgent and therefore "best" to spend one's life working for world peace. Of course an ultimate separation of these various concerns will not be possible. Nor can we say that every man (or Christian) must have the same concern. But this only complicates the problem. What is urgent to some is often of so little concern to others that it even seems "wrong."[13] But does this not then open the door to ethical relativism? In a certain way it does indeed, for it is difficult, to say the least, to judge that such and such an action is always right or always wrong. The influential standard works on ethics, e.g., those by Brunner, Bonhoeffer, Barth and Paul Lehmann, have each in its own way presented detailed discussions of this problem. We are concerned here merely with the question of the criterion, but primarily with the criterion for the discernment of what is *urgent*. We can learn from the Biblical writers that the question of *right* and *wrong* is less important than the question of what is *urgent*. The categories of right and wrong have come into theology from Greek philosophy and other sources, as has also the interest in the "motives" of a person's actions. The importance of these problems should not be

---

[13] An example is our present discussion: While we will not deny that a Christian is characterized by a new self-understanding and that it is *possible* to unfold theology in terms of categories of existence, it appears to us that today's political and social problems are of such enormous weight that the "less urgent" questions of the theology of existence even seem "wrong." This would not be the case if the advocates of this theology had concretely and convincingly shown their concern and involvement in the world's present problems.

belittled, but it must also be admitted that they have caused much confusion in the Church. In the following discussion we will leave aside the relation between theological and philosophical ethics. We presuppose that the vicarious function of the Church, the theme of the following chapter, compels us to assign to this problem an inferior position within systematic theology.

The history of theology has presented a variety of answers to the quest for the ethical criterion. Systematizing these answers, we can enumerate: (a) *"Pharisaism,"* the reliance upon the divine law for the purpose of pleasing God and man, (b) the *imitatio Christi* concept which portrays Jesus as the moral model and divine pattern according to which the believer's life must be shaped, (c) the reference to eternal *principles* which are deduced from what one supposedly knew of God and his will, (d) *idealism* as the theological form of the philosophical concept that man must constantly strive toward betterment, and finally (e) the *apocalyptic* denial of the value of any ethical concerns, or its counterpart, the idea that it is the task of Christians to create the kingdom of God on earth. There is of course a still greater variety of possible approaches, and those enumerated here can either be related to one another or split into more detailed subcategories. But all these answers to the quest for the ethical criterion cannot measure up to the theological depth of the Reformers' attempts to deal with the problem of the law. It is at this juncture in theology that the Old Testament, and especially the Pauline teaching of the relation between righteousness and law, personal and corporate responsibility, promise and hope, "Church and world," has again moved into the center. While Protestant theology can learn much from Roman Catholic dogmatics, there is little or nothing that Catholic theologians since the seventeenth or eighteenth century have produced in the field of ethics. "Modern theology," therefore, must not permit itself to lose contact with the positions of the Reformers in this matter. And it must be seen that authors like Gerhard Ebeling are deeply concerned with the modern interpretation of the Reformation heritage, whereas the advocates of the "New Morality" seem to be ignorant of their own heritage. The question is only whether the Reformers can really provide an answer to our quest concerning the criterion of ethics.

The Reformers' approach to ethics is based on the biblical categories of obedience over against disobedience. Indeed, the question

of what God wants man to do has priority over the question of what
is "good." We leave this supposition unchallenged and proceed to
the discussion concerning the "third use of the law" in Reformation
theology. It is here that the criterion is at stake. In short, the history
is this: While Luther taught a *duplex usus legis,* a twofold use of the
law (since 1522), *viz.* the political-normative use and the pedagogical use, Melanchthon added the much discussed *tertius usus legis,*
the third use of the law. This is the use and function of the law *"in
renatis,"* in the lives of those who are reborn. Calvin followed
Melanchthon in advocating the "third use of the law," but strict
Lutherans have denied the validity of this idea up to the present
day. Thus Reformation and post-Reformation theology faced in
principle the following alternatives: (a) The law is clearly distinct
from the Gospel: while the latter is strictly *forgiveness,* the former is
exclusively *accusation;* the law is *lex accusans* in its two forms, the
"political" and the "pedagogical" use (*usus elenchticus:* it shows
man his sin and leads him to the quest for forgiveness), *but the
Christian no longer is under the law,* "for Christ is the end of the
law," (Rom. 10:4). The Christian lives in faith and faith produces
works of love. Love is the freedom which only faith can provide.
The other alternative is (b) that the first and second use of the law is
accepted and explained as in Lutheran theology but that the "third
use" is added: the Christian *not only needs the law* as criterion for
his decisions but *he loves it* (Psalms 19 and 119) and sees it in its
fulfillment in Christ (e.g. Matt. 5:17) and obeys it voluntarily in
faith.

This alternative has occupied the minds of theologians and laymen
ever since the sixteenth century. (The still lively discussions in
American Protestantism, e.g. on the use of alcohol, are an indication
of it.) The Lutherans accused the Reformed Christians of legalism,
and generally rightly so. The Reformed in turn felt that the Lutherans had opened the doors to libertinism and to an ethics without
fixed criteria. The Lutherans felt justified in their position by the
Pauline passages on the end of the law and the liberation *from* the
law. The Reformed, however, had learned from Calvin to understand the law basically as the proclamation of God's good and
gracious will *for* his people. Thus the strong Lutheran fixation on
the Gospel as forgiveness of sins makes visible a lack of understanding of the "change of rulership" which has occurred in Christ's

coming; and the Reformed position may invite the thought that the coming of Jesus Christ is "merely" fulfillment but not the beginning of the "new creation."

Modern exegesis, e.g. Gerhard v. Rad's work on the Old Testament, has shown that the *Torah* is basically a help for Israel, rather than a "Power to death." Old Testament exegesis in general has vindicated the Reformed position, but some quarters in New Testament research still find the Lutheran denial of the "third use" confirmed by the observation that the admonitory passages of the Epistles are not a direct application of the Old Testament law. This is questionable, however, and some authors have already pointed out that the New Testament's application of Stoic and other extra-biblical ethical ideas is at least paralleled, if not overshadowed by the continuation of Old Testament concepts. Biblical scholarship at present is in the midst of this discussion. The only clear-cut position which can be recognized today is the strictly Lutheran denial of the "third use of the law" in the exegesis of Bultmann and his followers. The Old Testament is to them the "accidental" historical background of the New, a background which theoretically could have been Greek philosophy of history or Greek ethics. The newness of Christ is stressed at the expense of Israel's expectation and of the categories of promise and fulfillment in general. It follows that the *criterion* for ethics is for these theologians anchored not in history but in the *momentary encounter with the kerygma of Christ in whom I receive a radically new understanding of my existence.* The strong emphasis on faith permits only the sentence: Faith liberates me to works of love. The origin of this concept lies in Luther's *On Christian Liberty* of 1520, certainly one of the greatest works on theological ethics. But is the end result of this concept not perhaps the "New Morality," i.e. the consistent prolongation of the Lutheran denial of the "third use of the law"? Here faith tolerates no timeless and absolute regulations, instructions, laws and commands; everything must happen out of love, and love cannot be determined and defined in advance. Is this not perhaps the inherent problem and weakness of Lutheran and existentialist theology?

We would not suggest that the position which has grown out of the Lutheran stream of tradition be substituted by Melanchthon's and Calvin's "third use of the law." The time-boundness of theology, and the concreteness of the lives of Christians in and as the

Church, forbids this flight into timeless and always applicable laws. Lutheran theologians who have found themselves in disagreement with the results of the strict denial of the "third use of the law" have nevertheless carefully tried to avoid advocating the "third use." But not only they, e.g. Bonhoeffer, Gollwitzer and Ernst Wolf, but also Reformed theologians such as Barth[14] and Paul Lehmann have avoided a direct acceptance of the "third use."

How then can the problem be solved? We are neither able to agree with the traditionally Lutheran stress on the absolute newness of Christ's coming, which puts an end to the law as an ethical criterion (although this thought is tempting); nor are we willing to repeat and adopt Melanchthon's and Calvin's "third use of the law," although we may admit that at their time it was more justifiable than it would be today. The answer lies in the risk of referring to the *Christus praesens*. Inasmuch as God is not timeless and history-less, the "law" must not be conceived as a timeless authority hovering over history and its concrete situations. Only a timeless concept of the law, as it was expressed in the thinking of later periods of Israel's history, and subsequently in the Western Church, creates the problem as to whether there is a "third use of the law." If the Augustinian concept that the truth lies in the past and must be made relevant to the present applies to the Gospel, it applies also to the law. The climate of the later Roman culture within which the Western Church came into existence, supported this theological program. According to this way of thinking it is not only the "historical-risen Christ," as we have called him, who must be brought into "contemporaneity" with us, but also the law. But in the case of the law this operation is doubly difficult since the biblical texts seem to affirm that the coming of Christ has changed the function of the law. Thus Western theology has not in principle been troubled by the idea of "making relevant" the (risen) Christ of the past, but the undertaking of doing the same with the law has caused problems which are reflected in the Lutheran-Reformed discussion about the "third use of the law." Basically, however, the problem is the same in both instances. The neglect of the *Christus praesens* necessarily creates in

---

[14] Barth's classical reinterpretation of this problem was first presented in his *Rechtfertigung und Recht* in 1928 (3rd ed.; Zollikon-Zürich: EVZ-Verlag, 1948); Engl. transl. by G. Ronald Howe under the strange title *Church and State* (London: SCM Press, 1939).

theology the problems of the different uses of the law, not to mention the fatal separation between dogmatics and ethics.

There is no reason to disagree with existentialist theology and
other streams of tradition which have grown out of Reformation
theology when they affirm that the heart of the Good News is that
God is *for man,* and this is manifest in Jesus Christ's coming. It is
true that the general and all-embracing ethical criterion is oriented
on the creed: God intends man, God seeks man, God does not want
the death of man "but that he lives," *God is for man.* The orientation on this creed implies directly that man must also "intend" man,
and "seek" man, and want not man's death but his life; in short,
that man be *for man,* that he *hopes for man.*

The orientation on this creed remains in the realm of the abstract
as long as the individual who accepts this orientation has not found
his place in the *communio sanctorum,* the Church, where God in
Christ, of whom this creed treats, is *present.* The concrete orientation is possible only in the "assembly of the brothers," or at least in
remembering the asssembly and in hoping to find it again. For it is
in the assembly of the believers that the *Christus praesens* opens up
the dimensions of the past and the present, liberating the members
of the Church to solidarity with their fellow men, and enabling them
to be concretely *for man.* The decision of what is urgent and what is
good is neither based on the application of a timelessly understood
law, nor is it made without the law, for without the law the promise-
and-fulfillment character of God's history with his people would not
be understandable and the *Christus praesens* would become timeless. The ethical decision is based on the concrete insight into the
past, which is seen in forgiveness, and on the concrete expectation
for the *future,* which is seen in hope. The assembled congregation is
the place where the *Christus praesens* liberates and invites man to
this "historical view," which is the ethical criterion.[15] It goes with-

---

[15] The theme of our present study is only indirectly concerned with ethics. A
full discussion of the problems at issue can be found in Paul L. Lehmann,
Ethics in a Christian Context (New York: Harper & Row, 1963). My views
on the importance of the concept of the *Christus praesens* have developed over
a number of years, but the final formulation is indebted to what I have learned
from Prof. Lehmann in discussions and in reading his publications.

    I cannot follow Paul Ramsey's criticism of Lehmann ("Lehmann's Con-
textual Ethics and the Problem of Truth-Telling" in *ThToday,* Jan. 1965, pp.
466 ff.; cf. Lehmann's reply, *ThToday,* April 1965, pp. 119 ff.), suspecting that
Ramsey has quite basically misunderstood Lehmann's emphasis on the presence

out saying that the "historical view" is not the same in all places and
at all times. What is urgent and what is good differs from place to
place and from time to time. This insight is the correct aspect of
what is today called "contextual ethics." But while contextual ethics
seeks the criterion for ethics in the situations, an ethics which is
oriented on the *Christus praesens* finds its criterion in him. *He*
opens the eyes of those who seek and the ears of those who listen to
the understanding of the situation. Contextual ethics proceeds the
other way around.[16]

We have observed that certain trends in contemporary theology
speak easily of "man," but find it difficult to speak of "God"; that
the Augustinian interest in the individual's self-understanding can
lead to the dissolution of theology in the "New Morality," that the
Augustinian preparation of the idea of the Church's world domination is still present in hidden form when Christians call actions of

---

of Christ, a theological category of cardinal importance which is, so far as I
understand his position, alien to Ramsey's theological thought. I do not understand Lehmann's ethics as part of "contextual ethics" in the sense in which
this term is used in contemporary discussion.

Cf. also the clarifications provided by James M. Gustafson, "Context Versus
Principles: A Misplaced Debate in Christian Ethics," *HThR*, Apr. 1965, pp.
171 ff.

[16] We have no difficulties, of course, with the "situational" or "contextual"
ethicists' stress on the impossibility of an "ethical system" in the classical sense
of the term "system." But for theological as well as non-theological reasons
one would be well advised not to agree with the highly abstract emphasis on
"decision-making," so typical of situational ethics (and of Anglo-Saxon theological ethics in general). Joseph Fletcher, for instance, in his *Situation Ethics,
The New Morality* (Philadelphia: The Westminster Press, 1966), is a perfect
example of an ethicist who, in the attempt to be extremely *concrete*, operates
on the basis of the assumption that "decision-making" is a category which
adequately describes the reality of human life. This *abstract* assumption leads
Fletcher to such theoretical and not at all situational affirmations as, for instance, "Love only is always good" or "Love is the only norm" or "Life itself,
in fact, is decision" (pp. 57, 69, 154). The emphasis on the individual's decision and on his "will" is an Augustinian legacy which, even if separated from
its Platonic-idealistic origin, remains highly individualistic and can only in
rare cases serve as a description of or direction for complex ethical situations.
It certainly fails when applied to such important questions as: Why did Hitler
gain power in Germany? What ought to be done to overcome racial segrega-
tion? Fletcher's situational ethics gives *permission* to the *Christians* to feel
liberated from the "third use of the law," but it certainly does not give constructive directions to both Christians and non-Christians, directions which go
beyond generalities with which sensitive men in the West and in the East
(e.g. in Hindu thinking) have not been familiar for a long time. A more realistic approach is taken by Knud E. Løgstrup, *Die ethische Forderung* (Tübingen:

non-Christians "Christian," while they should simply admit that they are "good." Finally we have observed that the controversy over the "third use of the law" would not have occurred if the results of modern Old Testament exegesis had been known earlier and if the law had not been conceived as a timeless expression of God's will, parallel to the dogmatical idea of God's timeless existence. The widely accepted phrase that "God is for man" is removed from its abstract realm only when it is seen in its historical (i.e. embracing past *and* future) dimension, which we have called the *Christus praesens*. This will now be discussed in the final chapter.

H. Laupp'sche Buchhandlung, 1959; tr. from the Danish edition of 1958). Løgstrup, not quoted by Fletcher, concisely tries to depart from the traditional individualistic approach to ethics by conceiving of man in his involvements in obligations which are prior to his decisions and which make decisions appear as abstractions which are at best recognized in retrospect. This approach should be pursued further in order to bring out clearly the vicarious task of the Christians for others, of Christians who understand themselves as part of the history of the Church and of their culture. The excellent Czech film *Shop on Main Street* is an impressive example of the concreteness of man's involvement in *happenings* and *events*, and it serves better than a book the understanding of the limitations of "decision-making," which so often is a "bourgeois" abstraction concerning the reality of life.

VI

The High Priest and the Priestly
Task of the Church

In this final chapter we will utilize the findings of our preceding three historical and the two dogmatical chapters. Our aim is a tentative formulation of the *Christus praesens* concept. It cannot be more than a tentative formulation, for if our thesis is correct, it is just in this concept of the *Christus praesens* that all other aspects of theology and especially of Christology converge. But we must take up the questions which were left open in the first chapter, questions which have guided our criticism of Augustinianism and of characteristic aspects of contemporary Western theology. Our complaint was that under the direct or indirect influence of Augustinianism Western theology has not provided the categories for the understanding of the *Christus praesens*, and that therefore nature and grace, reason and faith, scholarship and piety, theology and doxology, historical past and existential present have been separated from each other. We must now risk a positive thesis which could help to bridge these gaps.

a) The Dilemma of Classical Christology

At the beginning of the first chapter we reiterated the results of recent New Testament research that *the post-Easter biblical books are not a commentary on the historical Jesus but on Easter,* and that *the resurrected Christ can be recognized only in the Church.* These affirmations represent nothing new, but we have seen that Western theology has had difficulties in combining the two. When speaking of the resurrected Christ it spoke of the "historical-resurrected Christ" who is to be made relevant to the Church at present. But this understanding is detrimental to the second affirmation, that Jesus Christ is recognized only in the Church. For the meaning of this second thesis is not that an event of the past should be reenacted in the present: on the contrary, it is Christ's self-presentation in the present which opens the eyes to the understanding of what happened in the past. The post-Easter appearances, recorded by various traditions in the first century, prove this point.

Whatever reservations and criticisms one may have, there is no denying that the Fathers of the Greek councils, whose formulations influenced all of later Christology, were aware of what our two affirmations intend to indicate. When speaking of Christ, the Greek Fathers *thought* and *prayed* at the same time. They praised and adored the presence of the One whose relation with the Father and with mankind they tried to define. Only they were unable to prevent the unfortunate development of the practice of making the definitions themselves the object of praise and adoration. But leaving aside this problem, why was it that their formulations ultimately presented an impasse? There is no doubt that a logical impasse accompanies all stages of the history of post-Chalcedonian Christology: Chalcedon itself, the monotheletic controversies, the Christological aspects of the iconoclastic controversies, the discussions on the Lord's Supper in early medieval theology in the West, Reformation Christology, the debates between Giessen and Marburg on the kenotic theory, and so forth.

The opinion is often heard that this impasse reflects the greatness or divinity of Jesus Christ himself. Popular piety has therefore even suggested that the theologians should not have tried to penetrate into the secret of Jesus Christ. But this is a very superficial view. How should those who try to understand something thereby show irreverence for what they desire to understand? On the contrary, the excuse that the matter is too complicated and too mysterious to permit the search for understanding is itself irreverent. Scholarly theology has therefore not abstained from trying to understand and to formulate christological questions. But is it true that the logical impasse in classical Christology is a reflection of the greatness and divinity of Christ? If this were true, it would presuppose that the Chalcedonian categories are correct and adequate. One would have to confirm the decisions of the early Fathers and accept in principle their categories, perhaps permitting some revisions and reinterpretations. This has been done, for instance, by D. M. Baillie,[1] who operates within the given framework of classical Christology, emphasizing the incarnation as a proper starting point. It is only consistent that Baillie ends up with a "paradox," and that he calls the "paradox" a reflection of the very being and nature of Christ himself. While this is a very respectable approach, we cannot refrain from expressing doubt as to whether the categories of classical Christology really present the "true paradox" of Christ. Instead of "true paradox" perhaps we should say what was stated at the beginning of the first chapter: that one cannot speak of Jesus Christ as an object, as though he were not the subject of our lives. It is doubtful whether a Christology that begins with the incarnation is capable of bringing to light this *mysterion*, or "paradox," or limit of theology. An Incarnation-Christology will probably present a logical impasse which is *no* true reflection of what we have tentatively called the "greatness and divinity" of Christ. The "scandal" of this impasse will be an intellectual-theological scandal or "paradox," but perhaps not a scandal to the faith and life of the Church. For *our* questions which we direct *to* Jesus do not merely end in logical paradoxes. Our questions result in questions which *he* asks of *us*. Jesus Christ is not the answer, however paradoxical, to our christological questions, but he is the calling into question of our questions, presuppositions and answers. It is doubtful whether an incarnation-Christology will make this clear. Such Christology may show the limits of theology at the wrong place so that a false paradox or scandal preoccupies the minds of the theologians and frightens the piety of the people in the Church.

The traditional description of the dilemma of classical Christology can be summarized in the following way.[2] From the beginning

[1] D. M. Baillie, *God Was in Christ* (New York: Charles Scribner's Sons, 1948), esp. chap. V.
[2] John McIntyre, *The Shape of Christology* (Philadelphia: The Westminster Press, 1966), presents an interesting categorization of "models" in Christology, and an openness to the choice between them ("according to the circumstance in the christological situation," p. 172). His discussion of the problems of two-nature Christology is found on pp. 82 ff.

the Church faced the alternative between a docetic and an adoption-ist understanding of the relation between God and man in Jesus. The incarnation is expressed either in terms of the Logos' move-ment from the Father into the form of the man Jesus, or else in terms of an elevation of the man Jesus into the form of Christ who is said to be equal with the Father. The first idea, which tends toward docetism, presupposes the knowledge of God; the second, which almost inevitably tends toward adoptionism, presupposes the knowl-edge of man. This is already an impasse. But the problem increases when the question is asked how the divine and the human "natures" are related to each other in the one man Jesus. Neither Apollinaris' nor Paul of Samosata's answers were considered satisfactory; the former made the divine nature so clearly his point of departure that the true humanity of Jesus was destroyed, and the latter did just the opposite. The positions of the Alexandrians and the Antiochians were more carefully elaborated, but the basic alternative between docetism and adoptionism was still noticeable in their approaches. Thus Chalcedon balanced the two incorrect views against each other by utilizing the "nature" concept which had served to clarify the quest concerning the "end product" of the incarnation, *viz.* the relation and connection between God and man in Jesus. Chalcedon, however, not only solved problems, it also created new ones. On the one hand it split the unity of the Church by hardening the already existing differences between the (predominantly white!) Greek Church and the Oriental churches. But on the other hand it not only left unanswered but opened anew the question of the integrity of each of the two natures. Leontius of Byzantium's and John of Damascus' doctrines of the *anhypostasis* and *enhypostasis* were the attempts to meet the problem: the human nature of Jesus cannot be thought of as having a separate existence (anhypostatically); in other words, there could not have been a Jesus who was not the Jesus Christ, but his human nature exists within the divine (enhypostatically) with-out ceasing to be human nature. Leontius' and John's doctrines did not merely express an interest in hairsplitting scholasticism, but were intended to grasp the soteriological aspect of Christology, because Jesus' human nature is *homoousios* with our nature. This doctrine is the best which could have been developed on the basis of Incarna-tion Christology, and it should not be dismissed lightly by those who agree with the presuppositions of this type of Christology. If one wanted to complain of the subtle docetism of the doctrines of the *en-* and *anhypostasis*, one would have to admit that the whole approach tended toward docetism long before Leontius and John developed their theories.

The usual criticism of classical Greek Christology refers to the problems which are connected with the employment of the concept of *nature*. But this is not really a convincing criticism. Although our present philosophical situation would certainly not facilitate the employment of the nature concept in theology, there is no theological reason as such to avoid the concept of nature. The Greek Fathers did not have as static an understanding of *physis* as did later theologians who had translated *physis* by the Latin *natura*. At least we can say that the nature concept is theoretically capable of expressing a non-static state of affairs. The problem of classical Christology does not lie in the use of the nature concept *but in the theological decision to speak of two natures*. But speaking of *two* natures follows necessarily when Christology takes the Incarnation as its point of departure.

The dilemma of classical Greek Christology is not the limited ability of theology and human understanding to comprehend the "greatness and divinity" of Christ, although subjectively the Fathers knew of the impossibility of describing and defining Christ, but rather it lies in the theological decision to make the Incarnation the point of departure and consequently to speak of two natures which embrace with the one notion "nature" that which cannot be embraced in one category, *viz.* God and man. The monophysites were aware of this impossibility, but their position is of course untenable on the basis of the presuppositions which they shared with the dyophysites.

When human nature and divine nature are conceived as the corresponding notions with which Christology must be unfolded, the result is not so much a "paradox" as rather an imbalance of the natures in Jesus Christ himself. One of the natures is stressed at the expense of the other, and it is only natural that it is the divine nature which outweighs the human. Not only the Biblical texts but also the adoration of Christ in worship seems to demand this. It is understandable that in the periods following the christological councils theology no longer saw the *oneness* of Christology and soteriology (cf. Augustine), of Christ's present high-priestly work and the priestly function of the Church (cf. medieval ecclesiology), of Christ's personal and "cosmic" work (cf. Luther), of the historical Jesus and the risen Christ (cf. nineteenth century), etc. Admittedly, theology has tried time and again to pull together what has fallen apart, but the incorporation of classical Christology, which was never seriously challenged in the mainstream of Church tradition, always presented problems. Most helpful were the various attempts to make the resurrection of Jesus the point of departure. The latest attempt along this line is W. Pannenberg's Christology. But his interpretation of the resurrection[3] is a direct expression of his problematical modification of Gerhard v. Rod's concept of history of tradition along with a quite new reinterpretation of Hegel, so that despite similarities with our theses his approach cannot be utilized here. His resurrected Christ is the "historical-resurrected" Christ who needs further transformation and transfiguration in order to "become" the *Christus praesens*. Nevertheless, Pannenberg's decision to take the resurrection as the point of departure for Christology is as such helpful, if only he did not base the statement that Jesus' resurrection is the confirmation of his oneness with the Father on the historical cognition of the details of Easter. But this he must do in order to remain faithful to his concept of history.

The proper starting point from which to unfold Christology will be the understanding of the resurrected Christ who is present in the Church. There are some passages in the Reformers which present this point of view.[4] But in general Western theology has shied away from it. The alternatives were seen elsewhere: in a Christology of ontological or personalistic character, in the emphasis on the *pro me* or the *extra nos*, etc. It appears that these problems are magnified when Christology is imprisoned by the questions of incarnation theories, e.g.: What is the relation of Christ's natures? What is the difference between the historical Jesus and the risen Christ? and the like. We could perhaps put it like this: There was a time in modern scholarship when it was discovered that the historical Jesus can be seen only through the eyes of the witnesses of the resurrection;

[3] W. Pannenberg, *Grundzüge der Christologie* (*vide* above, Chap. I, FN 10), pp. 47 ff.
[4] We have already cited Luther's statement, "He who wants to find Christ must first find the Church . . ." (above, chap. III, FN 37; cf. also WA, 40, I, 229, 233, 284 ff.), but later Reformation theology only discussed the presence of Christ in relation to the Lord's Supper.

today is the time when we must discover that the risen Christ can be seen only through the eyes of those who witness to the presence of Christ. Formally speaking, this means that no one would be seriously *interested* in Easter, in the historical Jesus and in the covenant with Israel if it were not for the concrete stimulus provided by the Church. The reception of the past is a question of one's interest in the present. This statement, however, is no more than a formal assertion.

b) The Function of Christology

Some further preconsiderations will be necessary before we venture to define the concept of the *Christus praesens*. It was Bonhoeffer[5] who criticized classical Christology for asking "What is Jesus Christ?" rather than "Who is he?" This is a more helpful distinction than the insistence that the use of the nature concept is false. The question must indeed be "Who is he?" for this requires an answer that does not tolerate a separation between his being and his work, or between his "person" and the "benefits" that come from him. Bonhoeffer said in the course of his argument:[6] "1. Jesus is man, and the *a posteriori* conclusion from the work to the person is ambiguous. 2. Jesus is God and the direct *a posteriori* conclusion from history to God is impossible. If this way of cognition is closed, there is left only one attempt to find access to Jesus Christ . . . to go to that place where the person . . . reveals himself. *This is the place of prayer to Christ.*" I would perhaps not repeat Bonhoeffer's "is-sentences"—he "is" man and he "is" God—because this dialectical parallelization is more valuable for refuting heresies than for making positive statements. But the main content of Bonhoeffer's statement is most helpful. Indeed, we cannot speak of Christ without loving him and we cannot think of Christ without praying to him. We cannot, as Bonhoeffer says in one place, meet him without dying. The function of Christology is that of clarifying what we can say about him *as well as* to him. Christology is the expansion and testing of the *logos* about Christ and to Christ. It is doctrine as well

---

[5] Dietrich Bonhoeffer, "Christologie" in *Gesammelte Schriften*, Vol. III, ed. Eberhard Bethge (Munich: Chr. Kaiser, Verlag, 1960); now Engl. transl., *Christ the Center* (*vide* above, Chap. I, FN 4).

[6] *Ibid.*, pp. 177 ff. (German text, my translation and my emphasis); p. 39 (Engl. text).

as *doxa*. Even such seemingly simple questions as What do you think of Jesus? are tested and judged as to their correctness and biblical validity in the light of his presence. This testing and unfolding is the function of Christology. Without it the *doxa* of his presence is misunderstood and spiritualized.

Since Christology begins with the presence of the one of whom it speaks and to whom prayers are offered, but not without remembering his past and hoping for his future, Christology has a function of "going before": it is *prior* to other thoughts despite the fact that it "follows" thoughts by testing and judging them. This strange fact is the manifestation of the time structure of Christ's existence. He is the past, present and hoped-for Christ. Only the separation between the presence of Christ and "Christ as such" could have made it possible that the Church reflected abstractly on the differences in the characteristics (the *idiomata*) of Christ in the various stages of his existence in time. The alternatives were: Should the post-existent Christ, i.e. the ascended Christ, be understood with the *idiomata* of the incarnate Christ? Or should the incarnate Christ be seen with the *idiomata* of the pre-existent Christ? The Church on the whole decided that the second view was to be preferred over the first. Thus the idea of the pre-existent *logos asarkos*, the fleshless Logos, became necessary. This is a speculation which suggests a Christ without Jesus and a Son of God without Jesus Christ. Again, this is a fruit of Incarnation Christology. But the third possibility, that the pre-existent, the incarnate, as well as the "post-existent" Christ is to be seen in the light of the *Christus praesens*, did not seriously enter into traditional Christology. The idea that God in Jesus Christ has a history frightened the theologians because it was seen as detrimental to the concept of the timelessness of God and because it appeared to be in proximity to the "economic" understanding of the Trinity. Thus it was "only" Jesus Christ who was conceived as having a history. This thought, however, permits a separation between God and Jesus Christ which makes meaningless or mythical the expression "Son of God." In order to bridge the gap between the three Sons of God that thus appeared as a logical necessity, *viz.*, the pre-existent Logos, the incarnate Christ and the risen Lord, the concept of the office (*munus*) of Christ was formulated. This office was subdivided into the prophetic, the priestly and the kingly office. This was done with the understanding that each of the *munera* was of like importance, although the sequence of the treatment of each of them varied. In Calvin,[7] for instance, the kingly office usually comes first and the priestly last. Can this doctrine of the *triplex munus Christi* be more than a pedagogical expression of what the believer must know when he begins to think biblically and historically about the Christ who is proclaimed and to whom he trusts his life? It can hardly be more than this, and the doctrine is in fact of little value altogether.[8]

The difficulty which arose in regard to the unity between God and Christ and between the work and person of Christ was treated in the doctrine of the "three forms of speaking" (*genera*) of the exchange of properties (*idiomata*), the exchange which is called *communicatio idiomatum* and which is based on the Chalcedonian concept of the two natures and their unity. The "three ways of speaking" of this exchange brought to light the inherent problem of the background of classical Christology, *viz*. the docetic and the adoptionist tendency. The three ways of speaking are: (1) the *genus idiomaticum*, which asserts generally that the *idiomata* belong to the whole person, not merely to one of the two natures; (2) the *genus apotelesmaticum* (from *apotelesma*-work), which indicates that in the *work* of the God-man both natures are effective; and (3) the *genus majestaticum*—not accepted by the Reformed[9]— which in a *one-sided* way states that the *idiomata* of the divine nature are also part of the human nature. The logical counterpart of this third *genus*, the *genus tapeinoticon*, was taught by only a few. It suggested that the properties of the human nature were also the properties of the divine nature.

Such is the end result of Chalcedon, and that means of a Christology which takes its point of departure with the Incarnation, a departure which necessitates the question: *What* is Jesus Christ? No one who intends to operate on this basis should dismiss the doctrine of the three *genera*, or of at least two of them. But do we want to end up at this point? The fact that this doctrine is complicated and

---

[7] Cf. Calvin, *Institutes*, III, 15; the doctrine also occurs (influenced by Calvin?) in the *Catechismus Ramanus*, I, 3, 7. Cf. John F. Jansen, *Calvin's Doctrine of the Work of Christ* (London: James Clarke, 1956), on the question whether Calvin had reduced the *triplex munus* to a *duplex munus* doctrine.

[8] Cf. Pannenberg's criticism of the *triplex munus*, *op. cit.*, pp. 218 ff.

[9] Cf. Calvin, *Institutes*, II, 12–14. Cf. also Thomas Aquinas, *Summa theologica*, III, 16, 8.

rather scholastic is in itself no reason to dismiss it or to ridicule it. A complicated question compels the asker to accept a complicated answer. But the answer is not only complicated, it is also problematical. The fact that the Reformed did not accept the third *genus* indicates that in midstream they gave up asking the question because they did not want to fall victim to the inherent docetism of this doctrine. But instead they fell into just the opposite of docetism; many of the Reformed Confession Books teach that it was only the human nature that died on the Cross! While the Lutherans tended toward monophysitism, the Reformed ended up with two Christs, one more of the Jesus-type, the other more of the Christ-type. The impasse can be illustrated by the following sample statements: According to both Lutherans *and* Reformed it is "orthodox" to say that when Jesus healed a man he was operating with both natures; when he returns in the last days, he will return in both natures. And according to the Lutherans it is fitting to say that when Jesus was at both sides of the lake at the same time, he was present in both divine and human nature. But according to the Reformed it is correct to say that when Jesus went through closed doors, it was only his divine nature that did this. And again Lutheran *and* Reformed would say that when Jesus was hungry only his human nature was hungry. More examples could be added. They are correct only in principle, for the individual authors in the sixteenth and seventeenth centuries went into great detail to define their special opinions. But all statements of this sort represent attempts to speak of Jesus Christ "as such," separated from the Church's co-existence with him. The differences between the Lutherans and the Reformed came to full expression only in the controversy over the Lord's Supper. It was at this point that the connection between Christology and the Church was seen most clearly.

One must give credit to the Reformers, however, for having came close to the *Christus praesens* concept in their emphasis on the *proclamation* of the Word. The original interest of the Reformers was not directed to statements about God or Christ "as such." Rather their interest was in God's coming to man in the liberating word of the Gospel. But their emphasis on the *Christus praedicatus* was expressed in terms of justification rather than in unfolding the presence of Christ who takes man into his possession. What was present, according to the Reformers, was the Holy Spirit, and the

Holy Spirit's function was understood as enabling the congregation to receive the grace of justification. Thus the third book of Calvin's *Institutes* refers already in its title to the "reception of grace." The presence of the *Word* is the presence of God in Christ in the *Holy Spirit* for the sake of receiving the grace of justification. What justification is in relation to the Word, the Lord's Supper is in relation to the ascended Christ. Of course the teachings of the Reformers regarding this point are not all alike. While Zwingli distinguished between the historical Jesus and Christ who is present in the congregation by saying that the historical Jesus is present in the *recordatio* of the faithful, Luther stressed the presence of Christ in word and sacrament to such an extent that he may rightly be accused of de-historicizing the historical Jesus. Luther's emphasis on the presence of Christ found its expression primarily in statements about the Lord's Supper, statements which sometimes indicate an "objectifying" tendency. Calvin, on the other hand, concentrated almost exclusively on the presence of the Spirit, almost to the point of substituting the Holy Spirit for the *Christus praesens*.

All of the Reformers were prevented from expounding their interest in the presence of Christ by their acceptance of the traditional framework of Chalcedonian Christology. As a matter of fact none of them added much to traditional Christology. None of them challenged the idea that *two* natures are an appropriate means of expounding Christology. Only post-Reformation theologians qualified traditional Christology by adding the complicated doctrines which we have mentioned. Their doctrines, however, merely made the answers to the traditional questions more differentiated and detailed, but they hardly provided satisfactory solutions to the basic problems. It is interesting that Karl Barth has restrained himself in the criticism of these doctrines. In the early christological passages of his *Church Dogmatics* he balances the Lutheran against the Reformed positions, and in the later parts, e.g. in the fourth volume, one can still trace the basic structure and outline of the classical categories, although it cannot be denied that his Christology goes beyond mere interpretations.

The theologian must receive with the greatest respect all the steps of the history of these admirable attempts to remain faithful to the Chalcedonian heritage. The interest in the "horizontal" unity of the Church in ecumenical contacts is devaluated and annulled if the concern for the "vertical" unity back into the tradition of the Fathers is sacrificed or neglected. But faithfulness to the Church's tradition does not mean that we must repeat or receive uncritically what the Fathers have contributed. To remain in conversation with them necessitates the risk of new approaches. Having pointed out the inherent dilemmas of classical Christology and having summarized the later attempts to combine the classical views with new theological insights, we can now proceed to present an outline of a tentative Christology of the *Christus praesens* as High Priest.

c) *Jesus Christ as Call and Response: the High Priest*

The term and the idea of a "Christology of Call and Response" grew out of conversations with Paul van Buren. But van Buren has dismissed it as "sadly mythological in form, if not in content."[10] His summary of it is indeed more "mythological" than it ought to be. The reason may be that he intended to unfold it as being in harmony with patristic theology, and he does this in order to bring out his new views all the more clearly. It seems to me, however, that the "sadly mythological" form or content is not at all necessary when one begins with the call and response concept in the same manner in which the Epistle to the Hebrews approaches it. Van Buren has not made use of this document at all, but it is precisely there that we can learn what theology is: a call to worship. "Since then we have a great high priest . . . let us hold fast our confession" (4:14), and "he holds his priesthood permanently, because he continues forever. Consequently he is able for all time to save those who draw near to God through him, since he always lives to make intercession for them" (7:24–25). And the certainly "non-mythological" interpretation of this confession is found in Hebrews 10:32 ff. where the believers who have lost their courage and faith are admonished: "recall the former days," i.e. the days when they

---

[10] *The Secular Meaning of the Gospel*, p. 55. The last part of chap. II, pp. 47 ff. presents van Buren's exposition of this Christology of which he says on p. 18 that "it represents my own position before I read Wittgenstein's *Philosophical Investigations*"; cf. his article "The Trinitarian Controversy Revisited" in *RelLife*, XXX (1960–61), pp. 71–80. My summary of it is contained in *Die homiletische Funktion der Gemeinde* (Zürich-Zollikon: EVZ-Verlag, 1959), pp. 21 ff., and in A *Theology of Proclamation*, chap. I as well as pp. 174 ff., and *Athanasius*, pp. 68 ff. and 73 ff.

suffered, days of suffering which they now understand in retrospect
as days of the presence of Christ. This *memory* of the Church
enables the Church to look forward into the future: "Therefore do
not throw away your confidence." This "historical perspective" of
remembering the past and of having confidence toward the future
indicates the dimension of the priestly work of Jesus, a work which
continues permanently and which is effective today. What does this
mean?

Leaving aside a detailed discussion of the titles of Jesus, and
also parenthesizing, as it were, the problem of ontology, one could
try in a merely phenomenological manner to reach a "synoptic
view" of the New Testament passages which speak of the function
of Jesus.[11] The fact that the New Testament writers do not for one
moment forget that "Jesus came from Yahweh" compels us directly to
understand the statements about his function in relation to the Old
Testament, i.e. to Israel's expectation. Any other "phenomenology"
of Jesus would be utterly abstract. Jesus is depicted in the New
Testament as being *simultaneously*:

YAHWEH'S		MAN'S
call	and	response
demand		fulfillment
invitation		prayer
will		obedience
revelation		understanding
word		reply
command		following
anointed		servant
help		cry
etc.		*etc.*

These terms are deliberately "neutral" in form and content in
order to express the impossibility of "getting hold of Christ" by
means of fixed terms or titles. The terms used above do not directly

---

[11] This is not to suggest that the various "models" of which McIntyre speaks, or
the stages of development within the New Testament, with which Reginald
Fuller's new book is concerned, are now synthesized into an all-embracing
christological concept. My suggestion to explore the "model" of a high-priest-
Christology cannot be more than one particular approach among others. I
would maintain, however, that this approach is today to be preferred over the
classical "models."

correspond to each other. What Jesus is "from Yahweh's side" can be expressed in many terms which are theoretically interchangeable, and the same applies to the designations of his functions on behalf of man. The decision as to which of these terms is most appropriate is *time-bound* and *situation-bound*. There is no criterion according to which one could decide in advance which designation is to be preferred over the other. Least of all do the biblical books suggest a preference, for the New Testament uses a much greater variety of designations of Christ than does the tradition of the Church. Church tradition has concentrated on "Son of God/true man" or on "Lord/servant." We could perhaps say that one general decision is possible and advisable in the light of today's "general" situation; one should avoid just these two pairs of terms because of their misunderstandability, which is partly due to the fact that the New Testament writers had a different conception of these titles than does modern man after two thousand years of Church history. But of course this cannot be more than a suggestion expressed with great care, for it would not be helpful to say that the terms "Son of God" or "Lord" are "wrong" as such. It is true, however, that these terms today require an extra effort of (historical) interpretation and explanation, whereas this is not true to the same degree with regard to the designations listed above. But the use and selection of designations is not our main point. More important is the contention that *Jesus should be described not in terms of being, location or relation of natures, but of functions.* We cannot discuss at this point the possible objection that this view merely substitutes a functional view for an ontic view. It suffices to say that the priestly work of Jesus indeed suggests an exposition in functional terms. The proximity to philosophical functionalism, so fashionable today, is no reason to avoid these categories.

What is the "priestly function" of Jesus? A priest is a man who works on behalf of others, though he may also work on his own behalf, as Hebrews 7:27 says; but the uniqueness of Jesus, according to Hebrews, is that he does not have to work on his own behalf and is therefore free to work on behalf of those whom he does not feel ashamed to call brothers. He does the works of another. Jesus does "the works of the Father," as John's Gospel says and reports him to have said. But he also does the works of man, standing as the One for many. It is an abstraction to speak of God apart from Jesus, and likewise it is an abstraction to speak of man apart from Jesus. If this is true, Jesus must be spoken of as the priest who works on behalf of God, so that God can be spoken of only through Jesus, and who works on behalf of man, so that man can be spoken of only through Jesus. Moreover, the denial of his priestly vicarious function would lead to the following abstractions which are not conceived as abstractions only if they are understood metaphysically and as "sadly mythological" in form and content; the statement that Jesus *is* God is as abstract as would be the statement that Jesus *is* mankind. He neither *is* God nor *is* he mankind, but he *works* on behalf of God and on behalf of man. The term "works," indicating his function, is understood exclusively and absolutely in the New Testament and in the confession of the Church. This is to say that *only he* performs the double function so uniquely that it is possible to speak of God and of man because of him. What this man did "from the side of Yahweh" is so exclusively authoritative that the insight into the fulfillment character of his life and death invited the statement that "he is one with the Father" and that the "Father is in him." And what this man did "from the side of man" invited the statement that "in him is the newness" and that he is for the rest of mankind God's righteousness. But these statements are confessions of faith, not "analytical judgments" but "synthetical judgments" which are doxological in character. In a word: *The assertion of the uniqueness of Jesus* regarding his "doing the works of the Father" and his "being the newness of men" *leads to prayer and flows from prayer.* In traditional language this means that the uniqueness of Jesus can only be preached in a worship service in which people pray. Preaching the uniqueness of Jesus on the street corners, i.e. without the beginning in prayer and the response in prayer, is "theoretically" absurd, and is possible "practically" only because the listeners on the street corner may still *remember* the prayer of worship services they once attended. This also applies to the first missionary activities of the Apostles: they went to the places where the expectation of the Old Testament promises were still remembered.[12]

[12] Conversations with young people in the Soviet Union indicate quite concretely that those who do not even abstractly "remember" worship cannot grasp statements about the uniqueness of Jesus even if they are willing to respect him as a man of high moral character and the like. Cf. my forthcoming article in *JES*, Fall 1967, "Theses Pertaining to Christian-Marxist Dialogue," related to my discussions with Marxist philosophers at the University of Prague in January 1967.

The concept of Jesus being God's call and man's response indicates that it is not "more difficult" nor does it demand "more faith" to accept and trust the creed that *he does the works of God* than the opposite creed that *he gives the reply that man owes God*. Conventional opinions regarding Jesus implicitly suggest that the "true miracle" is his being the Son of God, while his being true man is considered to go without saying (although his true manhood is often not fully accepted). But this is not true and not in accordance with the biblical witnesses. The implications of his being *vere homo* are as astonishing as are the implications of his being *vere Deus*, to use traditional language. His acts as man, his weeping, his being hungry, his ignorance, his "offering up prayers and supplications, with loud cries and tears" (Hebr. 5:7) are no less priestly, i.e. of "saving" effect, than are his manifestations of the works of God, e.g. his healings and authoritative teachings. Continuing for a moment with these traditional categories, we must add that the reception, acceptance and understanding of his "human actions" demand "faith," i.e. the understanding of the past in the light of the presence of Christ, precisely in the same way as do his "divine actions." This is another way of stating what we have concluded in earlier chapters, *viz.* that the "historical Jesus" can be understood only in the light of the *Christus praesens*.

"Doxological" statements, or at least those statements which lead open-endedly to doxology, are confessions of the Church. The Church confesses in them that all of mankind and in fact all of history is "intended" and addressed in this man Jesus. "Speaking of God" and of what he means when he addresses man in history is possible on the basis of the Old Testament, in which reference is made to the *expectation* which the believers have for the world. But when reference is made to the first and decisive *fulfillment* of what God means when he addresses Jews *and* Gentiles, "speaking of God" is restricted to what we see in the man Jesus who is understood against the background of the promises. In other words, neither the expectation character of the Old Testament nor the fulfillment character of the New Testament (concerning the man Jesus) can be superseded by any other thoughts that could authorize man to speak of God. Nor would it be possible to play the importance of the two Testaments against each other. No preconceived idea of who God could be can be useful for explaining who Jesus was or how God was in Christ. Only the memory of the promises and of the

first fulfillment in the coming of Jesus provide such a basis; but
Jesus, seen in the light of the promises of old, awakens expectation
anew. The Church can grasp who Jesus is only when she remembers
the promises and the fulfillment in Jesus and when she expects again
in hope the final fulfillment. But the Church is constituted ever anew
by the *Christus praesens* without whom she would have neither the
"interest," as we have called it before, nor the understanding of
what she remembers and hopes for.

Who then "is" the *Christus praesens? From the point of view of
the Church,* i.e. from the cognitive aspect within the matrix of what
we have called the "corporate intentionality" of perceiving in the
appropriate way the tradition of the Church, he is that "power" or
"interest" (formally speaking) which makes the Church see that she
is taken into possession, drawn into the history of promise and
fulfillment, used in service, invited to hope; and this "power" is
called Christ because the Church recognizes it in no one else than
the one whom she remembers as the earthly priest Jesus of Nazareth
and whom she expects in the future, though in no other terms than
those of the promises of the past. He who constitutes the Church
with these qualities enables her ever anew to see that his earthly
work as unique priest has not ceased but continues. This "historical
perspective," as I have called it, frees and enables the Church to
speak of the past in the knowledge of forgiveness and to look into
the future with hope. Or to put it more concretely: the Church's
recognition of the *Christus praesens* enables her to "hope backward," i.e. that the "High Priest" may change and remove those
elements of the past which still burden the present and destroy the
hope for the future, and to "remember forward," i.e. that the promises of the past may be fulfilled in the future. Memory and hope are
exchangeable, but past and future can never be exchanged, for it is
God himself who has a history. From the Church's point of view
this history is represented in the movements from promise to fulfillment, whereby fulfilled promises are again turned into promises that
wait for fulfillment (the occupation of the Land, the Davidic King-
ship, the coming of Jesus of Nazareth; these are the outstanding
examples). That which keeps together promises and fulfillments,
which permits the trust in the continuity and the denial of the idea
of a chain of accidental historical events, is called the "covenant,"
without which *hope* would not be possible, except in the unfortunate

form of a choice between hope "in God" or "in the world." This emphasis on the covenant is today especially necessary to counter-balance the speculative trends in part of recent "Process Theology": which speaks of a God who changes, but not of a God who has a history in the faithful covenant with his people.[13]

One may argue that this series of sentences is sufficient. It indeed suffices to derive from it the priestly service which the Church must perform, and to invite the Church to worship and prayer. There may be coming periods in history when the Church cannot say more than this. But on the basis of what we have concluded about Braun's and van Buren's theses in the fourth chapter, we can tentatively and with care venture a statement about the *Christus praesens "from God's side,"* as it were. Such speech, to be sure, presupposes that the transition can be made from "address language" to "report lan-guage," and this supposition would have to be examined carefully with reference to what is *necessary* in theology. This transition would result in such sentences as: The *Christus praesens* is "that" in Yahweh which was manifest in the man Jesus of Nazareth who performed his unique priestly task; and this "that" is nothing other than God's own covenantal will to remain man's partner through the course of his own history; it is "God's heart," "God's guts," which he has focused upon man, that which seeks man and stays restless until it has found man, that which makes God himself suffer for the sake of man.[14] God himself provides the priest who works

[13] E.g. John B. Cobb, *A Christian Natural Theology* (Philadelphia: Westminster Press, 1965), who utilizes Alfred N. Whitehead's philosophy of becoming as an alternative to a static conception of reality in classical theology. I appreciate Cobb's intent, but fail to see how he can avoid falling into Hegelianism since he does not operate with the categories of promise and fulfillment, i.e. the covenant. Existentialism still remains as an alternative and necessary corrective to Cobb's view, which means that the problem of theology today is not solved by "Process Theology." Pannenberg's Christology is philosophically more learned, though problematical too, and E. Jüngel's book is theologically deeper and more penetrating than "Process Theology." Cf. Langdon Gilkey's critical review article on Cobb's book in *ThToday*, Jan. 1966, pp. 530 ff.

Norman Pittenger summarizes well the present situation in American "Process Theology" in an article by this title in *RelLife*, Autumn 1965, pp. 500 ff., but his survey and the cited passages are only fully understandable if seen over against the background of Whitehead's (and also Hartshorne's) writings, which, so far as I am familiar with them, strike me as being of much greater intellectual brilliance and metaphysical depth than their theological descendents.

[14] After completion of this manuscript the book by Kazoh Kitamori, *Theology of the Pain of God* (Richmond: John Knox Press, 1965), came to my attention.

on God's as well as on man's behalf. The indication that God himself does not do this in a timeless manner is given by the resurrection of the man Jesus, the first man with whom the partnership has reached its fulfillment. But this fulfillment of the promise of partnership in *one* representative man is the beginning of the vicarious priesthood of God in Christ in the period after Jesus of Nazareth. The *content* of his priestly work is the implementation of Yahweh's righteousness, that is to say, of Yahweh's decision that his covenant with Israel would no longer be restricted to this one people but would be implemented for both Jews and Gentiles. Without this "gluing together" of Jews and Gentiles (and derived from it, of male and female, free and slaves), life in the covenant is not possible. Or positively speaking, because of this "gluing together" of Jews and Gentiles, the Church can and must consist of those people who think that by nature (race, sex, age, ideology, degrees of intelligence, etc.) they do not belong to each other. Thus, when the question is asked as to the actual accomplishment or "effect" of the priestly work of the *Christus praesens*, one would have to say: His ongoing action of implementing God's righteousness not only creates an "awareness" among the Christians that God's promises were true, or that the resurrection of Jesus is "meaningful," etc., but it actually *creates* the Church in which this "gluing together" of enemies is a reality. The Church not only *knows* of the *Christus praesens* and his work, she is also *being dealt with* by him. The Church can, therefore, *address* him in doxological language, al-

---

It contains many thoughts which would have been extremely stimulating in our discussion. Kitamori maintains that the dogma of God's impassibility, which was accepted from Greek philosophy, prevents our hearing the biblical insistence on God's suffering. The real analogy between God and man, Kitamori states, is that of pain: we serve God's pain with our pain, and it is this service which is the overcoming of pain. But we cannot begin with *our* pain, we discover the meaning of pain in the crucifixion of Jesus. It is here that the pain of God is received as the totality of God's communion with man and it is also here that pain is overcome. But the Cross is conceived by Kitamori strictly in the context of the resurrection. This tragic dialectic of existence, i.e. serving God's pain with our pain to overcome pain, is seen by the author as the peculiar responsibility of Japanese ethos in relation to the message of Easter and the crucifixion after the apocalyptic experience of the atom bombs. Kitamori clearly states that different cultural spheres and different times are given different responsibilities for the articulation of the Gospel. (The biblical basis for the theology advocated by Kitamori is expounded on pp. 151 ff. with special attention to Jer. 31:30 and Isa. 63:15).

though she is incapable of defining the peculiar mode of his existence. All she can say is that the present, risen Christ exists in a
mode peculiar to himself, but that his existence is certainly different
from being a mere representation or crystallization of the Church's
understanding, or of "authentic existence." Admittedly, he not only
creates, but also he *is* the Church's awareness of the ongoing stream
of promises and fulfillments. But the very fact of his physical absence after the resurrection indicates that he must be spoken of as
existing in a mode peculiar to himself. He too, not just the Church,
must have his mode of "intentionality" toward the Church, his "desire to be present," if this transposition of doxological language in
propositional statements is permitted for a moment. With the res-
surection he became what he was not before.[15] He has a history.
The risk of faith is to let oneself be taken into his history. If his
mode of existence were merely that of being the abstract summary
of the Church's self-understanding and faith, he could not *share* his
history and his presence. He would be dissolved into the community
of believers.

The biblical texts do not shy away from saying that Jesus Christ
had a history. Especially with regard to his designation as High
Priest it is made clear that he *became* High Priest. As the initial act
of the establishment and implementation of Yahweh's righteousness
for Jews and Gentiles, his resurrection is the fulfillment of Yahweh's
doings with Israel and at the same time the pledge of further fulfillments. To say this is nothing short of saying that God has a history.
To speak of it in this way is different from what the Arians had in
mind when they denied the co-eternity of the Logos with the Father,
for this denial implies that "there was a time when Yahweh had no
'heart' or 'guts,' " to use this metaphor once more. This is a useless
speculation. Rather we must say, again metaphorically, that God
has a history with this "heart" or "guts," because the resurrected
Jesus was the man Jesus and not the kerygma of God's goodwill,
as, in the final analysis, existentialist theology says.[16]

---

[15] This fact is related to, but not identical with the historical observation that
Jesus, after Easter, received titles and designations which he did not have
before. The application to such titles represents the primitive Church's awareness that Jesus was indeed the legitimate recipient of such titles which contained an eschatological open-endedness.

[16] The resurrection, however, cannot be understood apart from Israel's expectation
of the fulfillment of the promise that the Kingdom would come. If "resurrec-

These are problematical ways of expounding Christology. All we have said in this tentative quest for an exposition of the *Christus praesens* "from God's side" consisted of derived statements, derived not only from "analytical statements," as we have called them, but also from a combination of such with various doxological affirmations. The proximity to mere metaphorical speaking was also obvious. The Church has time and again risked such language. Could it be that without taking this risk the Church would deprive herself of the experience of *receiving* the *Christus praesens* as the one who really shapes the believers' thoughts, memories and hopes? By this I mean to suggest that the highly metaphorical speech about the *Christus praesens*, as seen "from God's side," expressed indirectly the never satisfied hunger to "see the face of the Lord" and, at the same time, the fear that it may really be true that the one who sees God will die. The risk of using this kind of language is indeed great, not only because of the criticism and scorn of the philosophers, but primarily because this kind of speech could indeed prove to be true. Metaphorical speech about the *Christus praesens* can "explode into directness," can lose its tentativeness, triviality and vagueness, and can burst into concreteness. This "directness" or "concreteness" will, however, hardly be similar to Augustine's and his mother's vision at Ostia; it will not be an "elevation" ad infinitum of man's highest qualities, but—if our understanding of the biblical texts is at all tenable—it will press man down to earth and show him his place in the community of those who freely serve their neighbors and love their enemies. It is at this point, too, that seemingly speculative thoughts, such as predestination, providence, and

---

tion" is separated from this background it is automatically reduced to a "confirming miracle" concerning a special status of Jesus, and this, in turn, would necessitate a concept of Jesus which utterly depends upon a non-understandable miracle. It is noteworthy that I Cor. 15:3 ff. gives account of the resurrection by emphasizing twice "in accordance with the Scriptures," whereas I Tim. 3:16 in its creed concerning Christ makes no mention of the resurrection (rather: "vindicated in the Spirit . . . taken up in glory . . ."). Should we too avoid using "resurrection" because of the absence of the proper understanding of it which originally was dependent upon the late Jewish *expectation* of the breaking in of the Kingdom? The only access *we* have to the resurrection is *backward* through Jesus' appearances; the *forward* access, coming from Israel's expectation, is no longer ours. Thus we must learn to receive the resurrection accounts as invitations to hope toward *new* actions of God. Easter is the earnest beginning (*arrabōn*) of the Church's hope.

prayers that are "answered," etc., will appear in a new light. The "directness" of doxological language will then become a reality.

By way of concluding this discussion of the possibility of speaking of the *Christus praesens* "from God's side," we can entertain one further thought. Our criticism of Augustine's concept of God, as well as our discussion of recent tendencies toward "atheistic Christology," and now our inquiry concerning the peculiar mode of existence of the *Christus praesens* have led us to reiterate "that God has a history." However, such a statement is only possible when one operates in one form or the other with the traditional trinitarian conceptual apparatus. It is possible, of course, to state in general terms that "changing" and "sameness" are not mutually exclusive notions. A covenant between two married people has a history too. While the two people obviously "change" in many ways, their covenant remains in its sameness. Being what they are because of their covenant, one can also say that they retain their sameness as persons despite that fact that they change. One could even say that sameness is only thinkable because of the change of certain factors within that which "stays the same." But whatever is changing (Aristotle mentions changes of quantity, quality, location, and substance), the *identity* must remain. All of this is true in a rather general way. Utilizing for our consideration concerning God's history the concept of *identity*, we must none the less employ more than general truths if we want to do justice to the problem at stake. Our implicit contention is itself a trinitarian thought: the *Christus praesens* is not other than God, rather, he *is* God's identity. Theology has never succeeded in circumventing the utilization of trinitarian concepts in discussing the relation between Israel, Jesus, the resurrection and the present Church. Without being able to enter into a full discussion of this problem, we can claim the following thought to be in harmony with our discussions about "Jesus and the Church," "Scripture and tradition" and the question of "Speaking of God"; the so-called heresy of modalism deserves reexamination for possible utilization. The stimulus which admittedly comes from Hartshorne's suggestions (our dissatisfaction with their application in "Process Theology" notwithstanding), makes this inquiry particularly urgent and interesting. Modalism, it seems, has at least one advantage, *viz.* its cognizance of the fact that God *has* a history which affects his people, and that any reflection about "the Trinity" in non-historical terms is based anyway upon an observation which is akin to modalism. After all, it was the modalists who tried to retain the contact with the accounts of Israel's and the primitive Church's history. However, a modalism regarding the relation between "the first and the second person of the Trinity," i.e. regarding the coming of Christ, would indeed lead to docetism, as it did in the third century. But would a modalistic view in respect to the so-called second and third persons of the Trinity not be a very adequate means of expression? Is the differentiation between the *Christus praesens* and the Holy Spirit more than a speculative prolongation of that which is historically known into the trans-empirical? The difficulties which the Western Church has had concerning the presence of Christ when speaking of the presence of the Spirit indicates at least that here is an unsolved problem. If faced with the choice between the idea that the Holy Spirit "makes relevant" the historical-resurrected Christ, and the somewhat unusual view that the Holy Spirit *is* the *Christus praesens*, I would not hesitate to choose the second. At least it seems problematical to use the same notion "person" (or any other notion) to designate Christ and the Spirit. The threefold use of such terms as "Person" only too quickly suggests a triangular conception of God which would be detrimental to the understanding of the union between Christ and the Church.[17] H. Berkhof's opinion regarding the relation between the risen Christ and the Spirit seems to be similar to the views advocated here.[18]

The ongoing work of the High Priest, the *Christus praesens*, whose dimensions are the memory of the promises and of the first fulfillment and the hope toward the final fulfillment, incorporates the Church into the High Priest's own work. This view, which is broader than the traditional concentration on justification or the modern exposition of the analysis of self-understanding, is the theme of the concluding part of this chapter.

[17] Pressing further this emphasis on God's history with his people within his own faithfulness, one could in exaggerated form say: The Church is "trinitarian" in regard to her memory, "binitarian" at the present and "unitarian" in hope. But such formulations are of no greater value or clarity than were the classical trinitarian formulations of the Early Church; they have their proper place within a given framework of thoughts.

[18] H. Berkhof, *The Doctrine of the Holy Spirit*, 1964 (*vide* above, Introduction, FN 12).

d) The Priestly Task of the Church: "Ora et Labora"

If the concept of a Christology of call and response were elaborated in detail, it would become clear that this approach takes care of the intentions of the traditional doctrines of the *triplex munus Christi* and of the three ways (*genera*) in which the *communicatio idiomatum* is expressed. It also does justice to the intent of the doctrine of Christ's exalted and humiliated *status*. The unfortunate distinction between the "person" and "work" of Christ could be avoided, and operating with the "two natures" would become superfluous. Christology and soteriology would again become one after the pattern of the New Testament statements.[19] Moreover, Christology and ecclesiology would be related so intimately that both the concept of a Jesus Christ "as such" and the idea of an autonomous Church would become impossible.

The Church has never completely forgotten that Christology shapes the understanding of the Church. The famous examples of this are Alexandrian Christology, which led to the concept of a diefied Church, sacramental Christology, which led to an institutionalized Church, moralistic Christology, which created a Church for the betterment of society, etc. What is said of Jesus Christ affects directly the definition of the Church and of its task. When he is defined in the categories of two natures, the designation of the function of the human nature is transferred to the Church, and the divine nature of Christ continues in its function which is now assigned to the heavenly Christ. This is already clear in Cyril of Alexandria, who taught that in Jesus the human nature *receives* while the divine *gives*. This concept was translated into ecclesiology: what the heavenly Christ *gives*, the Church *receives*.

We have sufficiently clarified our dissatisfaction with two-nature Christology. But at the point of translating this type of Christology into ecclesiology the disadvantages become even more obvious. The Christology of call and response will not tolerate the one-sided

---

[19] Bonhoeffer in his earlier writings repeatedly expressed his disagreement with the oneness of Christology and soteriology, e.g. *op. cit.* p. 37 (Engl. text). This is in line with classical theology which, however, presupposed a realistic (Platonic) thought structure, because of which the delicate questions concerning a "*beneficia* theology" versus a theology of the "Knowledge of Jesus Christ" became necessary. Bonhoeffer's own work, esp. the Christology lectures of 1933, mark the transition to new thought structures.

transference of the human nature of Christ to the Church. Both "functions" of Christ the High Priest become the functions of the Church. But here appears a point of considerable danger; the direct connection between the priestly work of Christ and of the Church could suggest that the Church is the "continuation" of Christ, or "another Christ," an *alter Christus*, as Roman Catholic dogmatics has called it. However, it should be clear by now that the ongoing work of the *Christus praesens* will not permit the idea that the Church has now become that which the incarnate Christ once was. On the contrary the Church is time and again constituted anew by the very work of the High Priest, and "constituted" means that she is ever anew called into participation in his work. No one in recent years has expressed this so convincingly as Bonhoeffer, whose academic and practical-political convictions have given an example of what he meant when he said that "Christ exists as the congregation," that he is the Church but that the Church is not Christ and that "the Church cannot be faster or slower" than Christ in his work. This thought appears again and again in his theological development from the early theological writings to the latest letters from prison; the Church cannot usurp the office of Christ. Jesus Christ alone is the officer-bearer, and the Church exists *because* she is ever anew called and invited to share in his work. The Church is not the *vicarius Christi*, but she participates in the whole ministry of Christ without degrading his work in times of her own passivity and without adding anything to it in times of obedient activity.[20]

Utilizing the neglected insight of what we have called "the best part" of the Greek Fathers' theology, we can say that the Church is *taken into possession*; the Church is used for a purpose. If it were meaningful to make a difference between justification and sanctification—but it is not meaningful—we would certainly say that sanctification is prior to justification. Sanctification means "being taken into possession" for a purpose. We have seen that Athanasius makes this thought clear, and even later stages of Eastern theology, stages which we are accustomed to observe with criticism, have preserved this insight, at least within the monastic movements. The

---

[20] I have tried to elaborate this further in *Christ Our Life* (Edinburgh: Oliver & Boyd, 1960), pp. 40–70, and in *A Theology of Proclamation*, pp. 117 ff. Cf. also T. F. Torrance, *Royal Priesthood*, *SJT*, Occasional Papers, No. 3, 1955, esp. pp. 35 ff.

purpose for which the Church is taken into possession is not the Church itself, rather it is the vicarious work of the Church on behalf of others.

Summarizing briefly what follows from a Christology of call and response: The vicarious work of the Church can be unfolded under the theme of the ancient Benedictine motto *Ora et labora.* The *Christus praesens* whose high-priestly function we have tried to describe by outlining a "synoptic view" of what the Church remembers of him, for the first time reported in the texts of the New Testament, *takes possession of the Church at present for the following purpose:* The Church prays (*ora*) on behalf of those who cannot pray; she gives adoration, thanksgiving and intercession only partly on her own behalf, but primarily on behalf of those whose priest she is; and she works (*labora*) because of God in Christ, from "the side of God" or "in his name" for the benefit of those whom God in Christ "means," the poor, the discriminated, the honorless, the hopeless, the dying, but also the joyful. The Church's task has clearly two sides, a doxological one and a social-political one. As times and situations change, the Church will always be inclined to stress one of these sides more than the other. If the analysis is permitted, we could perhaps say that today the Eastern Christians have often been and still are in trouble with the world and, while we Western Christians may think we are at peace with our world, we are in trouble with God.[21] But the limitation of one side of the Church's task does not mean that she ceases to be the Church. There may be times when parts of the Church can and must only pray or only work for others. It is for this reason that ecumenical contact is so vitally important; what one part of the Church omits is done by another part, and what ties the Church together is the confidence that each part is used in the same high-priestly task of Christ himself. Thus mutual *confidence* among the various parts of the Church is more important than *agreement.*

Those who take part in the Church's task of *ora et labora* are "saved." This understanding of the term "being saved" is expressed in Romans 9–11, for example. It is not a salvation which negates the lives of others, or which predicts the future of the Christians or of those who are not now participating in the *ora et labra* function. If this

---

[21] I have given examples of this observation in the article "The Priestly Church in Marxist Lands," in *Union Seminary Quarterly Review*, May 1965, pp. 333 ff.

were so, it would presuppose that belonging to the Church is based upon man's goodwill and free decision, and conversely that man's not-belonging to the Church would have to be considered as a decision for which he can be blamed. This view, however, would deny that it is the *Christus praesens* who in his freedom takes man into his possession for the purpose of man's sharing in his task.

If this is correct, it follows that (a) the individuals in the Church understand their own existence after they have become aware of the Church's task and not *vice versa*; their own justification is their constant hope in the memory of what they know of Jesus Christ, but their justification and the liberation of their "troubled consciences" does not initiate them into the Church (this would lead to Gnostic forms of perfectionism, or to Donatism). And (b) the whole Church and all its individual members (each of whom may have quite different tasks) have no excuse to withdraw from the not-Church and from their fellowmen; in both the doxological and socio-political aspects of their task they are intimately tied to those who are not the Church. They are not only the advocates and helpers of the unbelievers—much less are they their schoolmasters—but carrying in their bodies the death of Jesus they bear the burdens and guilt of those who do not know forgiveness. Yet this solidarity is no identity. They are in solidarity with others by freely accepting the *conditions of existence* of their fellowmen, not by agreeing with their opinions but often by contradicting them. Such disagreement and conscious contradiction may even lead to the breaking off of human contact, as has occurred in recent times, for instance during the Nazi regime and in America in relations with consistent segregationists. But such breach of contact is, rightly and not pharisaically understood, an expression of solidarity.

Without being prophets we can today predict that the established churches will decrease in numbers. The influence of the institutionalized churches will become weaker. We still talk too much and do too little, and our Western theology is crippled by the categories of the Constantinian-Augustinian tradition. The number of non-Christians who try to help themselves and to improve the conditions of the world with moral goodness and respectable intelligence will increase. The Church will learn that she is not permitted to waste her energies by working for her own self-preservation. It may be that what Bonhoeffer meant by the term *Arcanum* will be this: that the

Church tells her own members but not the world that she exists as the salt of the earth and the light of the world, as that vicarious priesthood which keeps the world from falling apart, as the "ten righteous ones because of whom the city is not destroyed." If this is said to those who are not the Church, it is demonic pharisaism; if the members of the Church say it to one another, in the memory and hope of what God in Christ in his history has done and will do, it is in praise of the *Christus praesens*.

"AND LO, I AM WITH YOU ALWAYS, TO THE CLOSE OF THE AGE" (MATT. 28:20)

1) The *coming of Jesus* is de-historicized when it is understood as separated from the history of Israel: either by making him the epiphany of the secrets of a hitherto unknown God, or by describing him as an example of "authentic existence," a model of "true faith" etc., or by referring to his person in terms of (however dynamically understood) "natures," i.e. by casting originally doxological affirmations into propositional language. Rather, the coming, the life, death and resurrection of Jesus are only adequately referred to in the awareness of the Church's confession in all ages that he is the fulfillment of the Exodus and of subsequent partial fulfillments, all of which were again turned into promises in Israel's worshipful understanding. This fulfillment of ancient promises, however, is understood by the Church as the beginning of the breaking down of the wall between the Jews and the Gentiles, i.e. as the establishment of the rule, right and righteousness of Yahweh over both Jews and Gentiles. Thus the Church's memory is the invitation to her hope for the world.

2) The Church, however, not only hopes because she *remembers* the promises, but she makes the accounts of Israel's and her forefathers' memory her own memory *because she hopes*, that is to say, she would not be "interested" in memories and hopes of previous generations if she were not prompted to do so by her own hope.

3) The Church's hope is her awareness of God's ongoing faithfulness. This awareness is the work of the *Christus praesens*. It is recognizable "from the point of view of the Church" in her willingness to accept her standing in the "stream of confessions" and to take seriously the doxological language of generations past, and also in her freedom to hope not only for the preservation of the Church but for the implementation of God's right and righteousness for the whole world. This hope is different from "wishes" and it frees the Church to understand and to accept the present; the more eschatological her faith, the stronger is her involvement in the present situation.

4) The Church's *freedom for the present* not only includes her solidarity with fellowmen and her free cooperation with non-Christians, it also liberates her from the selfish desire to experience "personal en-

counters," visions or epiphanies, which allegedly prove God's presence in Christ but which, in reality, if they ever happen, are only adequately interpreted in retrospect. By the same token, the Church knows that she is not compelled to provide direct interpretations of current events as "divine interventions" or as acts of god-less men. With the exception of possible charismatic interpretations, the "meaning" of current events is understood only in retrospect, in such fashion, however, that the Church's task to face the past with honesty and openness (because of her knowledge of forgiveness) is at the same time her invitation to anticipate realistically future developments, either by supporting or by preventing their coming about. This freedom in the presence of Christ, remembered and hoped for in the dimensions of past and future, is at the same time the *permission to worship* in vicarious praise and intercession and the *criterion for ethics.*

5) If compelled to give account of the ultimate content of her faith and hope, the Church will not merely refer to the "stream of confessions," to her "interest" in Scripture and tradition, or to the "shaping of her corporate intentionality" regarding her present task of *ora et labora.* It may become necessary to use "derived doxological language," often, though not always, metaphorically, in order to express the understanding that the *Christus praesens* is not the representation of the self-consciousness of the believing community, the personification of the kerygma, or the like, but that he *owns* his own mode of presence; that he had to absent himself in order to be present; that he has his peculiar "intentionality" of sharing his presence with man, perceived and praised by the Church on behalf of those who do not perceive and praise him; and that he must be spoken of as God's *identity,* as that which "stays the same" in God's own history. The articulation of this confession and praise has its own logic, determined and invited by the one whose presence and ongoing work is confessed and praised. Thus the high-priestly double function of the *Christus praesens* consists, firstly, of his owning his peculiar mode of being present as God's identity, of his sharing his presence with those with whom he is present, and, secondly and simultaneously, of his shaping the Church's "corporate intentionality" regarding his presence in past, future and present, expressed in the Church's *ora et labora* function.

Index of Names

Index of Subjects

Alexandrian-Antiochian controversy, 88, 99, 104, 183
Alexandrian theology, 88, 99, 183
Analogy, 58, 86, 105, 151, 173, 220
Anhypostasis-Enhypostasis Christology, 205, 206
"Anonymous Christianity," 181–202
Apologetic-ethical theology, 96–97
Apologists, 81, 96, 98
Aristotelianism, xv, 105
"Atheistic Christology," xv, 143–180, 223
Augustine
    influences on, 105–113
    Manicheism and, 107–109
    Neo-Platonism and, 109–113
    piety of, 113–115
Augustinianism, xii–xv, 6, 7, 42, 102–103, 104, 143, 144, 202
    atheistic Christology as, 143–180
    burden of, 17–140
"Authentic Existence," 7

Canon, 28, 47, 69, 70, 72–75
Chalcedon, 149, 203, 205
Christocentric-pneumatic theology, 96
Christology, xi, 12, 20, 24, 27, 28–30, 33, 34, 42, 43, 61, 78, 80, 97, 98, 99, 102, 115, 124, 138, 143, 146, 149, 150, 178, 181, 202–213, 219, 222, 225, 227
    Anhypostasis-Enhypostasis, 205, 206
    Antiochian, 99, 183, 205, 225
    call and response, 213, 225, 227
    communicato idiomatum, 210, 225
    Gnosticism and, 78–89
    Incarnation type, 204, 205, 206, 207, 209, 210
    Logos doctrine, 90–91
    status doctrine, 225
    triplex munus, 209–210, 225
    two-nature, 206, 210, 212, 225
Christus praedicatus, 27, 211
Christus praesens, xii, xiii, xv, 11, 13, 19, 27–28, 34, 41, 61, 63, 64, 65, 66, 68, 73, 74, 78, 84, 88, 98, 102, 124, 126, 136, 153, 154, 157, 167, 168, 178, 179, 186, 191, 198–200, 202, 207, 208, 209, 211, 212, 213, 217, 218, 219, 220, 222, 223, 224, 226, 227, 228, 229
Church
    future of, 228–229
    Jesus and, 20–34
    matrix of recognition of Christ, 20–34, 153
    priestly task of, 123, 202–230
Constantinianism, 136, 182, 192
Contextualism, 9, 200

Deification, 89–96
    doxology and, 89–91
    as redemption, 91
Docetism, 32, 57, 205, 211, 224
Doxology, 89–96, 166–176, 202
    deification and, 89–91
    language, 158, 166–176, 220–221, 223
Dualism, 108–109

Encounter, 133, 149, 151, 154–158
Epistemology, 55, 85–89
Eschatology, 27, 46, 122, 130–140, 163
Ethics, 185–201
    criterion of, 194–201
Exegetical theology, 50–51
Existentialist theology, 21–22, 35–45, 133–137, 164, 222

235